International Trade Agreements Before Domestic Courts

Maria Angela Jardim de Santa Cruz Oliveira

International Trade Agreements Before Domestic Courts

Lessons from the EU and Brazilian Experiences

Maria Angela Jardim de Santa Cruz Oliveira
Brasilia
Brazil

ISBN 978-3-319-13901-2   ISBN 978-3-319-13902-9 (eBook)
DOI 10.1007/978-3-319-13902-9

Library of Congress Control Number: 2015932773

Springer Cham Heidelberg New York Dordrecht London
© Springer International Publishing Switzerland 2015
This work is subject to copyright. All rights are reserved by the Publisher, whether the whole or part of the material is concerned, specifically the rights of translation, reprinting, reuse of illustrations, recitation, broadcasting, reproduction on microfilms or in any other physical way, and transmission or information storage and retrieval, electronic adaptation, computer software, or by similar or dissimilar methodology now known or hereafter developed.
The use of general descriptive names, registered names, trademarks, service marks, etc. in this publication does not imply, even in the absence of a specific statement, that such names are exempt from the relevant protective laws and regulations and therefore free for general use.
The publisher, the authors and the editors are safe to assume that the advice and information in this book are believed to be true and accurate at the date of publication. Neither the publisher nor the authors or the editors give a warranty, express or implied, with respect to the material contained herein or for any errors or omissions that may have been made.

Printed on acid-free paper

Springer International Publishing AG Switzerland is part of Springer Science+Business Media (www.springer.com)

Foreword

What is, or should be, the role of domestic courts in the enforcement of international law, more specifically, state-to-state trade commitments? This is the ambitious question masterfully tackled in this volume.

The work is unique in that it examines the interplay not from the conventional perspective of EU or US courts, but from the vantage point of developing countries, in particular, Brazil. It does so not in the abstract but with reference to rich jurisprudence before Brazilian courts, juxtaposing it, in particular, to the EU experience. The research also reaches a controversial conclusion: Brazil, which gives direct effect to trade agreement in its domestic courts, is not lauded as the champion of free trade. Instead, it is strongly advised to stop giving direct effect to trade agreements before its domestic courts.

The starting point of the book is an intriguing puzzle: Why is it that the United States, the EU, Canada, Japan and even China, India, and South Africa have refused to give direct effect to WTO and other trade agreements before their domestic courts, whereas Latin American countries like Brazil, Mexico and Argentina do continue to give such direct effect? What explains this "Latin American exceptionalism"? Does it make sense? The author provides a forceful case for Brazil to end this "exceptionalism."

States are free to decide how they will implement treaty commitments. Nothing under international law obliges them to give direct effect to treaties before domestic courts. Indeed, when looking at the largest trading countries, almost all of them have decided to create a wedge between (1) their international, state-to-state trade obligations before, for example, the World Trade Organization, and (2) what binds them vis-à-vis private parties under domestic law or before domestic courts. As a result, in neither the United States nor the EU can traders invoke WTO commitments of the state before domestic courts. The recently concluded Canada–EU Free Trade Agreement (CETA) goes as far as stating that "[n]othing in this Agreement shall be construed ... as permitting this Agreement to be directly invoked in the domestic legal systems of the Parties" (Chapter 33, Article 14.6). Also China, India and South Africa have done the same. In Brazil, in contrast, a rich jurisprudence exists where domestic courts have applied, interpreted and found violations of trade agreements binding Brazil at the request of (often non-protectionist-inspired) private parties.

Traditional international lawyers may applaud Brazil's commitment to international law. On their view, enlisting domestic courts in the enforcement effort of international law can compensate the flaws in the international enforcement of international law and thereby contribute to the effectiveness of the discipline. Dr. Oliveira tells a different story. In her view, and relying on rational choice approaches, allowing national courts to enforce trade agreements at the request of private parties is counterproductive, even for the effectiveness of international law. Building on the Brazilian experience, she points at a number of "unintended consequences": (1) a flood of individual cases, (2) diverse and inconsistent rulings among domestic courts within Brazil, (3) domestic courts' interpretation of WTO rules different from the international and foreign interpretation of trade rules, and (4) disequilibrium in international trade's concessions and rights. In the Brazilian experience, she argues, the executive, not courts (especially not lower courts) are more inclined to favor international law compliance. Direct effect shifts power from the executive to courts and is, on this view, more likely to harm rather than help the effectiveness of international law.

The book presents a nuanced theory of how countries should assess the role to give to their domestic courts in relation to international law: not a one-size-fits-all solution, but a calibrated one, based on the subject matter and type of treaty in question. A variable solution also that may change over time, depending on the needs of the country. New, relatively weak countries may find it attractive to tie their hands to international law through direct effect to signal their good citizenship in the world community, to attract foreign direct investment, or for internal purposes, e.g., for central governments to keep sub-federal levels of government under control or to tie in domestic reforms. In countries with a past of military rule, such hand tying enforced by domestic courts (not the rulers of the day) makes sense. It may be further explained by a country's colonial past, especially if it resides in continental Europe, where a strong "monist" commitment to international law prevailed at least until recently. However, in Dr. Oliveira's opinion, "as the Latin American economies grow, and their stance at the international trade system increases, it seems fairly reasonable to expect a move from traditionalism [direct effect] to the rational choice theory [no direct effect] . . . as it happened in European courts and US courts."

It remains to be seen whether this prediction will materialize. In any event, this book is an eye opening read, to be taken seriously by anyone interested in how emerging economies should structure their domestic engagement with international law, looking not only at theories but at practical experience, including unintended consequences.

Washington, DC, USA   Joost Pauwelyn
29 October 2014

Acknowledgments

This book would have never been completed without the generosity and wisdom of numerous people that supported me through this journey that I want to acknowledge and give my heartily thanks. I am greatly indebted to Joost Pauwelyn, who kindly encouraged me with insightful guidance and forward-thinking vision. Without him, none of this work would have been possible to achieve. I am also thankful to Andrea Bianchi, whose authoritative and challenging views stimulated me for academic dialogue and impelled me to deepen my argument with his invaluable insights. I would like to extend my gratitude to George Bandeira Galindo for his hard questions, thought-provoking comments and constructive feedback.

A special note must be made to Nuno Garoupa, for his illuminative perspective on judicial behavior, profound intelligence and straightforward conversations. His friendship and support has been invaluable to the development of this book.

I am grateful to the Honorable Justices Celso de Mello, Ellen Gracie Northfleet and Gilmar Mendes, for their kind support of my engaging in scholarly research. My gratitude also goes to Marcelo Kohen, for supporting my academic interest in international law, and Vera Thorstensen, for enlightening me about complex economic aspects of international trade and guiding me through the works of the World Trade Organization. I am also thankful to Deisy Ventura, for her insightful and thoughtful comments at the initial phase of this work.

I would also like to express my appreciation for the help and guidance that various people have given me in different capacities throughout this research. I would like to thank Carl Baudenbacher for his generous invitation to the 2nd Saint-Gallen International Dispute Resolution Conference, and Christine Peter da Silva for my attendance to the 2nd World Conference of Constitutional Courts in Rio de Janeiro. I am thankful to Francisco Acuña, Lorena Sander, and Armando Reina for their helpful insights of the Mexican legal system. My thanks to Adriana Dreyzin de Klor, Alejandro Perotti, and Juliana Peixoto Batista for their kind availability to share their knowledge about Argentinean courts. I also recognize the help of Celso de Tarso Pereira, Franz Stirnimann Fuentes, Luiz Eduardo Salles, Graziela Picinin, Mattias Bietti, Ángel Horna, and Eva Keszeliova. Further, thanks to Brigitte

Reschke, Julia Bieler and the Springer team for their valuable expertise and efficiency in the publication of this book.

Most importantly, I would like to express my infinite gratitude to my parents who have always supported my intellectual endeavors. My deepest appreciation goes to my beloved husband José Carlos Santiago for his adorable companionship during the writing of this book, and for his endless supply of patience and spirited conversations. I dedicate this book to him.

Contents

1	**Introduction**		1
	1.1 Outline of Argument		5
	References		10
2	**The Relations Between International Law and Domestic Courts**		13
	2.1	Comparative Studies on the Application of International Law by Domestic Courts	14
	2.2	The Role of Domestic Courts Regarding International Law: General Approaches in the International Legal Scholarship	17
		2.2.1 Ways Domestic Courts Usually Enforce International Law	20
		2.2.2 Traditional International Legal Scholarship on the Role of Domestic Courts Regarding International Law—or Traditionalism	25
		2.2.3 Rational Choice Theory in the Law and Economics Approach on the Role of Domestic Courts Regarding International Law	35
	2.3	The Role of Domestic Courts in International Trade Law: A Substantial Field Approach	38
		2.3.1 The Traditionalism v. Rational Choice Theory Debate on the Role of Domestic Courts Regarding the WTO Agreements	43
		2.3.2 The American Creation of the GATT and Its Leadership in the Adoption of the Rational Choice Theory in International Trade Agreements	47
	2.4	An Assessment on the Role of Domestic Courts in International Trade Agreements	50
		2.4.1 The Function and Objective of International Trade Agreements	51

		2.4.2	The Principle of Popular Sovereignty and Democratic Self-Government	54
	2.5	Conclusion		60
	References			61

3 The Relations Between International Trade Agreements and Domestic Courts in Brazil 67

	3.1	Constitutional Arrangements at the National Level: The Domestic Status of International Treaties in Brazil		67
	3.2	The Traditionalist Role of Brazilian Courts in WTO Agreements		71
	3.3	Brazilian Cases		76
		3.3.1	The Imports of Codfish Case: Extraordinary Appeal n. 229096	78
		3.3.2	The Retreaded Tires Case: ADPF 101	88
		3.3.3	The Radial Tires Case: Extraordinary Appeal n. 632250 ...	100
		3.3.4	The Thermo Bottles Case: Special Appeal n. 1105993	105
	3.4	Conclusion		107
	References			116

4 The Relations Between International Trade Agreements and Domestic Courts in the European Union 119

	4.1	The Domestic Status of International Treaties in the European Union		120
	4.2	The Rational Choice Theory Perspective of the European Court of Justice Regarding WTO Agreements		128
	4.3	ECJ Cases		133
		4.3.1	International Fruit Company Case	133
		4.3.2	Nakajima v. Council	136
		4.3.3	Germany v. Council	140
		4.3.4	Portugal v. Council	145
		4.3.5	Léon Van Parys v. Council	149
		4.3.6	Ikea Wholesale Ltd. v. Commissioners of Customs & Excise	152
		4.3.7	FIAMM v. Council	157
	4.4	Constitutional Pluralism: The Relationship Between the ECJ and National Courts Regarding WTO Agreements		161
		4.4.1	The German Jurisprudence	165
		4.4.2	The Italian Jurisprudence	169
	4.5	Conclusion		173
	References			174

5 Comparing the Role of Domestic Courts in International Trade Agreements 177
5.1 The Main Similarities and Divergences Between Brazilian and European Union Courts in International Trade Agreements ... 177
5.2 Thinking Beyond Brazilian Perspectives: The Patterns of Emerging Economies in Latin America 185
5.3 Conclusion 194
References 197

6 Conclusion 199
References 209

Chapter 1
Introduction

As economic globalization and free trade agreements make national economies more interconnected, business issues increasingly cross-affect more jurisdictions and nations. While trading systems expand at the international level, national courts are gradually more exposed to litigation involving international trade rules at the domestic level, increasingly in areas that involve domestic regulation and public policy. With the expansion of international law during the twentieth century, the number of international treaties increased even in areas previously never regulated by international agreements.[1] Such increase has made the relations between international law and domestic law more intricate by involving international law in domestic matters and policies, resulting in domestic judges being prompted to adjudicate on domestic litigation involving international treaties.

Domestic courts' litigation involving international law and the problems of interaction between domestic and international law have generated comparative studies on the interpretation of international law given by domestic courts' decisions from different countries. Debates on how domestic courts apply, or should apply, international law have flourished even among domestic judges themselves in various fields,[2] analyzing inconsistencies and consequences of such decisions.

The theoretical debate that contours the attitudes of domestic courts towards international trade law raises a primary question, that is, what should be the proper role of domestic judges regarding international law? Consider that the major economies of the world trade system, such as the United States (US), the European Union (EU), Canada, Japan, China, South Africa and India[3] do not allow domestic courts to review the validity of governmental policies by private parties based on the WTO agreements. Or, in the international trade parlance, these major economies do not give direct effect to WTO agreements. On the other hand, Latin

---

[1] Shany (2003), pp. 1–3.
[2] Breyer (2003), Scalia (2004), and Baudenbacher (2010).
[3] Van den Bossche (2008), p. 68.

American countries, such as Brazil, Mexico and Argentina, give direct effect to WTO agreements. From these contrasting patterns, this study aims to explore the role of domestic courts in international trade agreements, by analyzing the perspectives of the European Union and Brazil and drawing lessons from their experiences.

The debate on what should be the most appropriate role of domestic courts regarding international law has produced two contrasting currents in the international legal scholarship. The first and most widely accepted current in the international law scholarly debate promotes domestic courts as enforcers of international law. This current advances the argument that domestic courts should implement international law. Largely propounded by 1930s Scelle's theory of "role splitting" (*dédoublement fonctionnel*), this perspective considers that domestic judges, by applying international law, compensate for the lack of proper mechanisms at the international level for the enforcement of international rules.[4] This approach is the preponderant view in the international legal discourse on the role of domestic courts. It has influenced the legal profession in both Brazil and the European Union, and provides the theoretical background for the dominant practice in both Latin America and European Union courts. After all, in the European Union, the treatment of WTO agreements—which do not have direct effect—is a well-known exception to the preponderant judicial practice that fosters the application of international law by domestic courts. This study therefore refers to this prevailing approach as one of the traditional scholarship on the role of domestic courts in international law[5]—or "*traditionalism*"—because of this perspective's established influence in the international legal debate and its broad ascendancy in the domestic courts that are object of this research.

The second current on the role of domestic courts in international law considers that enforcement of international law by domestic courts may be counterproductive for the efficacy of international law. Grounded on the rational choice theory in the law and economics approach, this current reflects a minority view in the international legal scholarship. This perspective argues that greater domestic judicial involvement would not advance international law; instead, domestic courts would retard the development of international law.[6] Rational choice theorists propound that the executive supports international law more than the other branches of government.[7]

Considering that there is no universal answer for the role of domestic courts in international law, the aim of this study is to assess these contrasting approaches on the role of domestic courts upon the substantial field of international trade

---

[4] Dupuy (2007), p. 3.

[5] Previous works have also made reference to "traditional model of international law in domestic courts," "traditional international law scholars," "traditional scholarship," and even "traditional modes of international law scholarship" when addressing the role of domestic courts in determining a country's obligations under international law. *See* Knop (2000); Hathaway and Lavinbuk (2006), p. 1405, fn 4, 1407.

[6] Posner (2009).

[7] Ibid.

agreements, and to reflect on the significance of these approaches through the comparative study of domestic courts' decisions regarding international law. Therefore, this study elaborates on the specific debate about the role of domestic judges regarding international trade agreements. In particular, it examines the debate on the direct effect of international trade agreements, with the pros and cons discussed in international legal scholarship. This comparative study analyzes the diverse outcomes arisen in domestic adjudication to assess whether the traditional view that domestic judiciaries are an efficient venue where international law may achieve its full efficacy is valid for international trade agreements. To do so, it is necessary to recall the United States' paramount importance in the creation of the world trade system rules, and the American leadership in the adoption of the rational choice theory in the role of domestic courts regarding international trade agreements.

In examining the role of domestic courts regarding international trade agreements, this study is centered on the judicial decisions rendered by Brazilian domestic courts on WTO agreements—as a representative of an emerging economy in Latin America—in a comparative perspective with European Union courts, one of the major economies of the world. The choice to compare Brazil with the EU derives from the fact that the domestic legislation of both the Brazilian and EU domestic legal orders are silent on the legal effects of international trade agreements and therefore it is for their domestic judiciaries to decide on this matter. The two judiciaries, however, have taken opposing views. The Brazilian judiciary has given direct effect to WTO agreements, while the European Court of Justice (ECJ) has denied it. Such comparison is relevant because both the ECJ and the Brazilian Supreme Court have the ultimate say on the effect of international trade agreements in their respective internal legal orders. Although the United States created the GATT, the lack of direct effect of WTO agreements was instated by the U.S. Congress through statutory law, and therefore domestic courts are not responsible for such an outcome. For this reason, the United States courts are not object of this research, although references to U.S. courts' decisions are occasionally made in this study.

The choice of WTO agreements is a necessary one because they constitute the legal framework of the world trade system and are the only international trade agreements where both Brazil and the EU are members. Under the WTO agreements, the scope of this research is limited to the GATT and the Antidumping Agreement. The GATT is the most well-known agreement under the WTO umbrella as it exists since 1947, and contains the core rules of international trade law. The predominance of GATT is also visible at the international level in the WTO dispute settlement mechanism. Indeed, out of the 482 disputes brought by member states before the WTO dispute settlement system, 392 disputes cite GATT in their request for consultations.[8] The Antidumping Agreement is also important because it is the mechanism for regulating commercial defense, and directly affects

---

[8] WTO Dispute Settlement: Disputes by Agreement (2014).

interests of importers/exporters that are not satisfied with the imposition of the antidumping duties, and sets out clear rights and procedures, contrary to the GATT.

This study focuses on leading cases rendered by the highest courts of Brazil and the EU. Despite limitations of this research in terms of the number of leading cases found, because WTO agreements have not been frequently invoked before domestic courts in Brazil, there is potential for increase in private litigation invoking WTO agreements. For instance, international trade rules and rulings issued by international trade dispute settlement systems may go against national private businesses' interests or, more importantly, widely shared societal values, such as in the case of the European ban on hormone-treated beef, condemned by the World Trade Organization.[9] Because Brazil allows private invocability of WTO agreements, there is high potential for litigation of corporations in domestic courts against international trade policies based on the implementation of international trade rules or dispute settlement rulings at the domestic level. Brazilian domestic constituencies, in defending their private businesses' interests, are likely to challenge the merits of the existing government policy to implement a ruling from an international trade dispute settlement system. In case these constituencies are not able to change the government policy choices through government lobby, they may go to domestic courts to review the government measure that directly affects them. Domestic courts in Brazil and other Latin American countries can therefore be asked to decide on international trade policies at the domestic level.

In relation to the European Union, although in principle there is no potential for private litigation against trade policy choices in the domestic context, this comparative work is also relevant for the European Union and other WTO members' perspectives because it shows the potential effects that domestic private litigation in international trade rules may occasion. Therefore, a comparative empirical work may also inform other countries how direct effect of WTO agreements may develop in a domestic setting.

Now, add to that the possibility of conflicting rulings on the same trade dispute, one released by the WTO Dispute Settlement Body and another one issued by a regional trading system, both of which are also brought in the lawsuit before domestic courts. A paradigmatic case, which illustrates such tensions, is the dispute against Brazil on measures affecting imports of retreaded tires. Brazil imposed an import ban on used and retreaded tires in the year 2000. Nevertheless, Uruguay challenged the import ban under MERCOSUL dispute settlement mechanism and the arbitral tribunal found this measure was in violation with Brazil obligations under MERCOSUL rules.[10] To implement such ruling, Brazil issued a new measure excluding MERCOSUL countries from the import ban on retreaded tires. Later on, the MERCOSUL exemption of the Brazilian import ban on retreaded tires was

---

[9] WTO, *European Communities—Measures Concerning Meat and Meat Products (Hormones)*, WT/DS26/AB/R, adopted 13 February 1998.

[10] MERCOSUR, Ad hoc Arbitral Tribunal Award, *Import Prohibition of Remolded Tyres from Uruguay*, 9 January 2002.

challenged before the WTO dispute settlement system[11] by the European Union. The WTO Appellate Body found the MERCOSUL exemption was inconsistent with GATT.[12] At the same time, Brazilian retreaders went to domestic courts and obtained provisional injunctions against the import ban, therefore authorizing the import of used tires and retreaded casings from Uruguay. As a matter of fact, this case is of great importance because it is an example of conflicting rulings at the regional and multilateral trade systems, with multiple lawsuits at the domestic judiciary level that were finally decided after such rulings were issued. As a matter of fact, the coexistence of regional and multilateral dispute settlement systems requires the Executive to adapt domestically to conflicting rulings and negotiate a solution internationally. Such executive's prerogative may be severely restrained by domestic courts decisions that adopt traditionalism as a model.

As this study aims to prove, traditionalism in international trade agreements causes unintended consequences that do not advance international trade law as originally conceived. This study shows the unintended consequences of traditionalism in international trade agreements, and the unsuitability of domestic courts for unilaterally deciding on mutually accorded trade concessions and rights.

This book makes a normative argument that the function and objective of international trade agreements, and the principle of popular sovereignty and democratic self-government in choosing how international trade obligations are complied with require the adoption of the rational choice theory in the role of domestic courts regarding the WTO agreements. In this book's view, litigation based on international trade rules should be circumscribed to international adjudication at the WTO dispute settlement.

1.1 Outline of Argument

This book seeks to examine the normative claims of traditionalism and the rational choice theory in real world cases, and the consequences of adopting one or another approach by WTO members. Chapter 2 begins with a brief introduction on the comparative studies on the interpretation of international law given by domestic courts' decisions to situate the research as one that observes real cases and issues at work in domestic litigation. It then expounds the two general approaches in international legal scholarship on the role of domestic courts regarding international law, the traditional perspective and the rational choice theory approach. In identifying the foundations of these two main currents, some simplification is required, as there are particular views with nuances or more distinctions in each of these lines of thought. Nevertheless, they all share the same foundation, that is, one fosters the application of international rules by domestic courts, and the other

---

[11] WTO, *Brazil—Measures Affecting Imports of Retreaded Tires*, WT/DS332/R (2007).
[12] WTO, *Brazil—Measures Affecting Imports of Retreaded Tires*, WT/DS332/AB/R (2007).

does not favor the involvement of domestic courts in the interpretation and application of international law.

Next, while suggesting that there is no universal response to the most appropriate role of domestic courts, Chap. 2 elaborates on the specific academic debate on the role of domestic courts regarding the WTO agreements. To understand how the rational choice theory approach evolved regarding the WTO agreements, this study broadly addresses the conception of the GATT by the United States, and the non-self-executing character of WTO agreements before American domestic legal order.

With this background information, Chap. 2 sets out the main argument of this study. By building on the theoretical background found in Sykes' scholarship on the function and objective of international trade agreements, in conjunction with the principle of popular sovereignty, this book argues that traditionalism is not the most appropriate role for domestic courts in relation to international trade agreements. This book's argument continues that allowing individuals or private businesses to claim against governments' public policy choices before domestic courts for violations of WTO agreements does not advance the international trade system as it was originally conceived by WTO signatory parties and causes unintended consequences that do not foster international law to achieve its full efficacy.

With this theoretical framework established, Chap. 3 starts this comparative study by assessing the relations between domestic courts in Brazil and WTO agreements. Chapter 3 expounds that Brazil adopted a traditionalist approach. To assess the Brazilian perspective, Chap. 3 examines the constitutional arrangements at the national level on the domestic status of international treaties in Brazil, explores the traditionalist role of Brazilian courts with regards to WTO agreements, and finally goes to the core of this chapter which is the analysis of Brazilian cases on the GATT and the Antidumping Agreement. In this chapter, the Brazilian courts' cases are assessed and several disadvantages of traditionalism regarding WTO agreements took place. As a qualitative research, to avoid selection bias the cases chosen are primarily leading cases decided by the Brazilian Supreme Court that settled numerous similar cases over the same issue, starting from 1988—the year of entry into force of the current Brazilian Constitution after democracy was reinstated in the country, following a military dictatorship. The only exception is one case of the Superior Court of Justice, the highest court of Brazil for non-constitutional matters, as an example of how judicial activism in trade matters may develop differently than the perspective anticipated by traditionalism proponents.

This study is required to describe in detail all the arguments and votes in each Brazilian case for two main reasons. First, because there are not English versions of the Brazilian courts' cases and not much published in international legal scholarship about Brazilian courts' decisions. Second, the Brazilian courts' decisions have a particular feature whereby there is not only one single unified opinion written by only one member of the court. In Brazil, all members of a court present their individual opinion, which can be very different one from another specially when deciding a contentious leading case. Consequently, all individual votes are

1.1 Outline of Argument

important on their own to identify the reasoning behind the decision reached and therefore require much attention.

After examining the way Brazilian courts understand the GATT and the Antidumping Agreement, this comparative study then goes to analyze the European Union perspective. To do so, Chap. 4 assesses the relations between international trade agreements and domestic courts in the European Union, by first briefly exploring the domestic status of international treaties in the EU legal order. As widely divulged, the ECJ has a mixed position on international trade agreements in general and does not grant WTO agreements direct effect, as opposed to association agreements. The ECJ's mixed position on international trade agreements reveals relations of power between the EU and their former colonies or potential new members. Identified as "hegemonial" agreements,[13] association agreements are in line with EU domestic law, and therefore, the EU is in fact exporting EU domestic legislation to former colonies and aspiring EU members. Accordingly, potential conflict of association agreements with EU legislation is not likely to happen.[14] A shift of powers within EU bodies is also not relevant, as the EU executive bodies control the agreements' negotiations and drafting. In what concerns the other signatory parties of association agreements, however, the same might not be true. As a result, association agreements cannot be considered as standard international trade agreements, as envisioned by the world trade system, which assumes a relationship of equal status among the signatory parties.

Chapter 4 then continues to explore the main cases whereby the ECJ built its case law on the WTO agreements under the GATT and the Antidumping Agreement. Next, due to the unique features of the European Union legal order, Chap. 4 examines the degree of cooperation of national courts of the European Union Member States with the ECJ case law in relation to the WTO Agreements, through the lens of constitutional pluralism. The national constitutional courts' perspective is an important topic to address in relation to the ECJ case law because the constitutional courts of EU member countries have reiterated that they are guardians of fundamental rights and democratic principles in their national legal orders. Accordingly, these courts leave a door open for review of ECJ case law, if they find it necessary. As the GATT precedes the EU exclusive powers on international trade in goods, the way constitutional courts' prior jurisprudence evolved with the transfer of national powers to the EU on international trade matters is also relevant due to the following struggle of power between the ECJ and the national constitutional courts. As a result, constitutional courts of EU Member States may have the occasion to confirm or not the ECJ case law and therefore examining their views on the ECJ case law on the GATT/WTO agreements becomes relevant. Because it is beyond the scope of this research to examine all EU members, this study refers to the jurisprudence of Italian and German courts. The choice of Italy and Germany as representatives of the national domestic courts of EU Member States derives from

---

[13] Cottier (2009), p. 314.
[14] Ibid.

the circumstance that both countries were founding Member States of the EU that already had, at that time, constitutional courts.

Taking the Brazilian and the EU perspectives, Chap. 5 proceeds to compare them, and assess the differences and similarities found between Brazilian and EU courts. The main difference in the adoption of direct effect of the WTO agreements between EU and Brazilian courts reveals that private businesses are able to seriously impair public policy choices in Brazil. A flood of cases reached the Brazilian domestic judiciary neutralizing trade measures, and the domestic interpretation of trade rules was different from the international understanding of such rules. Conversely, the ECJ has avoided such outcomes by blocking private litigation against public policies over economic interests and better bargains. The question of reciprocity is also an interesting issue, as Brazilian domestic courts have never considered it in relation to international trade agreements, whereas the ECJ finds that reciprocity as one of the fundaments to deny direct effect of WTO agreements—a point that is disregarded for the EU association agreements. These differences indicate a question of power in trade relations, where weak economies tied their hands more easily at the international level, than rich economies, where diverse political and economic incentives are relevant in defining the role of domestic courts in international trade law. A point of convergence, however, is that neither perspective concedes WTO rulings with domestic legal status. On the other hand, both Brazilian and EU courts can be considered as having implicitly applied the doctrine of consistent interpretation in certain occasions involving WTO rulings, although there is not an explicit reference to such doctrine.

Chapter 5 then looks beyond Brazilian perspectives to suggest that the findings of the Brazilian experience can be extended to a high degree to other emerging economies in Latin America, namely Mexico and Argentina. Although this study compares two jurisdictions, the findings of this research may also be in a manner relevant to some degree to other countries in Latin America due to the region's traditional openness to international law.[15] In fact, as documented, Mexico and Argentina have considered that WTO agreements have direct effect in their domestic legal orders. Accordingly, the findings of this study in relation to the Brazilian cases may be relevant to the region's emerging economies because Mexico and Argentina, like Brazil, in principle interprets international trade agreements as creating trade rights to private actors. The opposing views of Latin American countries vis-à-vis world major economies indicate that there is an element of power in the adoption, or not, of direct effect of WTO agreements. Commentary remarked that weaker countries are more prone to tie their hands in relation to international trade law than powerful economies,[16] which seems to be a safe assumption to explain why Latin American countries have given direct effect to WTO law. Yet, Latin American emerging economies are growing and gaining influence in the world trade system. As the Latin American economies grow, and their stance at the international trade system increases, it seems fairly reasonable to

---

[15] Cassese (1985), p. 364.

[16] Guzman and Pauwelyn (2009), p. 77.

1.1 Outline of Argument

expect a move from traditionalism to the rational choice theory in Latin American countries, as it happened in European courts and US courts. However, whether this potential economic power shift towards Latin American economies will thrive and domestic courts will restrain themselves in trade matters remains to be seen in future years. So far, as this study will show, Brazilian courts have been very active in politically sensitive issues. To be sure, future field research is necessary to examine the usefulness of this study to Mexico and Argentina, but this is beyond the scope of the present research.

This book concludes on the basis of this analysis that the function and objective of international trade agreements, and the principle of popular sovereignty and democratic self-government in choosing how international trade obligations are discharged, compel the adoption of the rational choice theory approach on the role of domestic courts regarding WTO agreements. It puts in question the core assumptions of traditionalism which do not seem to be applicable to international trade agreements in emerging economies in Latin America.

Instead of direct effect, compliance with WTO rules at the domestic level seems to be more effective when courts are making use of the doctrine of consistent interpretation, through the highest domestic court's guidance to avoid international responsibility. If supervised by the Supreme Court, the political dimension of the role of domestic courts is more effective than left to lower courts, where conflicting decisions may arise when there are multiple private claims against governmental public policies.[17] Still, the doctrine of consistent interpretation has no answer when there are contradictory international trade obligations derived from regional and the multilateral trade dispute settlement systems, a question that has raised much concern at the international level.[18] In any case, domestic courts' proceedings are usually slow and it may take years before a time-consuming litigation finally reaches the Supreme Court level.

Regardless, domestic courts are not needed for addressing WTO-inconsistent domestic policies. Having the WTO system an effective rules-based dispute settlement mechanism at the international level with a 90 % compliance rate,[19] the main reason for the advancement of traditionalism—that international mechanisms are not sufficient to make member states comply with international law—is not compelling with reference to the world trade system. In addition, the WTO dispute settlement mechanism is the most appropriate venue for solving disputes in the application of WTO rules, because it provides a common forum for discussing the meaning of WTO rules while leaving open the possibility of negoationg a better solution among the countries involved. Thus, the WTO dispute settlement mechanism prevents disparate outcomes and conflicting interpretations, while still giving preference to a solution mutually acceptable between the parties.[20]

---

[17] Oliveira and Garoupa (2012).

[18] Hillman (2009), p. 205.

[19] Lamy (2011).

[20] WTO Understanding on Rules and Procedures Governing the Settlement of Disputes (DSU), Article 3.7.

This book aims to add to the scholarship on the relations between international law and domestic courts in the area of international trade. Most academic work on the interplay between the WTO law and domestic judiciaries is limited to studies on WTO deference to domestic courts' jurisprudence,[21] and on the question of direct effect of WTO laws in the European Union and United States[22] contexts because they have been the major players in the international trade arena. Indeed, international trade literature is mostly focused on the two most active members of the WTO dispute settlement system. As a result, more studies need to be done in relation to emerging countries that have been increasingly engaging in the international trade dispute settlement systems. With the proliferation of international trade agreements, domestic courts' views on international trade law become of particular importance due to its potential impact on domestic jurisdictions and on the executive's authority to negotiate trade concessions at the international level.

Hopefully, this book will enrich the understanding of the effects of domestic judicial interpretation of international trade agreements through the Brazilian and EU courts experiences, and will provide pathways for further research in other Latin America countries. More importantly, this study will raise awareness that the prevailing international legal scholarship advancing an increased role of domestic courts in the enforcement of international law should be revisited in relation to international trade agreements, although this perspective continues to harvest followers in Latin America.

References

Baudenbacher C (2010) International dispute resolution. Dialogue between courts in times of globalization and regionalization, vol 2. German Law Publishers, Stuttgart

Bhuiyan S (2007) National law in WTO law: effectiveness and good governance in the world trading system. Cambridge University Press, London

Breyer S (2003) The Supreme Court and the new international law. Proc Annu Meet (Am Soc Int Law) 97:265–268

Cassese A (1985) Modern constitutions and international law. Collected courses of the Hague Academy of international law, vol 192. Martinus Nijhoff, Leiden

Cottier T (2009) International trade law: the impact of justiciability and separations of powers in EC law. Eur Const Law Rev 5:307–326

De Búrca G, Scott J (eds) (2003) The EU and the WTO: legal and constitutional issues. Hart, Oxford

Dillon S (2002) International trade and economic law and the European Union. Hart, Oxford

Dupuy PM (2007) The unit of application of international law at the global level and the responsibility of judges. Eur J Legal Stud 1(2):3. http://www.ejls.eu/2/21UK.htm. Accessed 4 Sept 2014

Guzman A, Pauwelyn J (2009) International trade law. Aspen, New York

---

[21] Bhuiyan (2007).

[22] Weiler (2005), Ortino (2004), De Búrca and Scott (2003), and Dillon (2002).

References

Hathaway O, Lavinbuk A (2006) Rationalism and revisionism in international law. Faculty Scholarship Series. Paper 835. http://digitalcommons.law.yale.edu/fss_papers/835. Accessed 4 Sept 2014

Hillman J (2009) Conflicts between dispute settlement mechanisms in regional trade agreements and the WTO – what should the WTO do? Cornell Int Law J 42:193–208

Knop K (2000) Here and there: international law in domestic courts. N Y Univ J Int Law Polit 32:501–535

Lamy P (2011) WTO news: speeches – DG Pascal, International Chamber of Commerce in Oslo. http://www.wto.org/english/news_e/sppl_e/sppl192_e.htm. Accessed 4 Sept 2014

Oliveira MAJSC, Garoupa N (2012) Stare Decisis and Certiorari Arrive to Brazil: a comparative law and economics approach. Emory Int Law Rev 26(2):555–598

Ortino F (2004) Basic legal instruments for the liberalisation of trade: a comparative analysis of EC and WTO law. Hart, Oxford

Posner E (2009) The perils of global legalism. University of Chicago Press, Chicago

Scalia A (2004) Keynote address: foreign legal authority in the federal courts. Proc Annu Meet (Am Soc Int Law) 98:305–310

Shany Y (2003) The competing jurisdictions of international courts and tribunals. Oxford University Press, Oxford

Van den Bossche P (2008) The law and policy of the World Trade Organization. Cambridge University Press, London

Weiler J (ed) (2005) The EU, the WTO and the NAFTA: towards a common law of international trade? Oxford University Press, Oxford

WTO Dispute Settlement: Disputes by Agreement (2014) http://www.wto.org/english/tratop_e/dispu_e/dispu_agreements_index_e.htm?id=A9#selected_agreement. Accessed 4 Sept 2014

Chapter 2
The Relations Between International Law and Domestic Courts

This chapter provides the theoretical framework that supports this comparative study on Brazilian and European Union courts regarding international trade agreements. It first presents general lines on the comparative studies on the interpretation of international law given by domestic courts to locate this research as an empirical observation of real domestic litigation. Then, it expounds the general approaches in the international legal scholarship on the role of domestic courts in international law, drawing two main currents. The first and generally accepted current promotes that domestic courts should enforce international rules in domestic litigation, which this study identifies as one of the traditional perspectives of international legal scholarship, or "traditionalism." The second and less accepted current advocates that domestic courts should refrain from enforcing international rules in domestic litigation, called the rational choice theory approach. After considering these two contrasting perspectives, this chapter then suggests that, instead of a universal response, the proper role of domestic courts in international law should vary in accordance with the substantial field of international treaties.

That being the case, this chapter subsequently addresses the specific academic debate on the role of domestic courts regarding international trade agreements, expounding the pros and cons of direct effect of the WTO agreements. To assess the role of domestic courts in the specific case of the WTO agreements, this chapter makes reference to the idealization and drafting of the GATT by the United States. Understanding the origins of the world trade system provides evidence on the function and objective of the WTO agreements, an element that is relevant for the analysis of a substantial field for the purposes of defining the proper role of domestic courts. With the creation of the GATT in mind, this chapter turns attention to the American leadership in adopting the rational choice theory regarding the WTO agreements. The EU and the majority of the world trade players follow the American adoption of the rational choice theory, indicating therefore that the principle of self-government informs the world trade system. Nevertheless, Brazil and other Latin American countries do not share the same perspective, and adopted traditionalism, an aspect that will have specific attention in Chap. 5. Finally, building on the theoretical background found in Sykes' scholarship on the function and objective of international trade agreements and on the principle of popular sovereignty and self-government, this chapter develops this book's argument that traditionalism does not seem to be the most appropriate role for domestic courts in relation to international trade agreements.

2.1 Comparative Studies on the Application of International Law by Domestic Courts

This study focuses on the Brazilian and EU domestic courts' experiences regarding international trade agreements. The interpretation that domestic judges from different jurisdictions have given to international treaties has been object of academic research. Roberts identifies such studies as "comparative international law."[1] However, there is a lack of consensus over what comparative international law means and, therefore, for the purposes of this research, a brief explanation of the legal debate over the comparative studies on the decisions of domestic courts regarding international law is required. More importantly, this study focuses on the underlying question at the bottom of the comparative studies on the interpretation of international trade agreements by domestic courts, which is: what should be the proper role of domestic courts in relation to international trade law? This is the core question that emerges from the comparative studies debate that this study will address.

According to Roberts, comparative international law is a phenomenon whereby scholars are investigating and comparing the interpretation of international law given by domestic courts' decisions from different countries.[2] However, it is important to note that commentary has opposed this definition arguing that the more traditional and common sense use of comparative international law should be the description of competing approaches to international law, institutions and governance.[3] In an earlier work, another scholar has given the meaning of comparative international law as the study that first describes the similarities and differences in how *"international law is understood, contested, and implemented in diverse societies"* and second considers *"what connections, if any, exist across societies with respect to the politics and law of global legal norms,"* urging for inclusion of non-westerns and non-democratic contexts.[4] Ranging from a cutting-edge interpretation to a traditional description, and a mix of both approaches, the alternate definitions of comparative international law do not preclude one or another. After all, the comparative process encompasses international law as a

---

[1] Roberts (2011).
[2] Ibid.
[3] Mamlyuk and Mattei (2011), p. 389.
[4] Mednicoff (2007), p. 338.

matter of substance, along with comparative law as a matter of process of analysis.[5] On the comparative method, Sacco (1997) explains:

> The comparative method is thus the opposite of the dogmatic. The comparative method is founded upon the actual observation of the elements at work in a given legal system. The dogmatic method is founded upon analytical reasoning. The comparative method examines the way in which, in various legal systems, jurists work with specific rules and general categories. The dogmatic method offers abstract definitions.[6]

International law as the substance of the comparative process has increased in the last decade, mostly attributed to new critical approaches to international law.[7] Koskenniemi makes the case for comparative international law as a contribution to *"thinking the world no longer in terms of what Hegel used to call abstract universals but seeing all players as both universal and particular at the same time, speaking a shared language but doing that from their own, localizable standpoint."*[8] Such academic and practitioners' interest in comparative international law have brought commentators to note that the beginning of the discipline started in the 1970s,[9] tracing the terminology of comparative international law in scholarly production of the 1960s analyzing western and soviet international law.[10]

Regardless of the concept or origins of comparative international law, as a matter of fact, scholarly literature and academic writings have analyzed the application of international law by domestic courts, mainly in the international human rights area.[11] In a recent work, Sloss presents a comparative study on the application of international treaties by domestic courts from eleven countries from different regions of the world,[12] and classifies international treaties in three types: (1) horizontal provisions governing relations between states, (2) vertical provisions, regulating relations between states and private parties, and (3) transnational

---

[5] Roberts (2011), p. 57.

[6] Sacco (1997), pp. 25–26.

[7] Mamlyuk and Mattei (2011), p. 388.

[8] Koskenniemi (2009), p. 4.

[9] Mamlyuk and Mattei (2011), p. 388, asserting that William Butler, a Russian scholar, is the founder of the comparative international law as he taught a course on "comparative approaches to international law" in England in the 1970s, and citing his scholarly production, among them, a study on Russian, Chinese and American approaches to international law conducted at Harvard Law School in the late 1960s.

[10] Ibid. (2011), pp. 388–389.

[11] *See* Koh (1999) describing the British and the US judicial internationalization of the norm against torture in international human rights law; Warner la Forest (2004), p. 158, discussing the use of international and comparative human rights law in Canadian courts, and listing numerous academic writings on the parameters of the use of international law and comparative law by domestic courts; Waters (2006), with several individual writings considering the use of international law by British and Canadian national courts.

[12] Australia, Canada, Germany, India, Israel, the Netherlands, Poland, Russia, South Africa, the United Kingdom, and the United States. Sloss clarifies that at the outset of this comparative study, chapters on Argentina, Brazil, China, Mexico, Nigeria and South Korea were also included, but, for different reasons, such chapters never materialized.

provisions regulating relations among private parties that go beyond domestic frontiers.[13] Focusing on the question whether "*domestic courts provide remedies to private parties who are harmed by a violation of their treaty-based primary rights*,"[14] Sloss (2010) concludes that

> The conventional wisdom is wrong, insofar as the conventional wisdom holds that direct judicial application of treaties is a more effective means of treaty enforcement than indirect application. In countries such as Canada and India, where domestic law precludes direct application of treaties, domestic courts play an active role in treaty enforcement by applying treaties indirectly. In contrast, in the United States, for example, although domestic courts have the authority to apply treaties directly in some cases, they rarely use their judicial power to remedy treaty violations committed by government actors.[15]

The current scholarship is so extensive that, besides heavily discussing national courts in the developed world,[16] it has recently approached how international law has been used in African judiciaries,[17] reaching even into not so obvious fields such as normative beliefs in the role of domestic courts in the system of international responsibility for wrongful acts.[18] In addition to the comparison among domestic courts from different countries, numerous commentators have produced scholarly work on the interactions between international and domestic law from the perspective of one national jurisdiction—including the judges themselves —that is, how one country's judiciary has interpreted and applied international law, and also engaged domestic judges in the debate.

This study however does not aim to exhaust the scholarly and judicial discussion on the use of comparative studies of domestic courts' decisions. This study limits itself to the use of the comparative method to focuses on the role of domestic courts in relation to international trade law. To address this core question, this study will now turn to briefly expound the general approaches in international legal scholarship on the role of domestic courts in the interpretation of international law.

---

[13] Sloss (2010), p. 1.

[14] Ibid., p. 2.

[15] Ibid., p. 3.

[16] *See* Cataldi and Iovane (2009) and Fatima (2005), explaining how United Kingdom courts handles international law in domestic law; Klein and Hughes (2009), Eskridge Jr (2004), Rosenkrantz (2003), and Reinisch (2007).

[17] Panel on *The Rising Use of International Law by African Judiciaries* (2010).

[18] Nollkaemper (2007). Nollkaemper acknowledges that is not clear whether domestic courts have a role in the implementation of the international responsibility of states because, when domestic courts find that international law has been breached, "*they tend to apply domestic rules of attribution, defenses, and reparation, without considering what international law might have to say on the question of responsibility.*" Nollkaemper argues that domestic courts should apply principles of international responsibility as a practical way to develop international law, which otherwise would be exclusively confined to political processes.

2.2 The Role of Domestic Courts Regarding International Law: General Approaches in the International Legal Scholarship

The traditional schools of thought that aim to explain how international treaties apply in domestic legal orders are dualism and monism in the theory of international law. Although the relations between international law and domestic law have their starting point with the adoption of either the monist or dualist theory, such theoretical constructions have not clarified the existing complex relations in the real world,[19] and scholars have dismissed this debate as fruitless and anachronistic.[20] A minority view, however, noting that the main discredit of monism relies on theoretical inconsistencies and lack of capacity to explain "*a world where different legal orders (domestic, international, supranational and transnational) refuse to subordinate to each other*,"[21] has urged for a reborn of monism based on its ethical dimension.[22] As a result, it is necessary to briefly recall monism and dualism in a general overview as such concepts are continuously referred to in the literature and in domestic litigation, as well as for the sake of historical accuracy.

Dualism defends that domestic law and international law are two autonomous and independent legal orders, not derived from each other, which regulate different social relations.[23] According to the dualist theory, the validity of a domestic legal norm is not conditioned on its harmony with the international legal order; therefore there is no conflict or concurrence between them.[24] In this respect, dualist theorists sustain that international law regulates the relations between states by reciprocal rights and obligations based on the consent of the countries involved, while domestic law defines the rules among individuals in each country solely depending on the will of the country itself. As a result, the international legal order does not have the power to create or modify the rules of the domestic legal system, and vice-versa.[25] The main advocates of this approach were German and Italian theorists from the beginning of the twentieth century.[26]

Monism abolishes the separation of domestic law and international law as two independent realms, and claims the unity of the domestic and international legal order.[27] The supporters of the monist theory however differ in relation to the consequences of the unitary view of domestic and international law, that is, the question of

---

[19] Crawford (2012), p. 50.
[20] Conforti (1993), p. 26.
[21] Galindo (2012), p. 141.
[22] Ibid.
[23] Triepel (1920).
[24] Ibid., pp. 252–253.
[25] Kaczorowska (2010), p. 143.
[26] Ibid. These main theorists are Triepel, Jellinek and Anzilotti.
[27] Ibid.

hierarchy of the norms in case of conflict. One view argues for the primacy of international law over domestic law. This approach sustains that international law is superior to domestic law and because it is a higher law from which the subsequent levels of the domestic legal system are based. Consequently, in case of conflict, international law prevails.[28] An important practical consequence of the monist doctrine is that international treaties automatically become law of the signatory state, and are directly applicable in the national legal regime.[29] Another monist approach asserts that, in case of conflict between international and domestic law, domestic law prevails. This interpretation finds its grounds in the principle of the primacy of the domestic law of each sovereign state, under which international law represents a discretionary choice.

These theories, however historically important, have lost their relevance. Brownlie explains that jurists have escaped the clash between monism and dualism because *"the logical consequences of both theories conflict with the way in which international and national organs behave."*[30] Eeckhout states that the theories of monism and dualism are blunt and abstract concepts that are inadequate and outdated for an appropriate assessment of the relationship between legal systems,[31] while Petersen suggests that, rather than referring to the traditional dichotomy of monism and dualism, the relations between international law and a national legal order should be considered *"through the prism of how its constitutional court approaches the governance issue."*[32] Indeed, monism and dualism are not the most appropriate analytical frameworks to reflect on the relationship between international and domestic law, because such relationship has nowadays so many dimensions that monism and dualism cannot be much helpful anymore.[33]

There are several aspects one can consider to observe a domestic judiciary' approach towards international law. Bianchi highlights that there are various factors that influences the attitude of courts towards international law, and asserts that the attention given to the implementation of international law in domestic systems is not sufficient.[34] In this sense, Cassese suggests that a feasible approach to evaluate to what extent states have domestic mechanisms for implementing international law is to examine a state's national constitution.[35] National constitutions contain the basic principles of state action at the domestic and international levels, and set up the framework of the state functioning.[36] Indeed, national constitutions usually lay

---

[28] The most prominent legal scholars who supported this approach were Hans Kelsen, who based his theory on formalist logical grounds, and Lauterpacht, who sustained this theory based on moral purpose and justice. For more detailed information, *see* Shaw (2003), p. 122.
[29] Kaczorowska (2010), p. 148.
[30] Crawford (2012), p. 34.
[31] Eeckhout (2011), p. 1501.
[32] Petersen (2009).
[33] Eeckhout (2011), p. 1501.
[34] Bianchi (2004), p. 753.
[35] Cassese (1985), p. 343.
[36] Ibid.

down the internal guarantees of compliance of domestic legal orders with international law and are fundamental to the study of the relations between international law and domestic courts.

Starting in the eighteenth century, modern constitutions have established rights and guarantees that have increased the power of the courts at the domestic level and in international relations.[37] In 1803, John Marshall declared in the famous United States case *Marbury v. Madison* that *"it is emphatically the province and duty of the judicial department to say what the law is,"*[38] and established the authority of constitutional interpretations arisen out of judicial adjudications, and the courts' final word in constitutional interpretation.[39] In fact, U.S. Chief Justice Charles Evan Hughes affirmed in a 1907's speech *"we are under a Constitution, but the Constitution is what the judges say it is, and the judiciary is the safeguard of our liberty and property under the Constitution."*[40]

Because international law has gradually permeated domestic law in the last decades, domestic judges are increasingly confronted with international law arguments. In most democratic states, the legal status of international treaties is usually conformed by the national constitutional order. In analyzing the constitutional safeguards of compliance with international treaties, Cassese offers a general classification of the principal models of modern constitutions in relation to the implementation of international law in four groups as follows[41]: constitutions that are silent about the implementation of international treaties; constitutions that prescribe international treaties must be complied with, but do not grant international treaties a higher status than ordinary legislation; constitutions that establish that international treaties prevail over statutes; and constitutions that allow international treaties to modify or revise constitutional provisions. Although there are different levels of constitutional guarantees in relation to the implementation of international treaties, Cassese notes that the majority of countries of the world tend to comply with international agreements, which seems a logical consequence of their willingness to sign treaties and put them into practice.[42] Conversely, states are also willing to reserve the right to not comply with an international obligation in exceptional circumstances, and deal with the international consequences of such behavior such as accusations of international wrongdoing and the consequent international responsibility.[43]

Commentary notes that domestic courts, when faced with international law arguments, are not influenced by whether their country adopts monism or dualism[44]; instead, judges develop their own reasoning independently of this formal

---

[37] Petersmann (2007), p. 3.
[38] *Marbury v. Madison*, 5 U.S. (1 Cranch) 137, 177 (1805).
[39] Dorsen et al. (2003), p. 100.
[40] Hughes (1908), p. 139.
[41] Cassese (1985), p. 394.
[42] Ibid., p. 395.
[43] Ibid., pp. 395–396.
[44] Canor (2009), pp. 877–878.

dichotomy and may have recourse to judicial constructions to interpret, or not, international norms.[45] Therefore, it is necessary to briefly address the conventional ways upon which the debate in international trade law refers to the way domestic courts use international law in domestic litigation, namely the doctrines of direct effect or self-execution, and the doctrine of consistent interpretation.

2.2.1 Ways Domestic Courts Usually Enforce International Law

The application of international law by domestic courts has generated a vast literature about the role of domestic judges with respect to international law.[46] However, international trade law may be considered as a specialization field of which the necessary concepts and basic framework needs to be addressed specifically. Therefore, this section briefly defines in general terms the doctrines that inform the academic discussion on the role of domestic courts regarding international trade law, which are the doctrine of direct effect or self-execution, and the doctrine of consistent interpretation. The broad definitions of these doctrines are developed below, and are a necessary background for the analysis of the case studies that will be pursued in this book.

2.2.1.1 The Doctrine of Direct Effect or the Concept of Self-Execution of International Treaties

The expression "direct effect" of international treaties has been used interchangeably with self-execution[47] in the debate among legal academics in the international trade law field. That is, the doctrine of direct effect in the European Union context is equivalent to the concept of self-execution developed in the United States.[48]

For the purposes of this research, once incorporated, an international treaty has direct effect, or is self-executing, when private parties may directly invoke it before domestic courts. In general terms, the question of self-execution, or direct applicability of an international treaty *"is a matter of whether or not the rule by its content lends itself to be applied directly by the judge."*[49] The question of direct effect, or self-execution, addresses whether a treaty *"provides legal rules capable of*

---

[45] Ibid.
[46] Conforti (1993), Slaughter (1994, 2003, 2004), Benvenisti (1994), Conforti and Francioni (1997), Frowein (1997), Knop (2000), Betlem and Nollkaemper (2003), Posner (2009), Nollkaemper (2011), and Roberts (2011).
[47] Cottier and Schefer (1998), p. 91, explaining that there are some authors that make subtle distinctions between "direct effect" and "self-executing" doctrines.
[48] Brand (1997), p. 559; Cottier (2009), p. 308.
[49] Bianchi (2004), p. 759.

2.2 The Role of Domestic Courts Regarding International Law: General...

enforcement through litigation when private parties contend their rights have been affected, or simply provides rules applicable to sovereign relations."[50] Cottier and Schefer (1998) explain that

> 'direct effect' is used to mean that a private person in a state (or Union, respectively) may base a claim in, and be granted relief from, the domestic courts of that state against another private person or the state on the basis of the state's obligations under an international treaty. Such claims can be made without a transformation of the obligation by national or regional rule-makers. They may equally be made against implementing legislation on grounds that such legislation is not compatible with international law.[51]

In the international trade scholarly debate, "direct effect" is used interchangeably with private "invocability." Defining invocability when "*a determination may need to be made as to who is entitled to invoke or rely on treaty norms,*"[52] Jackson suggests that "invocability" should be distinguished from "direct application." According to him, it would be analytically preferable to separate the concept of "directly applicable or 'statutelike' application" from the concept of "invocability," and exemplifies by stating that "*direct application may primarily be a question of intent of one or more of the treaty parties, while invocability may depend on the precision of the language, definitions of categories of persons (e.g., 'citizen', 'adult male'), or concepts of justiciability or 'political question'.*"[53] According to Jackson, the doctrine of direct effect, or the invocability of WTO rules by private parties before domestic courts, is different from "direct applicability" of international rules. Van den Bossche (2008) explains that

> The issue of direct effect, i.e., the issue of direct invocability, is to be distinguished from the issue of direct applicability, i.e., the issue whether a national act of transformation is necessary for an international agreement to become part of national law. On the latter issue, it should be noted that WTO law is directly applicable in the EC legal order. It became part of EC law without any act of transformation.[54]

As mentioned above, the expression "direct effect" is also considered equivalent to "self-executing treaties." Generally speaking, self-executing treaties are those treaties that do not require prior legislative implementation to be enforced by domestic courts, as opposed to non-self-executing treaties that cannot be enforced by domestic courts without prior enactment of legislation by Congress.[55] The distinction between treaties that are self-executing and those that are non-self-executing has also brought about much scholarly debate and lack of concordance in its nature.[56] Commentary has noted that, to determine whether a treaty is self-

---

[50] Brand (1997), pp. 559–560.
[51] Cottier and Schefer (1998), p. 91.
[52] Jackson (1992), p. 317.
[53] Ibid., p. 318.
[54] Van den Bossche (2008), p. 66, fn 259.
[55] Vázquez (1995), p. 695.
[56] Ibid. (1995), Bradley (2008), Vázquez (2008), Moore (2009), Young (2009), and Golove and Huselbosch (2010).

executing or not, domestic courts may look at the intent of the contracting parties, consider if the treaty provisions are addressed to the judiciary as to confer individuals with rights, or yet examine if the treaty's rule simply urge the signatory states to take action.[57] Other than scholars, judges have also recognized that the doctrine of self-execution has raised much confusion in its application.[58]

The underlying stake on the doctrine of self-execution, just like direct effect, is the allocation of power between the judiciary and the legislative in what concerns the responsibility of implementing an international treaty at the domestic level.[59] This doctrine derives from the reluctance, or prudence, of domestic courts in enforcing international treaties only when there is an equivalent or compatible domestic law.[60] Even though the doctrine of self-execution has its origins and is applied in the United States, other courts of the world have implicitly or explicitly used this distinction regarding international treaties.[61]

2.2.1.2 The Doctrine of Consistent Interpretation with International Treaties

In the academic literature, the principle of direct effect is usually confronted with the alternative technique of the doctrine of consistent interpretation with international treaties. According to the consistent interpretation doctrine, whenever a domestic law has several possible interpretations, judges should apply the interpretation that conforms to international law. The doctrine of consistent interpretation, also known as "indirect effect," does not postulate that international law prevails over domestic law. Instead, it adjusts domestic law in accordance with international law as far as possible.[62] This doctrine is particularly relevant in the area of international law because *"this principle is only marginally influenced by constitutional provisions and can be used even when constitutional law otherwise seems to bar application of international law."*[63] In fact, the doctrine of consistent interpretation is used to interpret a domestic rule in light of international law. For this reason, the doctrine of consistent interpretation is also known as the doctrine of "indirect effect" of international law.[64]

Established in several jurisdictions,[65] like the United States, Switzerland and the European Union, the doctrine of consistent interpretation is recognized as a

---

[57] Brand (1997), p. 562.
[58] Vázquez (1995), p. 695.
[59] Ibid., pp. 695–696.
[60] Dupuy (2007), p. 3. See also Conforti (1993), p. 26; Canor (2009), p. 877.
[61] Conforti (1993), p. 25.
[62] Cottier (2002), p. 110.
[63] Betlem and Nollkaemper (2003), p. 571.
[64] Ibid., p. 572.
[65] Cottier and Schefer (1998), p. 88.

2.2 The Role of Domestic Courts Regarding International Law: General...

principle in trade regulation.[66] The doctrine of consistent interpretation operates in the United States since the U.S. Supreme Court reasoning in *Murray v. The Schooner Charming Betsy*,[67] known as "*Charming Betsy doctrine*." This doctrine states that "*an act of Congress ought never to be construed to violate the law of nations if other possible constructions were available.*"[68]

In Switzerland, the doctrine of consistent interpretation was applied in the case *Frigero v. EVED*,[69] where the Swiss Supreme Court stated that when there is incertitude about the interpretation of a domestic statute, national law must to be construed in conformity with the country's international obligations.[70] As for the European Union, the doctrine of consistent interpretation with international treaties is also present. The European Court of Justice stated that "*the primacy of international agreements concluded by the Community over provisions of secondary Community legislation means that such provision must, so far as possible, be interpreted in a manner that is consistent with those agreements.*"[71]

The doctrines of direct effect or self-execution and consistent interpretation will be used throughout this study regarding their application, or not, in relation to the WTO agreements. This section does not aim to exhaust the topic, but to provide the basic framework of the concrete application of international law by domestic courts.

After laying down the main instruments upon which domestic courts may refer to international law in concrete cases in domestic litigation, this study will now turn to the international legal scholarship. To assess the role of domestic courts in the concrete application (or not) of international trade rules, this study draws on the two general approaches in the international legal scholarship on what should be the proper role of domestic courts in international law, both of which will be further developed in the following sections. In brief, this study draws on the literature review about the role of domestic courts regarding international law to build a picture of currents in international legal scholarship that share the same foundation, although their particularities should not be disregarded.

Accordingly, this study has identified two broad contrasting currents on what should be the most appropriate role of domestic courts regarding international law. The first and broadly accepted current among international legal scholars promotes domestic courts as enforcers of international law. Reflecting the widely accepted viewpoint of international legal scholarship and influencing the dominant behavior of Brazilian and European Union domestic courts, this book will term this current as the traditional perspective on the role of domestic courts in international law, or

---

[66] Cottier (2007), p. 316.
[67] *Murray v. The Schooner Charming Betsy*, 6 U.S. (2 Cranch) 64 (1804).
[68] Ibid.
[69] *Frigero v. EVED*, BGE 94 I 669, 678 (1968).
[70] For more examples of Swiss cases, *see* Cottier and Schefer (1998), p. 268, fn 23.
[71] Case C-61/94, *Commission of the European Communities v. Federal Republic of Germany*, 1996 E.C.R. I-03989, Summary of Judgment, paragraph 3.

"traditionalism," as will be further elaborated in the following section. In the modern legal scholarship, traditionalism has produced three main variations. The primary one is Conforti's doctrine, advocating for the role of domestic legal operators in enforcing international law.[72] Another variation provides a supplementary perspective stating that domestic judges function not only as *"enforcers"* of international law, but also as *"creators"* of international rules based on the doctrine of sources.[73] The last variation is what Knop classifies as transjudicialism,[74] a less explicit alternative to the previews variations, which however argues for the persuasive value of international law before domestic courts, rather than its enforcement, through a decentralized dialogue between domestic judges all over the world.[75]

The second current on the role of domestic courts in international law, and a minority view in the international legal scholarship, considers that enforcement of international law by domestic courts may be counterproductive for the efficacy of international law, grounded on the rational choice theory in the law and economics approach.

A word of explanation is nevertheless needed regarding the description of these two main currents on the general approach on the role of domestic courts in international law. First, to capture the main foundations of these theories, some kind of simplification is necessary, for explanatory purposes. The description gathers the main rationale for each current, although particular views may provide for more distinctions or nuances in each of these two currents. For example, the rational choice theory approach is originated in the United States and, naturally, most of the debate is interconnected with specific domestic provisions that are not central to the debate at the international level. Therefore, specific domestic rules will not be elaborated, because the focus of this section is the normative considerations on the role of domestic courts as perceived in a broad way at the international legal scholarship, without specific reference to provisions that apply to one single jurisdiction only.[76]

The point of interest here is to have a broad panorama of the foundations of these general perspectives in international law to inform the following sections on the more specific debate over the question of direct effect of WTO agreements. The next section will now address the traditional, or conventional, perspective of international legal scholarship on the role of domestic courts regarding international law.

---

[72] Conforti (1993).

[73] Waters (2005) and Roberts (2011).

[74] Knop (2000), p. 520.

[75] Ibid., p. 520.

[76] The United States' position on the WTO agreements will be appraised in Sect. 2.3.2 below, because of its paramount influence in the world trade system.

2.2.2 Traditional International Legal Scholarship on the Role of Domestic Courts Regarding International Law—or Traditionalism

The most accepted and influential viewpoint in the scholarly legal debate propounds that domestic courts should implement international law,[77] and determine how states meet international obligations in their domestic legal orders. Broadly envisioned by Georges Scelle's 1930s theory of "role splitting" (*dédoublement fonctionnel*), this perspective considers that domestic legal actors have an important role in compensating for the deficiencies of the international legal order by providing it with their domestic mechanisms of enforcement.[78] The role splitting theory argues that domestic courts have a double role whereby they work as domestic legal actors operating their functions domestically and they work as international agents to ensure the enforcement of the international legal order that lacks sufficient enforcement mechanisms.[79]

Before elaborating on this point, explanation on the choice of the term "traditionalism" to identify Scelle's theory and its modern developments is necessary. This study chooses to identify the perspective that fosters the role of domestic courts in the application of international law as the "traditional" perspective or, for convenience purposes, "traditionalism," because of this theory's long-established influence in international legal debate and its territorial dominance in the domestic courts object of this research. Envisioned in the beginning of the last century, Scelle's scholarship flourished and the influence of his proposition favoring the role of domestic courts in enforcing international law transcended the boundaries of the international legal debate and is generally dominant in the work of domestic courts in Brazil and the European Union. Indeed, this perspective on the role of domestic courts in enforcing international law predominates not only in the Brazilian judiciary, but also in the European Union courts—being the WTO agreements the most famous exception in the European legal order—topics that will be developed in the subsequent chapters of this research.

More recent international legal scholarship has added to Scelle's foundation by developing and sophisticating the argument that domestic courts should function as international legal actors and are key to the implementation of international law. Among the leading exponents in this perspective, Conforti argues that it is necessary that domestic courts cooperate in the implementation of international law so that it can achieve its full efficacy.[80] In pointing out the disparity between the increasing normative content of international law vis-à-vis the lack of enforcement

---

[77] See Falk (1964), Conforti (1993), Benvenisti (1994), Conforti and Francioni (1997), Francioni (2001), and Nollkaemper (2011).
[78] Dupuy (2007), p. 3.
[79] Cassese (1990), p. 213, fn 5.
[80] Conforti and Francioni (1997), p. 3.

mechanisms at the international level,[81] Conforti suggests that compliance with international law should rely on domestic legal operators, mainly judges, who can navigate through the domestic mechanisms within the internal legal order to guarantee compliance with international law.[82] Conforti argues that domestic systems are responsible for the implementation of international law, through their own state actors. Accordingly, domestic judges are among these state actors, and their rulings can be considered as state practice at international level.[83]

Therefore, according to traditionalism, domestic actors have a function in the application of international law while performing their domestic framework of competence prescribed in their national legal system.[84] Conforti argues that "*only a State's internal system can act effectively to prevent the State from violating international law, and it does so by relying on the implementation mechanisms particular to international law.*"[85]

An important contribution of Conforti's work is that he catalogues the most common judicial doctrines that he considers, from a traditionalist viewpoint, as "barriers" to the full enforcement of international law by domestic courts. Conforti called such judicial doctrines—or limits to judicial enforcement of international rules—as "judicial avoidance techniques."[86] According to Conforti's catalogue, judicial avoidance techniques encompass several judicial doctrines, some of which are pertinent to this study. The first judicial doctrine that limits the enforcement of international rules by domestic courts is the political question doctrine. The political question doctrine has been used by domestic courts to explain that breaches of international law by the executive are non-justiciable. This doctrine propounds that the judiciary arguably does not have judicially manageable standards to decide a political issue and cannot substitute a political decision of another branch of government.[87] The political question doctrine derives from the core principle of separation of powers between the judiciary, the legislative and the executive. As the subsequent chapters will show, the political doctrine has not been used in litigation involving WTO agreements in the cases studied before Brazilian and EU courts, which indicates of the lack of relevance of this doctrine outside the United States. Yet, the principle of separation of powers, which is the basis of the political question doctrine, will be much discussed throughout this study, particularly with reference to the shift of power between the judiciary and the political branches in how a state may discharge its international trade obligation, as the following sections will detail.

---

[81] Conforti (1993), p. 7.
[82] Ibid., p. 9.
[83] Jiménez de Aréchaga and Tanzi (2001), pp. 364–365.
[84] Dupuy (2007), p. 3.
[85] Conforti (1993), p. 10.
[86] Ibid., pp. 13–47.
[87] Ibid., pp. 15–16.

2.2 The Role of Domestic Courts Regarding International Law: General...

Under Conforti's traditionalist view, the doctrine of judicial deference towards the executive branch is also considered a judicial avoidance technique. This is a doctrine that advances judicial self-restraint and claims that, whenever the meaning of a law has more than one interpretation, courts should give deference to a reasonable interpretation given to such law by governmental agencies. In other words, the judicial deference doctrine postulates that it is not for the courts to substitute its judgment for that of the executive—a viewpoint that traditionalism claims to be not beneficial to international law. An example of the application of judicial deference to the executive comes from the United Kingdom, where courts will consider whether or not they have expertise to decide a case, because it is for the legislature to choose one policy among several acceptable ones.[88]

In light of the analysis of the cases studied in this research, it will be clear that the concept that judicial deference to the executive breaches international trade law needs reconsideration. After all, it may be that the executive is actually complying with its international trade obligations and private litigants, unsatisfied with a legitimate trade measure's impact on their businesses, may eventually convince domestic courts to adjudicate the case in a way that will not follow trade rights and obligations, as will be discussed in the Brazilian *Thermo Bottles case* in Sect. 3.3.4. At the very least, it might be prudent to consider that there are cases where the executive is not recalcitrant and actually is complying with international trade rules and judicial deference towards the executive branch may turn out to be compliant with international trade law.

Another judicial avoidance technique in Conforti's perspective occurs when domestic courts, in assessing the self-execution doctrine explained above, end up by deciding that a treaty is non-self-executing. This topic is listed here for the sake of accuracy to Conforti's scholarly classification of what he understands as judicial avoidance techniques. However, the broad view of the concept of self-executing treaties, along with its counterpart of non-self-executing treaties, has already been discussed in Sect. 2.2.1.1 of this study because they are necessary concepts that require definition before entering the debate on the desirability or not of the role of domestic courts in international law. For reviewing Conforti's writings, it suffices to say that the negative response of domestic courts when assessing whether a treaty is self-executing qualifies as an avoidance technique.

Per Conforti's standpoint, the application of last in time rule (*lex posteriori* principle) to international treaties also classifies as a judicial avoidance technique.[89] The application of the *lex posteriori* principle in relation to international treaties entails that the international rule has already been incorporated at the domestic level, and prescribes that a conflicting supervening domestic law revokes the international treaty. The application of this principle implies that there is no superior hierarchy between an international treaties and domestic law, with both having equal status. However, Conforti himself acknowledges that, in reality, few

---

[88] *See* Lord Lester of Herne Hill (2007), p. 73.

[89] Conforti (1993), pp. 42–44.

judicial decisions have invalidated a treaty over revocation by a domestic rule.[90] In fact, most courts seem to manage to give interpretative solutions to uphold an international treaty, such as the principle of *lex posterior generalis non derogat priori speciali*, and the requirement of clear legislative intent to revoke an international rule.[91]

Conforti's classification of "judicial avoidance techniques" has an important expounding value in expressing the traditionalist perspective on the role of domestic courts when putting all these judicial doctrines together, extracted from real domestic cases involving international law.[92] Nevertheless, despite the expounding value of Conforti's classification, this study anticipates that it does not share Conforti's conclusions on the appropriateness of the effective role of domestic judges in relation to international trade law. Conforti's conclusion seems to be mostly based on enthusiastic and aspirational intentions to restrain powerful countries when they do not comply with their international obligations, as these countries are not substantially affected by international pressure when they do commit an internationally wrongful act.

Nevertheless, this study argues that the premises in Conforti's scholarship, although apparently accurate in relation to the behavior of powerful countries regarding international law in general, do not survive further scrutiny in what concerns international trade agreements to guarantee market access and commercial defense rights. State-to-state market access commitments for trade liberalization cannot supersede domestic higher societal values at the domestic level, as the domestic application of international trade law cannot be an end in itself, but a way to promote people's welfare. To be sure, by not complying with its international trade obligations, a state may of course incur into international responsibility and naturally take the consequences at the international level.

However, Conforti's argument seems superficially attractive when one implies that states will more likely comply with international law if they are subject to the jurisdiction of their own domestic courts. Accordingly, Conforti note that "*international law can and, therefore, must be applied domestically through municipal legal systems and the guarantees they provide.*" According to his views, international law would be enforced by domestic judges against recalcitrant governments that violate international law, as a way to address the issue of discretion of countries

---

[90] Ibid., p. 42.

[91] Conforti (1993), pp. 43–44.

[92] There are two "judicial avoidance techniques" per Conforti's classification that will not be addressed in this research. The first one is the "trend to deny that binding resolutions of international organizations are self-executing." Conforti himself recognizes (and heavily criticizes) that the dominant doctrine states that United Nations binding resolutions (like Security Council decisions or WHO regulations) cannot be enforced by domestic legal actors. The second one is the act of state doctrine. Even though the act of state doctrine may prevent courts from analyzing allegations of breach of international law, it refers to adjudication over official acts of another country issued within its own territory. Although very interesting t issues, these two categories are not pertinent to this study, and therefore are not further elaborated in this research.

2.2 The Role of Domestic Courts Regarding International Law: General...

to disregard international obligations based on alleged superior interests.[93] He concludes that *"adequate administration of justice within the States constitutes the only effective check from a legal point of view, to such discretion."*[94] Such perspective on the role of domestic judges vis-à-vis international law has been condensed in the 1993 Resolution of the Institute of International law, with Conforti as the Rapporteur.[95]

This approach seems convincing particularly in relation to international criminal law and human rights law, mainly due to its direct influence on individuals and its need for cooperation by domestic courts. Bianchi sustains that domestic courts should decide on cases involving individual crimes of international law.[96] According to Bianchi, *"[t]heoretical and practical considerations mandate this solution. The very notion of crimes of international law postulates that they constitute an attack against the international community as a whole and, therefore, any state is entitled to punish them."*[97] Regarding international human rights law, even in dualist settings, scholars have noted that international human rights law is indirectly being used in domestic courts through interpretive incorporation techniques.[98]

Although the most widely accepted approach among international scholars, traditionalism has raised a scholarly debate through which key assumptions and conclusions about the actual and proper role of domestic courts are revisited. Knop criticizes the traditional view whereby international law scholars have fostered domestic courts as enforcers of international law as an alternative to the weakness of sanctions at the international level.[99] She argues that the rhetoric of enforcement of international law by domestic courts as an attempt to supplement the lack of an effective enforcement system at the international level, goes beyond a strategic choice and *"reduces these courts to a simple compliance mechanism for international law; in effect, not judges, but police."*[100] She notes that traditionalism assumes that, once domestic judges are bound by international law, they do not have much discretion and leeway in its application, which would make international law the same everywhere,[101] leading to homogenization. Such proposal for homogenization—regardless if it is perceived as *"uniformity, universality or colonization"*[102]—implies that domestic courts, when interpreting international law,

---

[93] Conforti (1993), p. 10.
[94] Ibid.
[95] Institut de Droit International, *L'activité du juge interne et les relations internationales de l'Etat*, Session de Milan (1993).
[96] Bianchi (1999), p. 250.
[97] Ibid.
[98] Lord and Stein (2009), Waters (2007), and McGoldrick (2007).
[99] Knop (2000).
[100] Ibid., p. 503.
[101] Ibid.
[102] Ibid., p. 505.

function as a *"conveyor belt that delivers international law to the people."*[103] Knop observes that the traditional perspective of promoting international law as one disregards that there can be many interpretations from different domestic legal orders with possible complications of meaning in international law.[104] It therefore exposes international law to charges of hegemony due to the inequalities between states on international law-making.[105] Bindingness of international law has no answer to such imperialism charges.[106] From this perspective, Knop argues that domestic judges' interpretation of international law should be approached as a *"problem of translation"*[107] that is *"neither wholly international nor wholly national, but a hybrid that expressed the relationship between them."*[108] She suggests that the attachment international lawyers have to the traditional perspective on the role of domestic courts in the enforcement of international law *"may prevent them from seeing and evaluating what judges purport to do or are actually doing."*[109]

Knop observes that international lawyers perceive domestic courts' decisions as a way to solidify meaning in international law,[110] disregarding the potential for fragmentation of meaning due to the diversity of domestic courts.[111] Knop therefore points out that particularizations of an international rule by domestic courts are usually considered as isolable or biased, under the assumption that the international law is unconnected with its application.[112] In cases where domestic courts' decisions applying international law are contrary to the international consensus, Knop continues, such particularizations are imputed to the court's partiality and are deemed as weighting little or nothing to determine the meaning of the norm.[113] She questions the *"assumption or aspiration"* of straightforward and universalizing domestic courts' interpretation of international law, because it is analytically too simple and *"because it obscures the possibility that domestic interpretation might help to legitimate international law through a process of particularization and justification.*[114]

Aiming at revisiting the traditional analysis, commentators have proposed a new perspective of the role of domestic courts in applying international law based on the doctrine of sources.[115] According to the doctrine of sources, domestic judicial

---

[103] Ibid.
[104] Ibid., p. 517.
[105] Ibid., p. 503.
[106] Ibid., p. 504.
[107] Ibid., p. 506.
[108] Ibid., p. 506.
[109] Ibid., p. 504.
[110] Ibid., p. 517.
[111] Ibid.
[112] Ibid.
[113] Ibid.
[114] Ibid., p. 535.
[115] Knop (2000) and Roberts (2011).

2.2 The Role of Domestic Courts Regarding International Law: General...

decisions can be used as subsidiary means for the determination of rules of law.[116] Building on Knop's call for rethinking domestic courts' interpretation of international law, Roberts calls for attention to the dual role of domestic courts in the doctrine of sources of international law, under which domestic courts' decision can constitute state practice as well as a subsidiary means for interpreting international law. She argues that this dual role of domestic courts as *"law enforcers,"* and as *"law creators"* can be conflicting and complicates what she identifies as the *"comparative international law"* process. In her views, because comparative international law surveys the interpretation of different countries' domestic courts, *"the tendency to emphasize the importance of consistent interpretation* [of the application of international law in different courts] *may have the effect of overplaying the role of domestic courts as law enforcers and undermining their potential as law creators."*[117] In fact, commentary had already remarked that the scholarly debate had focused on the role of domestic courts as norm *"internalizers"* only, and not as norm *"creators,"*[118] indicating domestic courts as if primarily acting as *"passive conduits through which fixed and immutable international law norms become part of domestic law."*[119]

Roberts notes that scholarly literature on comparative international law focuses on the advantages of domestic courts as impartial international law enforcers, and do not discern courts' dual role as law creators.[120] She acknowledges the benefits of comparative international law when courts are looking for common interpretations and, at the same time, valuing productive normative contestation in the courts' role in creating and developing international law.[121] She advocates that, instead of analyzing whether domestic courts' decisions enforce or breach international law, one should focus *"on the way in which domestic courts nationalize substantive international law in diverse ways, resulting in a hybridity that is ripe for comparative analysis."*[122] Roberts further explains that *"hybridization"* of international law with domestic law during the process of nationalizing international law[123] can produce conflicting interpretations of the same international norm by different countries' domestic courts. In this case, then the question turns to which precedent other courts will decide to follow in relation to the content of an international rule.[124] One main criticism Roberts explains is that, like comparative law in general, most references allude to few countries with familiar language or legal systems, which often do not represent all systems and approaches.[125]

---

[116] Statute of the International Court of Justice, 1947 I.C.J. Article 38.
[117] Roberts (2011), p. 91.
[118] Waters (2005), p. 490.
[119] Ibid.
[120] Roberts (2011), p. 61.
[121] Ibid., p. 91.
[122] Ibid., p. 74.
[123] Ibid.
[124] Ibid., p. 70.
[125] Ibid., p. 88.

A less explicit complement to traditionalism and its variations on the role of domestic courts in international law is what Knop classifies as "*transjudicialism*,"[126] found in Ann-Marie Slaughter's scholarship.[127] Slaughter envisions a global community of courts, urging international and domestic judges to acknowledge common principles in their relations based on the phenomena of constitutional cross-fertilization and judicial cooperation in transnational litigation.[128] Slaughter also propounds that the relations between judges include "*not only horizontal relationships between national courts, but also vertical relations between national courts and their supranational counterparts.*"[129] Accordingly, transjudicialism offers an implicit alternative to traditionalism because it emphasizes the persuasiveness of international law—as opposed to its bindingness—whereby domestic courts can act not only as enforcers, but also as disseminators of international law.[130] Under this dissemination function, domestic courts' decisions can circulate horizontally and vertically, carrying weight due to their logic rationale or gaining legitimacy through association with a larger community of courts.[131] Transjudicialism assumes that domestic adjudication of international law is universalizing and gradually expands liberal democracy, by dialogue and engagement of domestic courts from different countries through judicial networks.[132] Transjudicialism therefore focuses on domestic judges, rather than international institutions, as the main instruments to establish an international rule of law.[133]

Slaughter's perspective is based on the concept of judicial dialogue, which has been used to signify different although related forms of communication among courts.[134] With variations in function and degree of reciprocal engagement, judicial dialogue may take place in several forms.[135] Judicial dialogue may represent the direct interaction between the European Court of Justice and the courts of the European Union member states.[136] This notion of judicial dialogue materializes through the use of the reference for a preliminary ruling, a procedure through which national judges of member states of the European Union may refer a question on the interpretation or validity of European law directly to the European Court of

---

[126] Knop (2000), p. 520.
[127] Slaughter (1994, 2003, 2004).
[128] Slaughter (2004).
[129] Slaughter (2003), p. 194.
[130] Knop (2000), p. 520.
[131] Ibid.
[132] Ibid., p. 524.
[133] Mills and Stephens (2005), p. 2.
[134] Slaughter (1994), p. 101.
[135] Ibid.
[136] Baudenbacher (2004), p. 358.

Justice.[137] Out of the European context, that is, in absence of a regional integration process, judicial dialogue among courts from different countries is considered as the way domestic courts are looking to the judgments rendered by other jurisdictions when making decisions in their domestic legal order.[138]

Knop criticizes however transjudicialism because Slaughter takes the United States law as paradigm for liberal democracy, from which others could draw inspiration, without a clear distinction between persuasion and power. In Knop's views, transjudicialism therefore does not provide a solid response to critics of *"politics of imposition."*[139] Instead of persuasiveness, the authority of American judicial decisions may represent *"the unchecked entry of Americanized international law into domestic law."*[140] According to her, transjudicialism does not answer how to distinguish political influence from persuasiveness.

Commentary has also opposed Slaughter's assertion that courts are forming a global legal system for the lack of evidence that, in the case of the United States, domestic courts are actually doing this.[141] Posner observes that the fact that judges are meeting in conferences around the world, and occasionally citing foreign courts' rulings as *obiter dictum* does not lead to the creation of a global legal system or to the enforcement of international law by domestic courts against their own governments.[142]

In general terms, traditionalism and its variations—the doctrine of sources approach and transjudicialism—favor and accept the role of courts in the application and enforcement of international law by domestic courts, although their particularities should not be overlooked. They do differ in how the role of domestic

---

[137] Article 267 of the Treaty on the Functioning of the EU prescribes:

The Court of Justice of the European Union shall have jurisdiction to give preliminary rulings concerning:

(a) the interpretation of the Treaties;
(b) the validity and interpretation of acts of the institutions, bodies, offices or agencies of the Union;

Where such a question is raised before any court or tribunal of a Member State, that court or tribunal may, if it considers that a decision on the question is necessary to enable it to give judgment, request the Court to give a ruling thereon.

Where any such question is raised in a case pending before a court or tribunal of a Member State against whose decisions there is no judicial remedy under national law, that court or tribunal shall bring the matter before the Court.

If such a question is raised in a case pending before a court or tribunal of a Member State with regard to a person in custody, the Court of Justice of the European Union shall act with the minimum of delay.

[138] L'Heureux-Dubé (1998), p. 16.
[139] Knop (2000), pp. 522–524.
[140] Knop (2000), pp. 522–524.
[141] Posner (2009), p. 48.
[142] Ibid.

courts would develop and their effects on international law. Yet, such differences do not prevent these variations from sharing the same foundation, that is, in their views, the necessary and beneficial role of domestic courts in determining how a given country should comply with its international obligations. Even though Roberts distinguished her doctrine of sources' approach from the "*traditional approach*" and from "*transjudicialism,*" this study will use the term "*traditionalism*" more broadly. This study will allude to "*traditionalism*" as the overarching umbrella concept that includes Conforti's domestic legal operators doctrine, Robert's doctrine of sources, and Slaughter's transjudicialism.

Whether or not Slaughter's perspective will develop as she envisioned remains to be seen in the years to come. Yet, the probability that domestic courts would create a community of courts applying international law through persuasive authority would be contingent to their capacity to influence other countries' domestic courts to follow their rulings, which would inevitably reveal former imperial powers relations with their ex-colonies as well as the influence of the major economies of the western world.

The doctrine of sources variation of traditionalism complements Conforti's work with a more updated and realistic reading of actual evidence emanated from the opinions issued by domestic courts when applying and interpreting international law. The major contribution of the doctrine of sources' variation is its description of the resulting hybridity when international law meets domestic law. The doctrine of sources variation, however, is not convincing in advocating that this hybrid result will create international law. For instance, it seems that international trade agreements are more prone to apply norms from their own legal framework, and more constrained to borrow rules that do not reside in their systems. This is certainly true in relation to the WTO, which is often referred to as a "*self-contained regime*." The WTO dispute settlement mechanism has a very tight institutional setup, and their rulings are very closely scrutinized for their rationales,[143] which would make it unrealistic to expect that the Statute of the ICJ can be used in a trade dispute to consider domestic courts decisions as subsidiary means for the determination of international trade law. Add to that the potential controversy over which countries' domestic courts decisions would originate and be considered as creators of international law. Like Slaughter's perspective, the doctrine of sources approach reflects a normative account of the future of international law that also remains to be seen.

---

[143] Abi-Saab (2010), pp. 13–14. Abi-Saab remarks that the WTO's atmosphere is encapsulated in the mantra that "this is a member-driven Organization," and the general feeling that it is the members themselves that take all the final decisions. It [the Appellate Body] had for mandate to interpret and apply very detailed treaty provisions, shoddily drafted, with the injunction that its rulings "cannot add to or diminish the rights and obligations provided in" these treaties; and with the political organs and the member states closely watching (not to say looking over its shoulder) how it interprets and applies them.

2.2.3 Rational Choice Theory in the Law and Economics Approach on the Role of Domestic Courts Regarding International Law

An opposing view to the previous perspective on the role of domestic judges in international law is the rational choice theory in the law and economics approach. The rational choice theory is grounded on the political science approach defined as *"rational-functionalism,"* whereby *"legal rules and institutions are explained as a result of the ex ante choices of rational agents who seek functional benefits ex post."*[144] Consistent with the mainstream approach in international relations,[145] yet a minority view in international law scholarship, rational choice theorists have sustained that the greater judicial involvement in international law would retard, rather than advance, international law, and have argued that the executive has given more support to international law than other branches of government.[146]

One of the leading proponents of the rational choice theory, Posner argues that judges should not have a role in implementing international law, and that *"domestic adjudication that seeks to advance international law can do little to address the global problems that one should care about."*[147] He claims that the costs of judicial implementation of international law at the domestic level are very high, and classifies such costs in two categories, namely, *"ex post"* costs and *"ex ante"* costs.[148] In relation to *"ex post"* costs, Posner explains that courts would need to make policy judgments about what measures the international treaty requires, by either ordering the government to pass implementing legislation, or by creating themselves such implementing regulation.[149] In this case, Posner argues that judges lack expertise to develop policy instruments and, most likely, do a poor job.[150] Regarding *"ex ante"* costs, Posner states that in countries where judges may adjudicate litigation involving international treaties, the executive would either choose to not enter any treaty at all or, most likely, to enter in treaties with weaker obligations than the government desires.[151]

Posner contends the common argument that judges are more impartial and trustworthy than elected policymakers as the former act for the long term, not political short-term goals.[152] He argues that this claim, although superficially attractive, is not solid because elected officials are accountable to their constituencies on the long-term impact of their choices. He further explains that it is not clear whether judges are more farseeing and, in any case, they are less sensitive to public opinion as

---

[144] Raustiala (2006), pp. 423–424.
[145] Ibid., p. 424.
[146] Posner (2009).
[147] Ibid., p. XV.
[148] Ibid., pp. 110–111.
[149] Ibid., p. 110.
[150] Ibid.
[151] Ibid., p. 111.
[152] Ibid., p. 111.

they do not depend on an electorate to achieve and retain office.[153] In addition, Posner asserts that judges are not good at setting policy as they are non-experts.[154] He highlights that the executive is more equipped to comply with international law, and underlines that, most of the times, the question on the implementation of international law is not an issue of *"overt violation versus compliance,"* but a matter of practice and interpretation of states. Posner (2009) explains:

> Here it is important to emphasize that the question is rarely one of overt violation versus compliance; the question is usually one of shades of meaning. International law, especially customary international law, is frequently vague, and it is very much a part of international relations for states to advance their particular interpretations of international law in the hope of persuading other states to agree to them. The preferred interpretation of a particular state will serve its interests more effectively than alternative interpretations. Often, an interpretation of international law or a general willingness to comply with a particular norm depends on what other states are doing – whether they recognize the norm, whether they comply with it, and whether they do so enthusiastically or minimally – so that knowledge about the attitudes and activities of dozens of foreign states is a key element in deciding how to comply with international law. Elected officials, assisted by bureaucratic experts, are in a better position to engage in these inquiries than are judges.[155]

Other accounts of the rational choice framework propound that international treaties should not have direct effect and should be considered as non-self-executing by domestic courts are based the notions of popular sovereignty and democratic self-government.[156] Because international law is frequently ambiguous, states may enter into international treaties and may choose how to translate such commitments into domestic practice.[157] Therefore, rational choice theorists argue that the

---

[153] Ibid., p. 112.

[154] Ibid., p. 112.

[155] Ibid., pp. 112–113.

[156] Yoo (1999a), p. 1961. *See also* Yoo (1999b), p. 2240.

[157] Posner (2009), p. 109. Posner exemplifies the way that countries may discharge their international obligations in domestic practice as follows:

> Suppose the United States and Canada agree to limit cross-border pollution. The United States might discharge this obligation by strengthening tort laws, while Canada issues an administrative order requiring factories to relocate farther from the border. As long as the United States and Canada are concerned only about the pollution, they should be indifferent to how pollution is reduced, in which case there is no reason for the treaty to provide rules governing how pollution is to be controlled.
> In a regime in which international law is incorporated into domestic law, we can imagine domestic courts responding to the cross-border pollution treaty in a number of ways. Suppose that a citizen of Canada (or the United States) sues the United States for failing to adequately implement the treaty through the strengthening of the tort system. A court would no longer have the option of holding, as it would probably do today, that the treaty is non-self-executing, and therefore, the claim fails. Instead, it might order the government to revise the tort system or undertake the revision itself. If, for example, the defect in the tort system is that the damages remedy is too low, the court could order the government to change the remedy or else, through ordinary litigation, change the remedy by holding that the treaty obligation supersedes the tort system.

political branches, and not the judiciary, should control how a country discharges its international obligations.[158] Because there are numerous ways to implement international obligations at the domestic level and, without clear implementing legislation, domestic courts would necessarily make decisions on public policy choices, which is a province of the political branches. Accordingly, as treaties consist of rights and obligations accorded between nations under international law, they should not have effect in domestic litigation brought by individuals, until the legislative passes a treaty's implementing legislation.

Moreover, the proliferation of international treaties, particularly the multilateral ones, has produced a significant change in the *content* of international law.[159] Multilateral treaties have been designed to regulate matters traditionally addressed as domestic affairs, and are usually vague.[160] To consider that international treaties may be enforced by domestic courts without any implementing legislation shifts authority to domestic courts, which will have a lot of discretion in the interpretation of international obligations, instead of leaving the deliberation on how to discharge international obligations in domestic law to the political branches. The new content of international agreements permeating domestic affairs seems to be an even more convincing argument to the requirement of implementing legislation to respect the principle of popular sovereignty and democratic self-government.

In summary, rational choice theorists argue that, at the domestic level, the judiciary is not the most appropriate branch to setting policy in discharging international obligations. Because there are several options on how to implement international law at the domestic level, and to choose which one is suitable reflects more a matter of public policy than of a legal choice.[161] In this line of thought, the political branches, mostly the executive, are more suitable to execute international legal obligations, based on "*ex post*" and "*ex ante*" costs of judicial implementation as well as the notions of popular sovereignty and democratic self-government. Accordingly, the political branches—the executive along with the legislative— are the ones legitimated to decide on how international obligations are complied with, urging for the need of implementing legislation before international obligations can create private rights of action before domestic courts.

From the review of the two contrasting approaches to the role of domestic courts in international law, while the law and economics approach has only recently been applied at the international level,[162] traditionalism is the major and widely accepted

---

[158] Ibid., p. 103. *See* also Yoo (1999a), p. 2220.
[159] Bradley (1998b).
[160] Bradley (1998b), p. 443.
[161] Posner (2009), p. 112.
[162] Dunoff and Trachtman (1999), p. 1.

academic theory on the role of the judges in international law, having Slaughter's perspective acquired many followers. Traditionalism and the rational choice theory propound irreconcilable answers to the role of domestic courts in international law, although nuances of these doctrines may be found. In practice, states have made simultaneous use of both these theoretical perspectives, with traditionalism prevailing and, whenever it does not, the doctrine of consistent interpretation has also been used. As this study will argue, each of these perspectives may not provide a unique answer to all matters regulated by international law. The next section will now develop the idea that the role of domestic courts may vary according to the substantial field of international law.

2.3 The Role of Domestic Courts in International Trade Law: A Substantial Field Approach

The discussion so far has demonstrated that there are two general approaches on the role of domestic courts in international law in the academic debate. Nevertheless, due to fragmentation of international law, commentary has proposed that it would be not accurate to promote uniform enforceability of all international treaties, as well as the effect of all international treaties at the domestic legal orders.[163] Some international treaties should be enforced by domestic courts, while some others should not.[164] Accordingly, this study considers that there is no universal and uniform answer for the role of domestic courts in the enforcement of all international treaties. Either traditionalism or the rational choice theory, each one standing in an isolated way, are not comprehensive, as they may not give definitive and exhaustive responses to the increasing complexity of international law in the last decades.

To define the role of domestic courts regarding international treaties, this study advances the idea that it is important to evaluate both the traditionalist and the rational choice theory approaches, with their values and limits, according to the kind of international treaty involved, instead of a unique and peremptory answer. Consequently, both traditionalism and the rational choice theory may be examined together to provide responses about the proper role of domestic courts in international law on a specific basis according to the substantial field of an international treaty. This specific analysis depends on how normative considerations are involved in the various existing fields, and in connection with certain norms.[165]

In this sense, the most appropriate role of domestic courts should be analyzed based on the substance field of an international treaty, which varies according to the

---

[163] Trachtman (2009), p. 224.
[164] Posner (2007), p. 513.
[165] Trachtman and Moremen (2003), p. 222.

type of treaty involved. International legal assistance, human rights and trade, just to name a few, are fields regulated by various international treaties and are very diverse in their context and their objectives and purposes. All these different fields require distinct analysis on the role of domestic courts to identify specifically the most appropriate approach in each substantial area. It may be that in a certain field, traditionalism can be the most efficient doctrine, while in another area it might not be the case. As a result, an analysis of the substantial field is necessary to draw lines in evaluating which of these doctrines represent the more appropriate role of domestic courts.

Thus, an interpretation according to the treaty's substantial area is necessary to analyze the utility of the role of domestic courts in international law because neither traditionalism nor the rational choice theory can be single out or presumed as the most beneficial one for international law as a whole. International treaties are increasingly demanding changes in domestic legislation and implementation of policies. Furthermore, each international treaty contracted by states has a function and an objective that need to be taken into consideration when determining whether the treaty is capable of creating private parties' rights enforceable before domestic courts. In this sense, there are international treaties where traditionalism is appropriate, whereas other international treaties will be better addressed according to the rational choice theory approach.

In some international treaties, the role of domestic courts in their enforcement is not only desirable, but also advantageous for international law. Commentary has noted that some international treaties usually require enforcement by domestic courts because they are directed to domains that are traditionally subject to the jurisdiction of domestic courts.[166] The purpose and objective of such treaties refer to assisting and cooperating with aspects of domestic public life that require involvement of domestic jurisdiction. Examples of international treaties where the role of domestic courts is paramount for their enforcement are international legal assistance treaties, extradition treaties and judicial cooperation with international criminal tribunals. Here, domestic courts are necessarily involved in assessing whether the conditions of legal assistance, extradition and surrender requests are met. International legal assistance treaties are designed to provide cooperation between domestic judiciaries in criminal and civil investigations that extrapolate the domestic realm, like international drug trafficking and corruption, by addressing international money laundering of illegal proceeds and strengthening assets recovery programs. In what concerns extradition treaties, the reason for the need of courts' intervention is based on the fact that extradition request claims criminal jurisdiction over a person with his or her consequent imprisonment, a restriction in the individual freedom and liberty of a person that requires judicial scrutiny. Similarly, the need for domestic courts' intervention is also important in the case of the Rome Statute of the International Criminal Court (ICC) regarding the surrender of persons, particularly if there are competing surrender requests from

---

[166] Posner (2007), p. 513.

ICC and any other state party for the extradition of the same person for the same conduct.[167]

Conversely, according to this line of thought, some other international treaties, in substantial fields that are not within the traditional domain of the judicial branch, should not be enforced by domestic courts.[168] These international treaties are not meant to be enforceable by domestic courts because they are directed to domains that are traditionally state-centered and regulated under international law, and are not subject to the jurisdiction of domestic courts. An example of these international treaties is the ones that regulate arms control, as the development of military armaments is not a province of domestic courts.[169]

When it comes to drawing lines to establish the most appropriate role of domestic judges in adjudicating matters involving international law, the substantial field of an international treaty is a relevant factor to take into consideration. For instance, in what concern human rights, the function and objective of international human rights treaties is to protect fundamental rights of individuals and therefore are different from other categories of international treaties that cover states' self-interested arrangements on technical cooperation or commercial bargains.[170] International human rights are understood as deriving from the inherent dignity of the individual,[171] and have been incorporated in many national constitutions.[172] In a general way, international human rights treaties are very broadly similar to national constitutional rights in modern constitutions.[173] Commentary has remarked that there is similarity of function and substance between international human rights law and national constitutional law in western liberal states.[174] Because of such similarity, the three most important international human rights treaties are commonly designated as the international bill of rights.[175] As a matter of fact, both international human rights instruments and domestic constitutional law protect the same

---

[167] Article 89 of the Rome Statute provides that the International Criminal Court may request states parties for the arrest and surrender of a person, and Article 90 regulates priority when there are competing surrender requests from the ICC and extraditions requests from other states parties of the same persons.

[168] Posner (2007), p. 513.

[169] Ibid.

[170] Neuman (2003), p. 1869.

[171] Ibid.

[172] Abul-Ethem (2002), p. 762.

[173] Gardbaum (2009), p. 235. The author points out that the major exceptions (of international human rights treaties that are not part of modern constitutions bill of rights) are parts of the International Covenant on Economic, Social and Cultural Rights and the Convention on the Elimination of All Forms of Discrimination against Women.

[174] Ibid., pp. 233–234.

[175] Ibid., p. 236. The international human rights treaties commonly referred to as the "international bill of rights" are the Universal Declaration of Human Rights, the International Covenant on Civil and Political Rights, and the International Covenant on Economic, Social and Cultural Rights.

object, that is, fundamental rights of individuals.[176] Because of this common characteristic, traditionalism might seem appropriate as domestic courts routinely adjudicate on cases related to individual rights based on domestic constitutional law. As result, in principle, the overlaps or potential additional rights that might emerge from international human rights obligations would not, at first glance, interfere with or depart too much from the regular developments of domestic jurisprudence on individual rights. Although commentary has argued for the integration of the human rights dimension into the WTO,[177] such stance reflects a normative perspective, not a description of the system as it is.[178]

In this sense, traditionalism, with its complementary variations on the doctrine of sources and transjudicialism, may have a relevant task in international human rights treaties. To understand how international human rights law seems to expect that domestic courts play a role in the international human rights at the national level, the various treaties that provide for an international court to address human rights violations require as a condition for admissibility of a complaint, the exhaustion of local remedies before domestic courts.[179] Usually referred to as the principle of subsidiarity,[180] the role of domestic courts, and their lack of success in addressing a human rights violation at the national level, is a prior condition to trigger international human rights courts' jurisdiction. In the international human rights scholarship, commentary has also argued that domestic courts also have a relevant responsibility in providing individuals with a forum for publicizing violations and generating attention to international violations at the national and world level.[181] The role of domestic courts in international human rights abuses has indeed remarkably grown in powerful countries' jurisdictions such as the United States during the past few decades, where American domestic courts have admitted claims of extraterritorial international human rights violations committed abroad under the Alien Tort Statute.[182]

However, commentary has also presented negative effects of the influence of international human rights treaties at the domestic level, particularly the enormous amount of power given to the domestic judiciary as opposed to the ordinary processes of representative government.[183] While bringing into question the desirability of the role of domestic courts in applying international human rights treaties at the domestic level, Tomkins (2001) exemplifies skeptical concerns in relation to the United Kingdom's Human Rights Act of 1998, which incorporated in the British

---

[176] Ibid.

[177] Petersmann (2001).

[178] Cass (2005), p. 21.

[179] Hilf (1997), p. 331.

[180] International legal scholarship has provided diverse meanings of subsidiarity in different contexts. For detailed information on the different concepts and usage of subsidiarity, see Carozza (2003).

[181] Bradley (2001), p. 459.

[182] Michaels (2011), p. 171. See also Bradley (2001).

[183] Tomkins (2001) and Fuentes Torrijo (2008).

domestic legal system substantive provisions of the European Convention on Human Rights:

> Why should it be the unrepresentative, overwhelmingly white male upper-middle-class judiciary of the UK's creaking courts who enjoy the emancipation that will come to them with the Human Rights Act? There are two questions here: why give power to these people, and why not give it to others? Even if the reasons for being skeptical about the rights can be overcome and, we decide that we do properly want rights-talk to play a greater role in our polity, why give the job of talking that talk to the judges? After all, what have they done to show either that they deserve, or that they are the appropriate body to enjoy this newfound role of constitutional referee?[184]

Although a fascinating debate, it is beyond the scope of this study to encompass and provide answers to the debate on the role of domestic courts in international human rights or other fields of international law, as this study specifically focuses on international trade agreements. This study is therefore agnostic regarding all areas of international law other than international trade agreements. The point of interest here is to show that, depending on the substantial field, domestic courts may, or may not, play a role in applying and interpreting international treaties.

After considering that the enforceability of international treaties by domestic courts may vary according to the substantial field involved, this section will now assess the specific discussion on the role of domestic courts regarding international trade agreements, from which this research's comparative work will assess the theoretical claims of traditionalism and the rational choice theory on the role of domestic courts. To address the question on the desirability of domestic judicial enforcement of international trade rules, this research selected the WTO agreements as the substantial field of study, particularly the GATT, because they are considered the core rules of the world trade system which comprise 160 member countries.[185] In addition, the WTO agreements are the only international trade agreement that both Brazil and the EU are members and, therefore, provide the necessary course of action for any meaningful comparative work to be pursued between these two jurisdictions.

This study will first address the specific trade scholarly debate on whether WTO agreements should, or not, have direct effect. Then, it will go back to the origins of world trade system as we know today to capture how the GATT was created, and the United States leadership in adopting the rational choice theory approach with regard to WTO agreements.

---

[184] Tomkins (2001), p. 2.
[185] WTO, *Members and Observers* (2014).

2.3.1 The Traditionalism v. Rational Choice Theory Debate on the Role of Domestic Courts Regarding the WTO Agreements

The current section aims to provide an overview of the policy considerations and legal rationales of the pros and cons of the direct effect of WTO Agreements. The direct effect of WTO Agreements, or lack of it, has been extensively discussed in European courts and academic literature. The refusal of the European Court of Justice to give direct effect to WTO Agreements, mostly criticized as displaying more of a political rather than legal rationale, constitutes an exception to the European approach towards international law.[186] However, because the European case is one of the main objects of this research, this study specifically discusses the pertinent case law in the European context and the following academic debate in Chap. 4. Other than the European Union debate, the question on the direct effect of WTO agreements has produced an extensive debate among international trade scholars in relation to major trading countries. The United States took a dualist perspective,[187] as the WTO Agreements are considered non-self-executing treaties and the US Congress enacted implementing legislation that do not give them direct effect. Similarly to the United States, the lack of direct effect of WTO Agreements is also the case for the most important trading nations in the world trade system such as Japan, Canada, South Africa, India,[188] and China.[189]

There are two main lines of thought in the international trade legal scholarship debate on the issue of direct of WTO law, one advocating it, and the other contrary to it. The main proponents of these two schools are Tumlir and Petersmann in favor of direct effect, and John Jackson, against it, with an intermediate position proposed by Eeckhout.[190] The underlying stakes on the policy choice of whether WTO Agreements should, or should not, create private legal rights directly enforceable by domestic courts involves mainly the principle of separation of powers: on one hand, whether judicial review should apply to international trade and, on the other hand, the executive's power to conduct international relations and flexibility to manage international trade fluctuations.

Table 2.1 provides a summary of the policy arguments involving whether direct effect of WTO law is desirable or not.

---

[186] Von Bogdandy (2008), p. 405.

[187] Reed (2007).

[188] Van den Bossche (2008), p. 68.

[189] *See* Qin (2007), stating that there is a consensus that WTO agreements do not have direct effect in Chinese law and require enabling legislation.

[190] Cottier and Schefer (1998), p. 93.

Table 2.1 Synopsis of arguments (Cottier and Schefer, 1998)

Arguments in favor of direct effect	Arguments against direct effect
1. In monist countries, direct effect has a long tradition. It is difficult to see why it should not apply to trade and economic relations	1. Trade regulation is special because it increasingly lends to intrude on domestic legislation more than other areas of international law
2. Direct effect is in the economic interest of each Member. Reciprocity based arguments follow the mercantilist tradition	2. The global system requires overall reciprocity of rights and obligations. Direct effect cannot be granted as long as dualism remains an option for WTO members
3. Direct effect is a powerful tool to render WTO rules effective and efficient	3. Direct effect takes away the option to grant temporary compensation and to prefer sanctions. It reduces the role of WTO as a negotiating forum
4. Most WTO rules are sufficiently precise to be given direct effect, the concept does not exclude denying the direct effect of programmatic rules	4. The problem lies with exceptions and safeguards that are too flexible to be considered justiciable. Application of WTO rules by multiple national judges will result in different, possibly inconsistent interpretations
5. The WTO offers a system of principles and exceptions which is capable of balancing diverging interests	5. The WTO agreements are not comparable to a constitution. They are based toward freer trade and do not allow for other policy goals to be considered on an equal footing
6. Direct effect stimulates effective negotiations because inadequate rules need to be changed on the international level	6. It is necessary to keep national law to remedy the deficiencies of WTO law which often cannot or will not be changed by members
7. Direct effect reinforces the global trading system as it grants rights to private actors to balance protectionist producer interests predominant in national regulations	7. Private actors should be limited to rights granted by national law, since otherwise they upset government foreign policy goals or restrict the effective pursuance of such goals
8. Direct effect stimulates legal education. WTO law will trickle into legal thinking and daily practice	8. The lawyers and judges are not sufficiently familiar with WTO rules to work with them effectively
9. Direct effect reduces the power of hegemons	9. If direct effect is mandatory, hegemons will refuse to ratify international rules in the first place. This will damage the international system more than would ratification without direct effect
10. Direct effect reinforces the role of courts of law. It is a check on protectionist interests and balances the system as above	10. Direct effect in international trade regulations fundamentally alters the balance of powers set out in national constitutions
11. Direct effect is not absolute. It does not exclude primacy of constitutional law, the later-in-time rule or other exceptions to primacy of international law. Direct effect does not exclude nuanced judicial approaches and doctrines of judicial restraint	11. Given the increasing degree of international trade regulation, courts will take on the duties of legislators and side-step the democratic rule-making process
12. Courts of law have learned to deal with domestic economic regulation. They will also learn to do so with international regulation	12. Foreign policy, including trade policy and international economic regulation is not a proper province of courts of law

(continued)

Table 2.1 (continued)

Arguments in favor of direct effect	Arguments against direct effect
13. The WTO rules are ratified upon approval by parliament negotiation by elected and accountable government. They are not inherently different from domestic rules	13. Democratic representation is largely absent in the negotiating process. Fast track and package deal approaches to procedures further limit the impact of elected representation
14. The WTO rules are negotiated by consensus, so smaller countries can block unacceptable propositions	14. In reality, the trade game is dominated by a small number of nations
15. The power and influence of lobbies is no different in the process of rule-making domestically or internationally	15. The WTO rules are being shaped by a few elite interests.
16. With increasing awareness of WTO law, the protection of trade rules will become available to individuals who are unable to make their voices heard internationally	16. Direct effect of WTO rules will only benefit the already-privileged large corporations, because individuals will not have the resources to bring arguments before the court based on sophisticated WTO law
17. Courts have judicial tools to ensure that only legitimate claims reach trial. These claims ought to be decided by a court to further social harmony, regardless of the costs to the judicial system	17. Allowing direct effect of WTO rules would cause a flood of individual claims to be filed (at least for some harassment purposes), further swamping the dockets of national and local courts

This table created by Cottier and Schefer (1998) summarizes the arguments in favor and against direct effect, with no particular order of presentation

The pros and cons of direct effect described above will serve as a benchmark against which the cases studied in this book will be assessed. To ponder the values and limits of both the traditional and rational choice approach to the role of domestic courts in international law, comparative studies becomes an important tool to describe the ways that such doctrines have actually operated in real cases involving WTO agreements at the domestic level, and appraise the empirical results.

As the alternative to direct effect, the doctrine of consistent interpretation may in principle be applied regarding the WTO agreements. To illustrate, in the case of the United States, where the doctrine of consistent interpretation was first created,[191] the application to WTO agreements is very complex and highly controversial. As will be further developed in the following section, the US Congress established that WTO agreements are non-self-executing,[192] which would in principle allow for the application of the doctrine of consistent interpretation. Nevertheless, it is not clear whether the doctrine of consistent interpretation apply in relation to WTO Agreements in the United States, as the implementing legislation prohibits private action based on allegations of breach of WTO Agreements, and prescribes that WTO

---

[191] *See* Jackson (1997) and Matsushita et al. (2006).

[192] Jackson (2006), p. 125.

agreements have no domestic effect at all in case they are not consistent with U.S. law. In *Suramerica de Aleaciones Laminadas, C.A. v. United States*,[193] the U.S. Federal Circuit Court of Appeals stated:

> [E]ven if we were convinced that Commerce's interpretation conflicts with the GATT, which we are not, the GATT is not controlling. While we acknowledge Congress's interest in complying with U.S. responsibilities under the GATT, we are bound not by what we think Congress should or perhaps wanted to do, but by what Congress in fact did. The GATT does not trump domestic legislation; if the statutory provisions at issue here are inconsistent with the GATT, it is a matter for Congress and not this court to decide and remedy.[194]

Indeed, commentary sustains that WTO agreements are not sufficient to overturn a governmental agency's statutory interpretation because the intent of Congress is crucial (US law prevail in conflict) in highly regulated areas.[195] Another scholar argues that, with proliferation of international treaties and their increasing influence in domestic affairs, the consistent interpretation doctrine becomes more important as a judicial canon in interpreting international law based on the separation of powers principle, which prevents domestic courts from encroaching on prerogatives of the other branches of government.[196] Such approaches seem to be the predominant attitude of US courts in relation to international trade obligations when interpreting US statutory law.[197]

However, an opinion asserts that the doctrine of consistent interpretation is very relevant to interpret WTO rules, and states that "*GATT agreements are international obligations, and absent express Congressional language to the contrary, statutes should not be interpreted to conflict with international obligations.*"[198] Cottier highlights that the doctrine of consistent interpretation is an important first step for sensitization of WTO rules in the legal community[199] and that it can be an effective tool in the way domestic courts use international trade law.

After drawing attention to the pros and cons of direct effect, and the potential use of consistent interpretation in relation to the WTO agreements, these doctrines will inform the empirical studies on the Brazilian and EU courts' cases in a comparative way, and will be the benchmarks against which such cases will be investigated. After setting out the specific description of the debate between traditionalism and the rational choice theory on the role of domestic courts in the particular case of the WTO agreements, this section will now explore the origins of the GATT to

---

[193] *Suramerica de Aleaciones Laminadas, C.A. v. United States*, 966 F.2d 660 (Fed. Cir. 1992). This statement was also quoted in a more recent decision *Cummins Inc. v. United States* 454 F.3d 1361, 1366 (Fed. Cir. 2006).

[194] *Suramerica de Aleaciones Laminadas, C.A. v. United States*, 966 F.2d 660, 667–668 (Fed. Cir. 1992).

[195] Restani and Bloom (2000), p. 1542.

[196] Bradley (1998a), p. 536. For a critique of this position, *see* Harvard Law Review (2008).

[197] Brennan (2003), p. 320. *See* also Reed (2007).

[198] *Federal Mogul Corp. v. United States*, 63 F.3d 1572, 1581 (Fed. Cir. 1995).

[199] Cottier and Schefer (1998), pp. 90–91.

understand the function and objective of the world trade system as envisioned by its idealizers. It will expound the United States leadership in the adoption of the rational choice theory approach regarding the WTO agreements as evidence of the principle of self-government that informs the world trade system.

2.3.2 The American Creation of the GATT and Its Leadership in the Adoption of the Rational Choice Theory in International Trade Agreements

To inform the discussion on the role of domestic courts regarding international trade agreements, it is necessary to understand the origins of the GATT in the 1940s, because the GATT is the basis of what we know today as the world trade system. The original intent of the contracting parties of the GATT is relevant for the analysis of the role of domestic courts because it provides evidence on the object and purpose of international trade rules contained in the GATT and in the subsequent WTO agreements.

The GATT was designed by the United States in a bilateral negotiation with the United Kingdom after the World War II. At that time, the United States conditioned American financial assistance to the United Kingdom in exchange of an agreement on trade policy, aiming at eliminating imperial trade preferences the United Kingdom had with its former colonies.[200] With a small team of Anglo-American economic officials responsible for negotiations, the United States proposed the draft agreement after the most important divergences between the two countries were appeased.[201] After that, negotiations proceeded in various stages to include

---

[200] Irwin et al. (2008):

Imperial preferences continued to be the most contentious issue and the United States handled it very clumsily. Clayton repeatedly tied American financial assistance to the elimination of imperial preferences, implicitly threatening that U.S. aid would not be forthcoming if Britain insisted on keeping preferences. Congress, he insisted, would not approve a loan unless Britain promised the complete abolition of discriminatory preferences. However, State Department civil servants took a softer line than Clayton, assuring their counterparts that there was no quid pro quo between preferences and financial assistance. Indeed, the U.S. Embassy in London warned the State Department that a heavy-handed American demand for an immediate and complete abolition of preferences as a condition for a loan would create a severe backlash in the United Kingdom. Whereas the United States thought the linkage was simply a form of conditionality, the United Kingdom viewed it as blackmail, as exploiting the country's weak economic position for America's advantage. However, Clayton and his staff were sending different signals to the British, and hence the U.S. message was somewhat contradictory: on the one hand, they wanted the two issues discussed in the same forum, but they did not insist that one depended upon the other.

[201] Irwin et al. (2008).

other "nuclear countries"[202] that were important trading partners, to be concluded at the United Nations Conference on Trade and Employment in 1947 in Havana. It can be safely assumed that the original intent of the GATT was to promote international economic cooperation and to provide government-to-government commitments in market access, which does not create corporations' rights to challenge governmental public policy based on such agreements. The original intent of the creation of the GATT also reverberated over time reaching even the creation of the WTO. During the Uruguay Round, the signatory parties never agreed to give direct effect to WTO rules, and the idea of giving private rights of action at the domestic level was promptly dismissed at that occasion. In making a statement as a matter of fact, a WTO panel asserted that "*[n]either the GATT nor the WTO has so far been interpreted by GATT/WTO institutions as a legal order producing direct effect. Following this approach, the GATT/WTO did not create a new legal order the subjects of which comprise both contracting parties or Members and their nationals.*"[203] It is not surprising therefore that the major economies of the world trade system do not give direct effect to WTO agreements.

Here, the point of interest is to capture the United States leadership in creating the world trade system[204] and the original intent of the GATT members, along with the corresponding United States' stance on the role of domestic courts. The GATT and the supervening WTO agreements undertake the rational choice theory approach in the role of domestic courts, because it deals with state-to-state commitments at the international level with no intention to create individual rights or private rights of action. As the proponent of the international trade system, and responsible for drafting the GATT, the United States affirmed the non-self-executing character of WTO agreements before American domestic courts through Congress' legislation. Jackson explains that U.S. Congress has made clear in several occasions that WTO agreements are not self-executing.[205] The U.S. Congress regulated the relationship of the WTO agreements to the United States law through the Uruguay Round Agreements Act (URAA), whereby the WTO agreements have no direct effect in U.S. law.[206] Besides stating that domestic law prevails over

---

[202] Ibid., p. 96, pointing out that the first time a small group of countries—or "nuclear countries"—were invited to participate in the discussion of the international trade system was in the UN Preparatory Committee for the International Conference on Trade and Employment in London, 1946 (the London Preparatory Meeting).

[203] WTO, *United States—Sections 301–310 of the Trade Act of 1974*, WT/DS152/R, adopted 27 January 2000.

[204] For a detailed account of the creation of the GATT, *see* Irwin et al. (2008).

[205] Jackson (2006), p. 125.

[206] Uruguay Round Agreements Act (URAA), Section 102(a)(1), 19 U.S.C. § 3512(a)(1) reads:
Relationship of agreements to United States law
(1) United States law to prevail in conflict.
No provision of any of the Uruguay Round Agreements, nor the application of any such provision to any person or circumstance, that is inconsistent with any law of the United States shall have effect.

2.3 The Role of Domestic Courts in International Trade Law: A Substantial...

conflicting provisions of WTO agreements, the URAA does not allow that private parties seek remedies grounded on alleged violations of the WTO agreements.[207] Only Congress or the Executive may withdraw or modify the measure that conflicts with WTO agreements or rulings. In addition, Vagts clarifies that *[b]ecause WTO rulings lack direct effect as domestic law, they do not 'bind' domestic courts in the way, for example, that United States Supreme Court rulings bind state courts in the American national system.*[208]

The United States conceptualization of the world trade system and its leadership in the adoption of the rational choice theory in the role of domestic courts regarding international trade agreements seem to explain the ascendancy of WTO members' practice in adopting the same approach. As earlier mentioned, other than the United States, major WTO members do not give direct effect to WTO law, including the European Union, Canada, Japan, China, South Africa and India.[209] Conversely, Latin American countries, such as Brazil, Mexico and Argentina, give direct effect to WTO agreements.

However, the amount of WTO members that do not consider domestic courts as a proper venue to adjudicate cases based on WTO rules is so numerous that the Latin American predominance of traditionalism seems to be largely ignored.[210] The Latin American exceptionalism on the role of domestic courts regarding WTO agreements is not connected with other WTO members' perspective on the original intent of the creation of the international trade system. The rational choice theory approach is so widespread in the WTO members' practice to the point that, as Bronckers remarked, the WTO secretariat insisted that Latin American WTO members passed implementing legislation for antidumping regardless of the fact that these members had adopted traditionalism.[211] Accordingly, commentary has argued that the WTO negotiators implicitly considered that WTO agreements do not have direct effect.[212]

Therefore, this contrasting perspective between Latin American countries and the major economies of the world raises a lot of questions. Commentary has drawn attention to the Latin American countries' position and questioned why weaker countries tie their hands to international obligations more easily than powerful economies,[213] a phenomenon that may partially explain traditionalism in Latin America, as will be later discussed. The lack of WTO direct effect in rich economies as opposed to direct effect in weaker economies indicates that there exists an element of power regarding the adoption of direct effect of WTO law by Latin American countries. At the same time, Latin American legal culture seems to bear a

---

[207] Grimmet (2011).
[208] Vagts et al. (2003), p. 130.
[209] Van den Bossche (2008), p. 68.
[210] *See* Hilf (1997), p. 337.
[211] Kuijper and Bronckers (2005), p. 1315.
[212] Ibid.
[213] Guzman and Pauwelyn (2009).

great responsibility for the adoption of traditionalism in relation to WTO agreements. All these questions and the possible reasons why Latin American countries adopted traditionalism will be developed below in Chap. 5.

Understanding the world trade system through the GATT's conception by its idealizers provides evidence on the function and objective of WTO agreements. Similarly, the United States leadership in adopting the rational choice theory regarding WTO agreements gathered the majority of the world trading players, which reveals states' intent in the sense that the principle of WTO members' self-government informs the world trade system.

The next section will develop this study's argument that, despite the enthusiasm of traditionalism in relation to the application of international trade agreements at the domestic level, the rational choice theory approach seems to be the most appropriate model because it conforms with the function and objective of trade rules to concede government-to-government market access and respects the principle of popular sovereignty and democratic self-government in choosing how international trade obligations are discharged.

2.4 An Assessment on the Role of Domestic Courts in International Trade Agreements

This section now develops this study's argument that, in relation to international trade agreements, while traditionalism apparently contributes to an immediate application of international trade agreements at the domestic level, it is normatively undesirable. This study argues that there are two main reasons why giving private rights of action based on WTO rules at the domestic level would not be appropriate regarding international trade agreements, which should be considered as not having self-executing character or direct effect. The first reason why the rational choice theory approach seems to be more suitable in relation to the role of domestic courts regarding international trade agreements is grounded on the function and objective of international trade agreements, as it maintains the balance of rights and obligations accorded under the WTO agreements, and allows the prevalence of higher societal values over businesses' interests. The second reason is based on the principle of popular sovereignty and democratic self-government in choosing how international trade obligations are discharged domestically. These two arguments are developed below.

2.4.1 The Function and Objective of International Trade Agreements

The first reason why the rational choice theory perspective on the role of domestic courts regarding international trade law seems compelling is based on the function and objective of international trade agreements. To understand why traditionalism may not be the most appropriate approach, one needs to consider Sykes' explanation on the function and objective of international trade agreements, indicating that governments are the most suitable and efficient branch to negotiate and solve disputes on international trade issues. In Sykes' description, international obligations arisen from international trade agreements are best interpreted as a government-to-government commitment, than government to corporations.[214] From a political economy view, Sykes explains why private parties are not allowed to have standing at the WTO level considering the function and objective of international trade agreements. Sykes (2005) notes:

> the function of international agreements is to make credible government-to-government commitments regarding market access and thereby to raise mutual political welfare relative to an environment without bilateral or multilateral cooperation. For the enforcement of such agreements, it can suffice to provide standing and remedy only to governments, and indeed a private right of action for damages may prove politically counterproductive for reasons that I will explain. Governments can then achieve mutual gains by reserving standing to themselves and becoming political filters for enforcement action, especially when ex post legislative action to reverse problematic adjudicative decisions is infeasible.[215]

Although Sykes's commentary addressed standing in trade disputes at the WTO level, his reasoning and arguments can also be extended to the discussion in cases involving international trade agreements at the domestic level. Sykes's rationale can be projected to the domestic plane because it focuses on the critical difference between international trade agreements and other international treaties, a distinction also valid when trade agreements are incorporated at the domestic level. Sykes explains that *"importing nations do no enter trade agreements out of a desire to lower the price of imports. They view any reduction in their own trade barriers, and the attendant price of their imports as a concession that is attractive only in return for concessions by trading partners."*[216] Indeed, trade agreements consist of reciprocal trade concessions towards trade promotion and, for this distinguished nature, private standing in trade disputes is not attractive and is potentially counterproductive.

At the WTO level, Sykes notes that *"[o]fficials concerned with their political welfare must worry that precedents established in an enforcement action brought on behalf of their exporters will come back to haunt them in an action brought*

---

[214] Sykes (2005), p. 631.

[215] Ibid., p. 633.

[216] Ibid., p. 646.

against them by foreign exporters."[217] As a result, the only way governments can make sure that their exporters do not develop legal theories that lack political value is by retaining control over the legal arguments in trade-related cases.[218] Hence, it is theoretically preferable that members of an international trade agreement should not grant private rights of action especially when such trade agreement creates a mechanism of dispute resolution.

The signatory parties of an international trade agreement create rules to achieve mutual gains and provide state-to-state commitments in the international trade area that do not involve private parties' rights, and to solve any potential conflict, there exists the international dispute settlement mechanism. That being so, whenever member states decide themselves to create trade rights and obligations for private individuals in a given international trade agreement, such intention may be given effect through implementing legislation at their domestic legal orders through their own ordinary processes of representative government.

However, there was never the intention to create rights and obligations to private individuals in relation to the WTO agreements. WTO members did not agree to grant private rights of action at the international or domestic level. The relationship of international law and national law was rarely discussed during the Uruguay round and, when this relationship was addressed, the question was swiftly dismissed.[219] Commentary understood this silence as leaving the member countries to decide individually how WTO obligations would be discharged in their domestic system.[220] However, Kuijper and Bronckers stated that "*the treaty drafters implicitly considered the WTO Agreement and its annexes as non-self-executing.*"[221]

Therefore, it can be objectively perceived that the common intent and the subsequent practice of the signatory parties during the Uruguay round was not to provide WTO agreements with direct effect, while not impeding member states that may wish to do so to grant this effect in their internal legal system. After all, it is a principle of international law that states are free to decide how to implement international obligations in their domestic legal orders, but clearly intentions to give direct effect to WTO agreements was never seriously considered. As a result, in principle, WTO member states could choose whether or not to implement traditionalism or the rational choice theory approach, that is, whether to allow, or not, the private invocability of WTO rules in their domestic legal order as a basis for litigation before domestic courts.

However, corroborating the common intent expressed during the Uruguay round, the overwhelmingly majority of WTO members have decided not to allow

---

[217] Ibid., p. 651.
[218] Ibid.
[219] Cottier and Schefer (1998), pp. 83–84.
[220] Ibid.
[221] Kuijper and Bronckers (2005), p. 1315.

2.4 An Assessment on the Role of Domestic Courts in International Trade Agreements

the private invocability of WTO rules in their domestic legal systems,[222] which indicates that Bronckers' perspective is a closer assessment. The number of countries not considering domestic courts as a proper venue to adjudicate cases based on WTO rules is so significant and taken for granted as a unanimity that even lead a prominent international scholar to state, in the early years of WTO, that *"[t]here seems to be virtually no national legal system which would consider GATT rules to be directly applicable in domestic law."*[223]

Moreover, considering that self-government informs the world trade system, economic interests for profits and market access may not supersede higher values in the way societies base their identity and unity. The WTO Understanding on Rules and Procedures Governing the Settlement of Disputes (DSU) prescribes that, in case measures inconsistent with WTO rules are not withdrawn, there is the possibility of mutually acceptable solution and suspension of concessions.[224] Accordingly, if a WTO Member State, under its self-government discretion, decides not to withdrawn the inconsistent measure shall suffer the suspension of concessions while keeping its higher societal values intact. This is what happened in the *EC-Hormones* case,[225] in which the European Union ban on the imports of meat from cattle treated with hormones for growth was found inconsistent with the WTO rules. Such import prohibition was maintained—attributed to the European view that such products would increase health risk for consumers—while a mutually acceptable solution was found with the complaining party, the United States. To be sure, there are serious issues deriving from the current system of compensation and

---

[222] For a survey of arguments for and against direct effect of WTO agreements, *see* Table 2.1 at Sect. 2.3.1 above.

[223] Hilf (1997), p. 337.

[224] DSU, Article 22 reads:

Article 22 – Compensation and the Suspension of Concessions

1. Compensation and the suspension of concessions or other obligations are temporary measures available in the event that the recommendations and rulings are not implemented within a reasonable period of time. However, neither compensation nor the suspension of concessions or other obligations is preferred to full implementation of a recommendation to bring a measure into conformity with the covered agreements. Compensation is voluntary and, if granted, shall be consistent with the covered agreements.
2. If the Member concerned fails to bring the measure found to be inconsistent with a covered agreement into compliance therewith or otherwise comply with the recommendations and rulings within the reasonable period of time determined pursuant to paragraph 3 of Article 21, such Member shall, if so requested, and no later than the expiry of the reasonable period of time, enter into negotiations with any party having invoked the dispute settlement procedures, with a view to developing mutually acceptable compensation. If no satisfactory compensation has been agreed within 20 days after the date of expiry of the reasonable period of time, any party having invoked the dispute settlement procedures may request authorization from the DSB to suspend the application to the Member concerned of concessions or other obligations under the covered agreements.

[225] *European Communities—Measures Concerning Meat and Meat Products (Hormones)*, WT/DS26/AB/R, adopted 13 February 1998.

retaliation in the DSU system, particularly when weaker economies face richer violating Members. The DSU remedies of suspension of concessions may prove ineffective as it has been the case for Antigua and Barbuda against the United States in the *US—Gambling*[226] dispute. Such issues are nevertheless under discussion at the DSU review for the improvement of the system.[227]

To sum up, WTO members have predominantly not granted the direct effect of WTO, evidenced by the common intent of the parties during the negotiations, as well as by the subsequent state practice regarding the interpretation of WTO agreements, with the apparent exception of Latin American countries. After arguing that Sykes' description of the function and objective of international trade agreements may be projected to the domestic level, the next section will develop the second reason why traditionalism regarding international trade agreements is not appropriate, as such agreements are not meant to regulate the activities of private parties and individuals.

2.4.2 The Principle of Popular Sovereignty and Democratic Self-Government

Proponents of traditionalism claim that, to advance international law, domestic courts should circumvent the local political branches to choose public policies based on international agreements. This book argues that, instead of fostering international law, the direct application of international trade agreements by domestic courts reinforces the perception that international law is not connected with popular sovereignty and self-government, because domestic courts generally are not elected by direct vote and are not politically accountable for their decisions.

The association of a non-democratic power like the judiciary with unaccountable international law makers to circumvent the domestic political branches and choose public policies reflects a subversion of people's power. Traditionalism, as a result, increases the lack of connection between international law and the domestic population and therefore builds against the trust of local population in international law. In the long run, although with the most laudable intentions, traditionalism may do more harm than good to the development of international law, because accountability of domestic public policies is a fundamental expression of popular sovereignty and democratic self-government. When domestic courts impose public policies through the interpretation of international rules without the participation of the local representatives, it will increase the gap between the domestic popula-

---

[226] *United States—Measures Affecting the Cross-Border Supply of Gambling and Betting Services*, WT/DS285.

[227] For an overall account of these negotiations, *see* Evans and Tarso Pereira (2005).

2.4 An Assessment on the Role of Domestic Courts in International Trade Agreements

tion and political accountability[228] in matters that directly affects the domestic arena.

When domestic legislators and the executive discuss the actual implementation of international trade obligations at the domestic level, international law is internalized in a way that accountability is present through an open political process. As a result, the population participates in the implementation of international rules through their accountable representatives and, consequently, the result is that the efficacy of international trade agreements becomes stronger in the long term. If the political branches discuss and decide the implementation of international trade obligations within the domestic legal order, international law will become compelling and persuasive, and will most likely have efficacy and success in its effectiveness. Creating a stronger relationship between a country's population and international trade obligations through the regular domestic legislative processes makes international law more legitimate and certainly more respected with lasting effects at the domestic level. In this sense, both international law and democracy would be strengthened if domestic courts assume that international treaties are not judicially enforceable in the domestic legal order unless and until implementing legislation is passed through the ordinary domestic processes of representative government.

Critics of the rational choice theory perspective argue that popular sovereignty and self-government are expressed in the incorporation process of international treaties by means of the legislative approval of an international treaty submitted by the executive. Indeed, the legislative participation after the executive has negotiated an international agreement is a very important step to legitimate the entry into international legal commitments. Nevertheless, the process of entering into an international treaty, through the executive's negotiation and the subsequent legislative's approval, does not supplant the need for implementing legislation before domestic courts may adjudicate on domestic legislation and public policies based on such international rules. The legislative's approval of international treaties is much looser than the legislative processes of domestic legislation, as it involves commitments and benefits that derive from the country's entry in an international agreement that goes beyond the domestic legislative's capability of altering an international negotiation.

Therefore, when the content of an international agreement requires changes in domestic legislation, the approval of an international treaty by the legislative should not suffice to render an international rule self-executing at the domestic level. The implementation of such an obligation is to be decided by the domestic legislative processes, as international law grants signatory parties the freedom to decide how to implement such obligations, not domestic courts. The implementation of an international obligation, undertaken at the national level, requires the participation of the political branches, not domestic courts.

---

[228] Bradley (1998a).

Domestic courts' application of international trade agreements that directly changes domestic law may cause difficulties for international trade in the long term, such as increasing the executive's resistance to enter into new international agreements, or even prompting the denunciation of a treaty in force. To understand why domestic courts should refrain from interpreting international trade rules to change domestic law without the implementing legislation by the political branches, one needs to look at the actual consequences of judicial implementation of international obligations for the future of international law. Judicial implementation of international rules without domestic political accountability can indeed produce *ex post* costs that undermine the willingness of the executive to enter in new international treaties and even denounce certain treaties.

To illustrate the point that the domestic courts' decisions may hamper the development of international law by prompting the executive to denounce an international treaty in force, consider the impact of judicial implementation of the Termination of Employment Convention of the International Labor Organization (ILO Convention n. 158) in the Brazilian domestic legal system. ILO Convention n. 158 provides for international standards on termination of employment at the initiative of the employer and states that the employment of a worker may not be terminated unless there is a valid reason. Incorporated in the Brazilian domestic legal system in April 1996, the text of the ILO Convention n. 158 did not provide for direct effect of its content and established that its provisions shall be given effect by laws or regulations at the national level.[229] Therefore, the ILO Convention n. 158 provided a margin of maneuver in its implementation by domestic legislation. At the time Brazil ratified the ILO Convention n. 158, the national legislation permitted dismissal without just cause, but required that the employee received the severance money and compensation.[230] At that time, some Brazilian labor courts interpreted the ILO Convention n. 158 as self-executing, and ordered the reinstatement of workers who were fired without a justified explanation,[231] based on Article

---

[229] ILO Convention concerning Termination of Employment at the Initiative of the Employer, Art. 1:

Article 1. The provisions of this Convention shall, in so far as they are not otherwise made effective by means of collective agreements, arbitration awards or court decisions or in such other manner as may be consistent with national practice, be given effect by laws or regulations.

[230] According to Brazilian legislation, an employer is required to monthly pay 8 % of the employee's salary to a severance bank account in the name of the employee. In case of termination without good cause by the employer, the employee has the right to claim the balance of such payments with an additional compensation of 40 % of the accumulated balance since the beginning of the employment.

[231] JT/MG, Processo n. 428/96, Patos de Minas, Juíza Alice Lopes Amaral, 29.4.1996; JT/MG, Processo n. 490/96, Patos de Minas, Juíza Alice Lopes Amaral, 15.5.1996; JT/MG, Processo n. 399/96, João Montalverde, Juíza Vânia Maria Arruda, 6.5.1996; JT/MG, Processo n. 373/96, João Montalverde, Juíza Vânia Maria Arruda, 9.5.1996; JT/RS, Processo n. 410/96, Alegrete, Juiz José Renato Stangler, 22.5.1996; JT/RS, Processo n. 697/96, Canoas, Juíza Maria Joaquina Carbunk Schissi, 4.6.1996.

2.4 An Assessment on the Role of Domestic Courts in International Trade Agreements

4 and 10 of the ILO Convention n. 158.[232] More importantly, the Labor Appellate Court of São Paulo—with jurisdiction over the most industrialized state of Brazil, with more than 40 million inhabitants—declared that ILO Convention n. 158 was self-executing.[233] The constitutionality of the Article 4 and 10 of the ILO Convention n. 158 was then challenged before the Brazilian Supreme Court.[234] The Supreme Court, by majority, did not invalidate the treaty, but invoked the "interpretation in conformity with the Constitution" method to decide that the text of the ILO Convention n. 158 was not self-executing. The Supreme Court considered that the ILO Convention n. 158,[235] besides containing rules that already existed in the Brazilian legal order, did not impose the mandatory reinstatement as the only consequence of an arbitrary dismissal. In the Court's majority view, the ILO Convention n. 158 *simply* urged the signatory parties to adopt rules of protection to employment, including the mandatory reinstatement among other possibilities in accordance with each country's domestic legislation. Nevertheless, by the time the Supreme Court reached its decision, the Executive had already denounced the ILO Convention n. 158.[236]

Critics of the rational choice theory perspective may argue that the lack of private invocability of international trade agreements would constitute a violation of the right of action, or a denial of access to courts. However, the argument that the lack of private invocability of international treaties before domestic courts would consubstantiate a denial of access to courts has already been rejected at the international level. The European Court of Human Rights, in the case *Markovic*

---

[232] ILO Convention concerning Termination of Employment at the Initiative of the Employer, Article 4 and 10:

> Article 4. The employment of a worker shall not be terminated unless there is a valid reason for such termination connected with the capacity or conduct of the worker or based on the operational requirements of the undertaking, establishment or service.
>
> Article 10. If the bodies referred to in Article 8 of this Convention [*an impartial body, such as a court, labor tribunal, arbitration committee or arbitrator*] find that termination is unjustified and if they are not empowered or do not find it practicable, in accordance with national law and practice, to declare the termination invalid and/or order or propose reinstatement of the worker, they shall be empowered to order payment of adequate compensation or such other relief as may be deemed appropriate.

[233] TRT/SP, Acórdão SDC n. 257/96-A, Relator: Juiz Floriano Corrêa Vaz da Silva, 13.6.1996.

[234] STF, Ação Direta de Inconstitucionalidade n. 1480-DF, Relator: Ministro Celso de Mello, 4.9.1997, D.J.U. de 18.5.2001. To be sure, the dispute over the application of the ILO Convention n. 158 was not only circumscribed to whether its text was self-executing; the controversy was also aggravated by the fact that the Brazilian Constitution Article 7, I, prescribes that the protection against arbitrary dismissal or against dismissal without just cause is to be regulated by supplementary law, which necessitates a qualified vote of absolute majority of Congress to be passed.

[235] Justice Celso de Mello, the Rapporteur of the case, cites Articles 4, 5, 6 and 8 of the ILO Convention n. 158 as examples of provisions that were similar to already existing provisions of Brazilian domestic law.

[236] The denunciation of Convention n. 158 was registered at ILO headquarters on 20 November 1996. At the domestic level, the denunciation was made public through Decreto n. 2100, de 20 de dezembro de 1996, D.O.U. de 23.12.1996.

and others v. Italy,[237] set aside allegations that there would have been denial of justice when Italian domestic courts did not find admissible an action in damages against the Italian government for the death of relatives of the applicants caused by NATO air strike in Belgrade in 1999, a military mission that Italy provided for political and logistical support in its air bases. The Italian Court of Cassation found that the reparation claim was inadmissible because the Italian decision to participate in the air strikes was a political one and, therefore, it could not be reviewed by domestic courts. In the Italian Court of Cassation's wording:

2. The claim seeks to impute liability to the Italian State on the basis of an act of war, in particular the conduct of hostilities through aerial warfare. The choice of the means that will be used to conduct hostilities is an act of government. These are acts through which political functions are performed and the Constitution provides for them to be assigned to a constitutional body. The nature of such functions precludes any claim to a protected interest in relation thereto, so that the acts by which they are carried out may or may not have a specific content – see the judgments of the full court dated 12 July 1968 (no. 2452), 17 October 1980 (no. 5583) and 8 January 1993 (no. 124). With respect to acts of this type, no court has the power to review the manner in which the function was performed.

3. While the purpose of the provisions of international agreements governing the conduct of hostilities – the Protocol Additional to the Geneva Convention (Articles 35.2, 48, 49, 51, 52 and 57) and the European Convention on Human Rights (Articles 2 and 15 § 2) – is to protect civilians in the event of attack, they are rules of international law, and so also regulate relations between States.

   These same treaties lay down the procedure for finding a violation and the sanctions in the event of liability (Article 91 of the Protocols and Article 41 of the Convention); they also designate the international courts and tribunals with jurisdiction to make such a finding.

   However, the legislation implementing these rules in the Italian State does not contain any express provision enabling injured parties to seek reparation from the State for damage sustained as a result of a violation of the rules of international law.

   The notion that provisions to that effect may implicitly have been introduced into the system through the implementation of rules of international law is at odds with the converse principle that has been mentioned which holds that protected individual interests are no bar to carrying out functions of a political nature.

   Indeed, in order to enable reparation to be provided in the domestic system for loss sustained as a result of a violation of the 'reasonable-time' requirement under Article 6 of the Convention on Human Rights, [the State] introduced appropriate legislation (Law no. 89 of 24 March 2001).

4. No entitlement to a review of the Government's decision concerning the conduct of hostilities with respect to the NATO aerial operations against the Federal Republic of Yugoslavia can be found in the London Convention of 1951.

   The fact that the aircraft used to bomb the Belgrade radio and television station were able to use bases situated on Italian territory constitutes but one element of the highly complex operation whose lawfulness it is sought to review and is not therefore relevant to the application of the rule laid down in paragraph 5 of Article VIII of the Convention,

---

[237] *Markovic and Others v. Italy* [GC], n. 1398/03, Eur. Ct. H.R. (2006).

2.4 An Assessment on the Role of Domestic Courts in International Trade Agreements

which on the contrary presupposes the commission of an act that is amenable to review.[238]

As per the excerpt above, the European Court of Human Rights rejected the argument that the Italian Court of Cassation denied *"the applicants access to a court by disregarding the provisions of domestic and international law on which the applicants had based their claim for compensation for damage."*[239] Considering that the right of access to courts *"secures to everyone the right to have a claim relating to his civil rights and obligations brought before a court"*[240] and assessing whether there were a civil right involved, the European Court of Human Rights corroborated the finding of the Italian Court that the 1977 Protocol regulated relations between States and, therefore, no civil right arose from this international treaty. The European Court of Human Rights concluded that the Italian Court's decision could not be considered as an arbitrary removal of the courts' jurisdiction and that the applicants had access to Italian domestic courts, although such access was limited because it did not allow them to reach a decision on the merits of their request.[241] Similarly, international trade agreements are state-to-state commitments that do not create individual rights. In this sense, the lack of direct effect of WTO agreements may not be considered as an impediment of right to access of courts, as corporations may seize courts but may not claim a legal instrument that does not create rights to private businesses.

Nevertheless, as this study will show, the legal systems of emerging countries in Latin America have considered domestic courts as a venue to adjudicate on international trade agreements' obligations. Latin American countries are not central in the international trade scholarship and are, most often than not, overlooked in the international scholarly debate. Predominant in Latin America, traditionalism regarding WTO agreements provides a valuable scenario for comparative work vis-à-vis the European perspective based on the rational choice theory perspective.

This comparative study will analyze the theoretical claims on the role of domestic courts, as envisioned by traditionalism and the rational choice theory, against empirical evidence provided by Brazilian and European domestic courts in relation to the WTO agreements. Accordingly, the comparative method is a helpful mechanism for inquiring into the effects of the actual practice of member states on how WTO agreements are interpreted domestically, particularly the GATT for it is the oldest and most well-known treaty under the WTO umbrella before domestic courts. Comparing the Brazilian judiciary experience with the European courts perspective on the GATT provides an empirical study on how emerging economies in Latin America and developed countries approach the same international trade

---

[238] Excerpt of the Italian Court of Cassation ruling quoted in *Markovic and Others v. Italy* [GC], n. 1398/03, Eur. Ct. H.R. (2006), pp. 6–7.

[239] *Markovic and Others v. Italy* [GC], n. 1398/03, Eur. Ct. H.R. (2006), p. 26.

[240] Ibid., p. 32.

[241] Ibid., p. 38.

agreement. Based on the evidence provided by actual court litigation based on WTO agreements, this comparative study may show the actual effects of traditionalism and the rational choice theory in these settings.

2.5 Conclusion

This chapter intended to define the theoretical framework that will support the research on how Brazilian domestic courts have adjudicated cases involving WTO law, specifically the GATT and the Antidumping Agreement, in a comparative perspective with European courts. Quite significantly, the comparative method, as a means to observe the way international rules are actually applied (or not) by domestic judges in different legal systems, provides an important tool to check how dogmatic theories work in the real world, and their impact on the function and objective of international law.

Second, this chapter endeavored to first lay out the two general approaches in international legal scholarship on the role of domestic courts in international law, with the values and limits of each of these theories. In view of the complexity and vastitude of the scholarly debate on the most appropriate role of domestic courts in international law, this chapter identified two polarized viewpoints, namely, traditionalism vis-à-vis the rational choice theory. Traditionalism has long been the most accepted approach in international legal scholarship, although recent literature has embraced the rational choice theory at the international level. In complementing Conforti's traditionalism, the doctrine of sources variation provides a more realistic view on the hybrid results that emerge from the application of international law by domestic courts, while transjudicialism, as a prediction of a global community of courts, remains to be seen. The rational choice theory approach, on the other hand, clearly advocates that the political branches advance international law, as opposed to domestic courts.

Third, this chapter aimed to provide the foundation of the argument developed throughout this study by asserting that the role of domestic courts in international law should not be viewed as having a uniform answer to the whole range of areas covered by international treaties. Moreover, this chapter suggests that the role of domestic courts should be examined according to the substantial field of a given international treaty. Therefore, this chapter addresses the specific academic debate over the pros and cons of direct effect of the WTO agreements. Then, this chapter investigates the origins of the world trade system through the idealization of the GATT by the United States, which substantiates the function and objective of the WTO agreements. In the sequence, this chapter examines the American leadership in adopting the rational choice theory approach regarding WTO agreements, a practice followed by the major trade players' practice, which indicates that the principle of self-government informs the world trade system.

Most importantly, by taking into account that each specific area requires a distinct analysis, this chapter advances this book's argument that international trade agreements, particularly the GATT, should be considered as non-self-executing until there exists implementing legislation passed by the domestic political processes. Building on the theoretical background found in Sykes' scholarship on the function and objective of international trade agreements and on the principle of popular sovereignty, this chapter argues that traditionalism does not seem to be the most appropriate role for domestic courts in relation to international trade agreements. To be sure, the rational choice theory does not preclude the application of consistent interpretation, whenever possible.[242]

Potential conflicts of treaty interpretation or lack of compliance with the WTO Agreements should be circumscribed to international adjudication at the WTO dispute settlement system, and not before domestic courts. The WTO dispute settlement system is the proper forum for the discussion over the balance of rights and obligations arisen out of trade obligations, as it also ensures the possibility that the parties involved find a mutually agreed solution.

Based on this intellectual framework, this research will show the diverse ways the judiciary of Brazil, an emerging economy in Latin America, and the European Union courts, a developed economy, have interpreted the GATT, and will demonstrate, through these contrasting patterns, the actual effects and impact of the traditionalism and rational choice theory. With this comparative analysis, this research will suggest that the findings of the Brazilian experience can be extended to a high degree to other emerging economies in Latin America. With this conclusion, the next chapter will turn attention to the perspective of the Brazilian judiciary regarding international trade agreements.

References

Abi-Saab G (2010) The normalization of international adjudication: convergence and divergencies. N Y Univ J Int Law Polit 43:1–14
Abul-Ethem F (2002) The role of the judiciary in the protection of human rights and development: a middle eastern perspective. Fordham Int Law J 26:761–770
Baudenbacher C (2004) The EFTA: an actor in the European judicial dialogue. Fordham Int Law J 28:353–391
Benvenisti E (1994) Judges and foreign affairs: a comment on the Institut de Droit International's resolution on 'the Activities of National Courts and the International Relations of their State'. Eur J Int Law 5:1–439
Betlem G, Nollkaemper A (2003) Giving effect to public international law and European Community law before domestic courts: a comparative analysis of the practice of consistent interpretation. Eur J Int Law 14:569–589
Bianchi A (1999) Immunity versus human rights: the Pinochet case. Eur J Int Law 10:237–277
Bianchi A (2004) International law and US courts: the myth of Lohengrin revisited. Eur J Int Law 15:751–781
Bradley C (1998a) The Charming Betsy canon and separation of powers: rethinking the interpretive role of international law. Geo Law J 86:479–537

---

[242] Bradley (1998a), p. 536.

Bradley C (1998b) The treaty power and American federalism. Mich Law Rev 97:390–461
Bradley C (2001) The costs of international human rights litigation. Chic J Int Law 2:457–473
Bradley C (2008) Intent, presumptions, and non-self-executing treaties. Am J Int Law 102:540–551
Brand R (1997) Direct effect of international economic law in the United States and the European Union. Nw J Int Law Bus 17:556–608
Brennan DJ (2003) Retransmission and US compliance with TRIPS. Kluwer Law International, The Hague
Canor I (2009) The European Courts and the Security Council: between *dédoublement fonctionnel* and balancing of values: three replies to Pasquale de Sena and Maria Chiara Vitucci. Eur J Int Law 20(3):853–887
Carozza P (2003) Subsidiarity as a structural principle of international human rights law. Am J Int Law 97:38–79
Cass D (2005) The constitutionalization of the World Trade Organization – legitimacy, democracy and community in the international trading system. Oxford University Press, Oxford
Cassese A (1985) Modern constitutions and international law. Collected courses of the Hague academy of international law, vol 192. Martinus Nijhoff, Dordrecht
Cassese A (1990) Remarks on Scelle's theory of "role splitting" (dédoublement fonctionnel) in international law. Eur J Int Law 1:210–231
Cataldi G, Iovane M (2009) International law in Italian courts 1999–2009: an overview of major methodological and substantive issues. Italian Y B Int Law 19:3–29
Conforti B (1993) International law and the role of domestic legal systems. Martinus Nijhoff, Dordrecht
Conforti B, Francioni F (eds) (1997) Enforcing international human rights in domestic courts. Martinus Nijhoff, Dordrecht
Cottier T (2002) A theory of direct effect in global law. In: Bogdandy A, Mavroidis P, Mény Y (eds) European integration and international co-ordination. Studies in transnational economic law in honor of Claus-Dieter Ehlermann. Kluwer Law International, The Hague
Cottier T (ed) (2007) The challenge of WTO law: collected essays. Cameron May, London
Cottier T (2009) International trade law: the impact of justiciability and separations of powers in EC law. Eur Const Law Rev 5:307–326
Cottier T, Schefer K (1998) The relationship between world trade organization law, national and regional law. J Int Econ Law 1:82–122
Crawford J (2012) Brownlie's principles of public international law. Oxford University Press, Oxford
Dorsen N, Rosenfeld M, Sajó A, Baer A (2003) Comparative constitutionalism: cases and materials. Thomson West, St. Paul
Dunoff J, Trachtman J (1999) Economic analysis of international law. Yale J Int Law 24:1–59
Dupuy PM (2007) The unit of application of international law at the global level and the responsibility of judges. Eur J Legal Stud 1(2):3. http://www.ejls.eu/2/21UK.htm. Accessed 4 Sept 2014
Eeckhout P (2011) The growing influence of European Union law. Fordham Int Law J 33:1490–1521
Eskridge W Jr (2004) United States: Lawrence v. Texas and the imperative of comparative constitutionalism. Int J Const Law 2:555–560
Evans D, Tarso Pereira C (2005) DSU review: a view from the inside. In: Yerxa R, Wilson B (eds) Key issues in the WTO dispute settlement: the first ten years. Cambridge University Press, New York
Falk R (1964) The role of domestic courts in the international legal order. Syracuse University Press, Syracuse
Fatima S (2005) Using international law in domestic courts. Hart, Oxford
Francioni F (2001) International law as a common language for national courts. Tex Int Law J 36:587–598

References

Frowein J (1997) International law in municipal courts. Proc Annu Meet (Am Soc Int Law) 91:290–295

Fuentes Torrijo X (2008) International law and domestic law: definitely an odd couple. Rev Jur U P R 77:483–505. http://www.law.yale.edu/documents/pdf/sela/XimenaFuentes__English_.pdf. Accessed 4 Sept 2014

Galindo G (2012) Revisiting monism's ethical dimension. In: Crawford J, Nouwen S (eds) Select proceedings of the European society of international law. Hart, Oxford, pp 141–154

Gardbaum S (2009) Human rights and international constitutionalism. In: Dunoff J, Trachtman J (eds) Ruling the world? Constitutionalism, international law and global governance. Cambridge University Press, New York

Golove D, Huselbosch D (2010) A civilized nation: the early American constitution, the law of nations, and the pursuit of international recognition. N Y Univ Law Rev 85:101–228

Grimmet J (2011) World Trade Organization (WTO) decisions and their effect in U.S. law. Federal Publications Paper 807. http://digitalcommons.ilr.cornell.edu/key_workplace/807. Accessed 4 Sept 2014

Guzman A, Pauwelyn J (2009) International trade law. Aspen, New York

Harvard Law Review (2008) The Charming Betsy canon, separation of powers, and customary international law. Harv Law Rev 121:1215–1235

Hilf M (1997) The role of national courts in international trade relations. Mich J Int Law 18:321–356

Hughes CE (1908) Address before the Chamber of Commerce, Elmira, New York. In: Addresses and papers of Charles Evan Hughes, G. P. Putnam's, New York. http://www.archive.org/stream/paperscharlesevan00hughrich#page/n7/mode/2up. Accessed 4 Sept 2014

Institut de Droit International (1993) The activities of national judges and the international relations of their State, Session of Milan, Rapporteur Benedetto Conforti. http://www.idi-iil.org/idiE/resolutionsE/1993_mil_01_en.PDF. Accessed 4 Sept 2014

Irwin D, Mavroidis P, Sykes A (2008) The genesis of the GATT. Cambridge University Press, New York

Jackson JH (1992) Status of treaties in domestic legal systems: a policy analysis. Am J Int Law 86(2):310–340

Jackson JH (1997) The world trade system: law and policy of international economic relations. MIT, Massachusetts

Jackson JH (2006) Sovereignty, the WTO and changing fundamentals of international law, Hersch Lauterpacht memorial lectures. Cambridge University Press, London

Jiménez de Aréchaga E, Tanzi A (2001) International state responsibility. In: Bedjaoui M (ed) International law: achievements and prospects. Martinus Nijhoff, Dordrecht

Kaczorowska A (2010) Public international law. Routledge, New York

Klein N, Hughes N (2009) National litigation and international law: repercussions for Australia's protection of marine resources. Melb Univ Law Rev 33:163–204

Knop K (2000) Here and there: international law in domestic courts. N Y Univ J Int Law Polit 32:501–535

Koh H (1999) The 1998 Frankel lecture: bringing international law home. Houston Law Rev 35:623–681

Koskenniemi M (2009) The case for comparative international law. Finnish Y B Int Law 20:1–8. http://www.hartpublishingusa.com/pdf/samples/9781849460712sample.pdf. Accessed 4 Sept 2014

Kuijper PJ, Bronckers M (2005) WTO law in the European court of justice. Common Mark Law Rev 42:1313–1355

L'Heureux-Dubé C (1998) The importance of dialogue: globalization and the international impact of the Rehnquist Court. Tulsa Law J 34:15–40

la Forest W (2004) A domestic application of international law in charter cases: are we there yet? UBC Law Rev 37:157–218

Lord Lester of Herne Hill (2007) Human rights and the British constitution. In: Jowell J, Oliver D (eds) The changing constitution. Oxford University Press, Oxford

Lord JE, Stein MA (2009) Social rights and the relational value of the rights to participate in sport, recreation and play. Boston Univ Int Law J 27:249–281

Mamlyuk B, Mattei U (2011) Comparative international law. Brooklyn J Int Law 36(2):385–452

Matsushita M, Schoenbaum T, Mavroidis P (2006) The World Trade Organization: law, practice and policy. Oxford University Press, Oxford

McGoldrick D (2007) Human rights and humanitarian law in the UK courts. Israel Law Rev 40:527–562

Mednicoff D (2007) The importance of being quasi-democratic – the domestication of international human rights in American and Arab politics. Victoria Univ Wellington Law Rev 38:317–339

Michaels C (2011) Global problems in domestic courts. In: Muller S et al (eds) The law of the future and the future of the law. Torkel Opsahl Academic Publisher, Oslo

Mills A, Stephens T (2005) Challenging the role of judges in Slaughter's liberal theory of international law. Leiden J Int Law 18:1–30

Moore D (2009) Law (makers) of the Land: the doctrine of treaty non-self-execution. Harv Law Rev 122:32–47

Neuman G (2003) Human rights and constitutional rights: harmony and dissonance. Stanford Law Rev 55:1863–1900

Nollkaemper A (2007) Internationally wrongful acts in domestic courts. Am J Int Law 101:760–799

Nollkaemper A (2011) National courts and the international rule of law. Oxford University Press, Oxford

Panel on The Rising Use of International Law by African Judiciaries (2010). Am Soc Int Law Proc 104:329–336

Petersen N (2009) The reception of international law by constitutional courts through the prism of legitimacy. Max Planck Institute Collective Goods Preprint 39. http://ssrn.com/abstract=1532110. Accessed 4 Sept 2014

Petersmann EU (2001) Time for integrating human rights into the law of worldwide organizations. Lessons from European integration law for global integration law. Jean Monnet Working Paper 7/01. http://www.jeanmonnetprogram.org/archive/papers/01/012301.html. Accessed 4 Sept 2014

Petersmann EU (2007) Do judges meet their constitutional obligation to settle disputes in conformity with 'principles of justice and international law'? Eur J Legal Stud 1:1–38. http://www.ejls.eu/2/22UK.pdf. Accessed 4 Sept 2014

Posner E (2007) Book review of the limits of leviathan: contract theory and the enforcement of international law by Robert Scott & Paul Stephan. Am J Int Law 101:509–514

Posner E (2009) The perils of global legalism. University of Chicago Press, Chicago

Qin JY (2007) The impact of WTO accession on China's legal system: trade, investment and beyond. China Q 191:720–741

Raustiala K (2006) Refining the limits of international law. Ga J Int Comp Law 34:423–443

Reed P (2007) Relationship of WTO obligations to U.S. international trade law: internationalist vision meets domestic reality. Geo J Int Law 38:209–249

Reinisch A (2007) International relations of national courts: a discourse on international law norms on jurisdictional and enforcement immunity. In: Reinisch A, Kriebaum U (eds) The law of international relations: Liber amicorum Hanspeter Neuhold. Eleven International Publishing, Utrecht

Restani J, Bloom I (2000) Interpreting international trade statutes: is the Charming Betsy sinking? Fordham Int Law J 24:1533–1547

Roberts A (2011) Comparative international law? The role of national courts in creating and enforcing international law. Int Comp Law Q 60:57–92

Rosenkrantz C (2003) Against borrowings and other nonauthoritative uses of foreign law. Int J Const Law 1(2):269–295

Sacco R (1997) Legal formants: a dynamic approach to comparative law. Am J Comp Law 39:1–34, quoted in Kennedy D (1997) New approaches to comparative law: comparativism and international governance. Utah Law Rev 1997(2):545–637

Shaw M (2003) International law. Cambridge University Press, London

Slaughter AM (1994) A typology of transjudicial communication. Univ Richmond Law Rev 29:99–137

Slaughter AM (2003) A global community of courts. Harv Int Law J 44:191–219

Slaughter AM (2004) A new world order. Princeton University Press, Princeton

Sloss D (ed) (2010) The role of domestic courts in treaty enforcement: a comparative study. Cambridge University Press, London

Sykes A (2005) Public versus private enforcement of international economic law: standing and remedy. J Legal Stud 34:631–666

The World Trade Organization. WTO Members and Observers (2014) http://www.wto.org/english/thewto_e/whatis_e/tif_e/org6_e.htm. Accessed 4 Sept 2014

Tomkins A (2001) Introduction: on being sceptical about human rights. In: Campbell T, Ewing KD, Tomkins A (eds) Sceptical essays on human rights. Oxford University Press, Oxford

Trachtman J (2009) Constitutional economics of the World Trade Organization. In: Dunoff J, Trachtman J (eds) Ruling the world? Constitutionalism, international law and global governance. Cambridge University Press, New York

Trachtman J, Moremen P (2003) Costs and benefits of private participation in WTO dispute settlement: whose right is it anyway? Harv Int Law J 44:221–250

Triepel H (1920) Droit international et droit internet. Collection Les Introuvables Paris, translation by René Brunet. Panthéon-Assas, Paris

Vagts D, Dodge W, Koh H (2003) Transnational business problems. Foundation Press, New York

Van den Bossche P (2008) The law and policy of the World Trade Organization. Cambridge University Press, London

Vázquez CM (1995) The four doctrines of self-executing treaties. Am J Int Law 89:695–723

Vázquez CM (2008) Treaties as law of the land: the supremacy clause and the judicial enforcement of treaties. Harv Law Rev 122:599–695

Von Bogdandy A (2008) Pluralism, direct effect, and the ultimate say: on the relationship between international and domestic constitutional law. Int J Const Law 6:397–413

Waters M (2005) Mediating norms and identity: the role of transnational judicial dialogue in creating and enforcing international law. Geo Law J 93:487–574

Waters C (ed) (2006) British and Canadian perspectives on international law. Martinus Nijhoff, Leiden

Waters M (2007) Creeping monism: the judicial trend toward interpretative incorporation of human rights treaties. Colum Law Rev 107:628–705

Yoo J (1999a) Globalism and the constitution: treaties, non-self-execution, and the original understanding. Colum Law Rev 99:1955–2094

Yoo J (1999b) Treaties and public lawmaking: a textual and structural defense of non-self-execution. Colum Law Rev 99:2218–2258

Young E (2009) Treaties as "part of our law". Tex Law Rev 88:91–144

Chapter 3
The Relations Between International Trade Agreements and Domestic Courts in Brazil

While there is an extensive academic literature debating the relationship between international trade agreements and national courts in developed countries, mostly the interconnection with the European Union legal system and the United States,[1] very little has been written about emerging economies in Latin America, particularly regarding Brazilian domestic courts. This chapter therefore analyzes the relations between international trade agreements and domestic courts in the specific case of Brazil. It first examines the constitutional arrangements on the domestic status of international treaties in Brazil. It then explores the traditionalist role of Brazilian courts with regards to WTO agreements. It finally analyzes Brazilian cases on the GATT and the Antidumping Agreement having in mind the theoretical framework established in Chap. 2. This research will return to the elements found in the Brazilian perspective to proceed to the comparison with EU courts in Chap. 5.

3.1 Constitutional Arrangements at the National Level: The Domestic Status of International Treaties in Brazil

To understand the limits and leeway that Brazilian courts have in deciding cases on international trade agreements, the hierarchy of international rules vis-à-vis the domestic law within the Brazilian legal system is considered a major aspect to be taken into account. In general, the higher hierarchy international treaties have in relation to domestic law, the more internationalist-friendly reputation a country has. The Brazilian Constitution however does not have a general provision stating the domestic status of all international agreements, with one exception on human

---

[1] Weiler (2005), Ortino (2004), De Búrca and Scott (2003), and Dillon (2002).

rights. Therefore it was for the Supreme Federal Court of Brazil [*Supremo Tribunal Federal*] to decide on the relations between international treaties and domestic law.

As the highest court of Brazil, the Supreme Federal Court has maintained for decades that international treaties or conventions, if incorporated into domestic law, have the same validity and efficacy of federal law. The leading case affirming such interpretation was decided in 1977—the extraordinary appeal 80004.[2] The Supreme Court's interpretation derived from the provision in the Brazilian Constitution that attributes to the Supreme Court extraordinary appellate jurisdiction over judicial decisions that declared a treaty or federal law unconstitutional. This constitutional clause was interpreted as allowing the judicial control of the constitutionality of an international treaty in the same way as judicial review of a federal law, without giving a higher status to international treaties. Consequently, the Court affirmed the parity of status between international treaties and federal law, with one dissenting vote in the sense that international treaties would have a higher hierarchy than ordinary federal law.

However, the Brazilian Constitution has recently provided an exception regarding international human rights treaties. In 2004, Constitutional Amendment 45 on the judiciary reform inserted paragraph 3 into Article 5 of the Constitution, prescribing that international human rights treaties, if approved in each House of Congress in two rounds with a three-fifth vote, will be hierarchically equivalent to constitutional amendments. So far, the only international human rights treaty that has gone through this special quorum incorporation process is the Convention on the Rights of Persons with Disabilities and Optional Protocol.[3] Following this distinct treatment in the Brazilian Constitution regarding international human rights law, the Supreme Federal Court, in a 2008 decision,[4] conferred supralegal status to international human rights treaties, meaning that human rights treaties which were incorporated into the Brazilian legal system through regular incorporation process of simple majority, that is, without Congress three-fifth majority vote, are considered above federal law, but below the Constitution.

In Brazil, to achieve the same hierarchy of federal laws, all international treaties have the same incorporation process into domestic law, including WTO agreements and regional economic integration treaties such as MERCOSUL. The incorporation process of international treaties has the same voting thresholds for federal law making, which means simple majority in both Houses of Congress. The incorporation of international treaties in Brazil has the following procedure. After signing an international treaty, the President sends treaty text to Congress for approval. If

---

[2] STF, Recurso Extraordinário 80004, Relator para o acórdão: Ministro Cunha Peixoto, 1.6.1977, D.J.U. 29.12.1977.

[3] Decreto n. 6949, de 25 de agosto de 2009, D.O.U. de 26.8.2009.

[4] STF, Recurso Extraordinário 349703, Relator para o acórdão Ministro Gilmar Mendes, 3.12.2008, D.J.U. 5.6.2009; Recurso Extraordinário 466343, Relator Ministro Cezar Peluso, 3.12.2008, D.J.U. 5.6.2009; Habeas Corpus 87585, Relator Ministro Marco Aurélio, 3.12.2008, D.J.U. 26.6.2009; Hábeas Corpus 92566, Relator Ministro Marco Aurélio, 3.12.2008, D.J.U. 5.6.2009.

approved in both houses by simple majority, the President may then ratify the treaty at the international level. After ratification at the international level, the President may issue a domestic decree to put into effect the international treaty as part of the Brazilian domestic legislation, with status of federal law.

In the Brazilian system, the ratification of an international treaty at the international level by the President of Brazil in itself does not confer to such treaty any legal status in the internal legal order. It is necessary that the President enacts a decree to finalize the incorporation process at the domestic level. This presidential decree is generally very short and only makes few considerations such as that Congress had approved the treaty, that the instrument of ratification had been deposited, and that the treaty had been in force for Brazil at the international level. After such considerations, the President decrees the enforcement of the international treaty. The text of the treaty itself, as ratified internationally, is usually annexed to the presidential decree, and is not copied into the decree. The date of publication of the presidential decree, with the text of the treaty annexed, is then considered the official date of entry into force of the treaty into the Brazilian domestic legal order.

Regarding the incorporation process of international treaties in Brazil, Justice Celso de Mello, of the Brazilian Supreme Court, stated the following in a case reviewing the constitutionality of the International Labor Organization Convention n. 158[5]:

> It is in the Brazilian Constitution – and not in the doctrinal controversy that antagonizes monists and dualists – that one should search for the normative solution for the question of incorporation of international acts in the Brazilian internal positive law system.
>
> The examination of the current Federal Constitution allows proving that the enforcement of international treaties and their incorporation in the internal legal order derive, in the system adopted in Brazil, from a subjectively complex act, resulting from the conjugation of two homogenous wills: one of the National Congress, which decides, definitively, through legislative decree, on international treaties, agreements or acts (Fed. Const., Art. 49, I), and one of the President of the Republic, who, besides the power to celebrate these acts of international law (Fed. Const., Art. 84, VIII), also has – as being the Chief of State – the competence to promulgate such acts through decree.[6]

As it can be seen in the excerpt above, the Brazilian Supreme Court in this case has not extended itself to major doctrinal discussions and put the Constitution above the theoretical questions of monism and dualism that, in fact, do not provide an adequate account of the relations between domestic and international law.[7]

To illustrate the treaty incorporation process, there is a well-known case on MERCOSUL agreements' incorporation process in Brazil. The Supreme Federal Court refused to give effect to the Ouro Preto Protocol on Provisional Measures

---

[5] STF, Ação Direta de Inconstitucionalidade (Medida Liminar) 1480, Relator: Ministro Celso de Mello, 4.9.1997, D.J.U 18.5.2001.

[6] STF, Ação Direta de Inconstitucionalidade (Medida Liminar) 1480, Relator: Ministro Celso de Mello, 4.9.1997, D.J.U 18.5.2001.

[7] Crawford (2012), p. 50.

[*Protocolo de Medidas Cautelares de Ouro Preto*] because such agreement, although approved by Congress and ratified at the international level by the President, had not been subject to a presidential decree to give it effect at the domestic level at the time the request of enforcement was filed.[8] The Ouro Preto Protocol on Provisional Measures states that provisional measures to prevent irreparable damages to private litigants issued by a judge of a MERCOSUL member state are to be enforced by the other members states' judiciaries. In this case, an Argentinean judge[9] requested the Brazilian judiciary to seize goods belonging to Coagulantes Argentina S/A transported in a ship that was moored at the city of Belém, as well as the ship itself, and to prevent the ship from navigating. The Court found that the ratification of an international agreement at the international level is not enough to promote the incorporation of such treaty in the Brazilian domestic law, and rejected the arguments that the Brazilian Congress approval sufficed to give effect to MERCOSUL agreements.

As for the incorporation of the WTO agreements in the Brazilian legal order, the National Congress approved the Final Act of the Uruguay Round and the Brazilian schedule of concessions on 15 December 1994.[10] Two weeks later, the Presidential decree that officially incorporated WTO agreements into Brazilian domestic legal order was enacted. It limited itself to state that the Final Act of the Uruguay Round was to be enforced in the Brazilian domestic legal order in its terms.[11] The whole process of incorporation of the WTO agreements was approved in a very expeditious way, if one considers that the Uruguay Round was concluded on April 1994, and that the time-length of Brazilian Congress deliberation of other international treaties made by the government can take years before a final decision. This process

---

[8] STF, Carta Rogatória (Agravo Regimental) 8279, Relator: Ministro Celso de Mello, 17.6.1998, D.J.U. 10.8.1999.

[9] Argentina, Juez Nacional de Primera Instáncia en lo Civil y Comercial Federal n. 4 de Buenos Aires.

[10] Decreto Legislativo n. 30, de 15 de dezembro de 1994, D.O.U. de 19.12.1994.

[11] Decreto n. 1355, de 30 de dezembro de 1994, D.O.U. de 31.12.1994, which reads:

THE PRESIDENT OF THE REPUBLIC, in the exercise of his attributions, and
Considering that the National Congress approved, by Legislative Decree N. 30 of 15 December 1994, the Final Act Embodying the Results of the Uruguay Round of Multilateral Trade Negotiations of GATT, signed in Marrakech on 12 April 1994;
Considering that the instrument of ratification of this Final Act by the Federative Republic of Brazil was filed in Geneva with the Director of GATT on 21 December 1994;
Considering that the referred Final Act comes into force for the Federative Republic of Brazil on 1 January 1995,
DECREES:
Art. 1 The Final Act Embodying the Results of the Uruguay Round of Multilateral Trade Negotiations of GATT, of which a copy is attached to the present Decree, shall be executed and enforced as entirely as it is.
Art. 2 This Decree shall enter into force on the date of its publication, revoked the provisions on the contrary.

shows the importance given by Brazilian public authorities, the legislative included, to trade negotiations in the context of the WTO agreements.

To sum up, in Cassese's framework discussed in Chap. 2,[12] the Brazilian constitution falls under three of the four systematized groups. The Brazilian constitution is silent for international treaties in general, provides that international human rights treaties prevail over statutes, and allows international human rights treaties to amend the constitution. The possibility of amending the Brazilian constitution by an international human rights treaty, the supralegal status of international human rights treaties, and the status of federal law for the other areas covered by international law show the different status of international treaties in the Brazilian system according to the substantial field of the treaty. More importantly, it shows the influential status of international human rights treaties vis-à-vis other international treaties. Although a very interesting topic of debate, the special status of international human rights treaties are not going to be further developed, as it would fall outside the scope of this research, which focuses on international trade agreements. WTO agreements as mentioned, fall under the category where the Brazilian constitution is silent and, according to the Brazilian Supreme Court's interpretation, have the status of ordinary federal law in the Brazilian legal system.

With these preliminary notes, the next section will show how Brazilian domestic courts have interpreted their role regarding WTO agreements, where traditionalism predominates over other approaches.

3.2 The Traditionalist Role of Brazilian Courts in WTO Agreements

Traditionalism is the predominant approach on the role of domestic judges regarding international law in Brazil. Brazilian courts have generally granted private invocability of international rules in domestic litigation—or direct effect of international treaties as in the international trade law parlance. This is also the case in relation to international trade agreements, including the GATT. According to Conforti's typology developed in Chap. 2, the Brazilian judiciary, as a domestic legal operator in the application of international law, shows a high level of enforcement of international obligations at the domestic level by (1) adopting the direct effect of WTO law, (2) interpreting domestic law in a consistent way with international law, and (3) not using the political question doctrine as a matter of

---

[12] As mentioned in Sect. 2.2, Cassese provides a general classification of the main models of modern constitutions in relation to the implementation of international law: (1) constitutions that are silent about the implementation of international treaties; (2) constitutions that prescribe international treaties must be complied with, but do not grant international treaties a higher status than ordinary legislation; (3) constitutions that establish that international treaties prevail over statutes; and (4) constitutions that allow international treaties to modify or revise constitutional provisions. *See* Cassese (1985), p. 394.

interpretation to avoid deciding on highly controversial issues involving governmental trade policies.

On the other hand, under Conforti's classification, traditionalism regarding WTO law does not prevent the Brazilian legal order from being qualified as nationalist due to the ordinary federal law domestic status of international treaties, with the consequent application of the last in time rule (*lex posteriori* principle). It is true that, at first glance, the consideration of the *lex posteriori* principle as an "avoidance technique" against international law indicates a nationalist attitude towards international law. However, Conforti also notes that many domestic courts have not strictly interpreted the last in time rule.[13] Instead, Conforti remarks, numerous domestic courts have interpreted inconsistencies between a treaty rule and a supervening domestic rule through "*the presumption of conformity of the domestic law to international law*"[14]—or as, most widely known, the doctrine of consistent interpretation. Conforti also observes that, while few domestic courts have also used the concept that an international treaty is a special law and therefore the principle *lex posterior generalis non derogat priori speciali* applies, the most favorable criterion for solving potential conflicts between an international treaty and a subsequent domestic law is the American and Swiss standard whereby "*a subsequent law prevails only if there is a "clear indication" of the intention of the law-maker to derogate from the treaty or other international commitment in force.*" [15]

With this general perspective, the case studies below demonstrate that Brazilian courts have applied GATT/WTO rules at the domestic level for a long period of time, even when confronted with supervening constitutional rules. Judicial respect for the international rule of law is shown in several excerpts of the opinions, and confirm so far the self-executing character of GATT in the Brazilian legal order. As a result, the *lex posteriori* principle, although formally considered a hindrance to international law application, loses its force while potential conflicts between domestic and international law are implicitly solved in the Brazilian context by the doctrine of consistent interpretation, as shown in the *Imports of Codfish* case. After all, the *lex posteriori* principle should not be considered *per se* as a lesser protection to international law, as the Brazilian courts have proven to be the case. It can be concluded therefore that Brazilian courts have taken an internationalist approach when adjudicating on international law matters, despite Brazil would, in principle, qualify as a nationalist regime due to the ordinary domestic status of international law.

A particular feature of traditionalism in the Brazilian judiciary is that, if WTO agreements are invoked before domestic courts, Brazilian judges usually interpret them, or any other international treaty, as they would interpret any ordinary federal law. With a legal profession's culture immersed in legal positivism,[16] such

---

[13] Conforti and Francioni (1997), p. 11.
[14] Ibid., p. 11.
[15] Ibid., p. 12.
[16] Faro de Castro (1997), p. 244.

3.2 The Traditionalist Role of Brazilian Courts in WTO Agreements

formalist view whereby international treaties in Brazil are interpreted as any ordinary federal law is not surprising. This formalist perspective on the interpretation of international treaties is reflected in the fact that the Brazilian judiciary does not rely on the question of reciprocity from other countries signatories when confronted with litigation based on an international treaty. The only exception so far refers to international treaties on international transportation, as the Brazilian Constitution is clear in stating that domestic legislation shall observe international treaties on the subject matter, with due regard to the principle of reciprocity.[17]

To disregard the question of reciprocity when an international treaty is invoked in domestic litigation is certainly not the practice of other countries, notably France. The French Constitution, while stating that international treaties prevail over acts of the parliament, conditions such prevalence to the requirement of reciprocity from the other countries involved.[18] After all, the lack of reciprocity would place a country's *"own citizens and government at the disadvantage of having the rules applied against them at home and yet not being available for application abroad."*[19]

As this study next shows, direct effect of WTO agreements has not been questioned in Brazilian domestic litigation arguments, and is taken for granted. One of the possible reasons why direct effect has not been questioned may be that the new democratic Constitution of 1988, aiming at enhancing access to the judiciary, determined in Article 5, XXXV, that *"the law shall not exclude any injury or threat to a right from the consideration of the Judicial Power."* This constitutional guarantee has been understood as not allowing judges to refrain from adjudicating on governmental trade policy matters, more so if involving international treaties, which have status of federal law. Therefore, the constitutional guarantee of access to courts in principle seems like a strong constitutional argument in favor of judicial review of international trade policy.

However, the right of access to courts does not hinder the application of the non-self-executing treaties' doctrine. Domestic courts may accept to review a claim grounded on an international treaty and then conclude that such international treaty contains programmatic rules that require further domestic legislation to be applicable. Or, in the case of the WTO agreements, domestic courts may conclude that international trade rules per their function and objective are not self-executing and necessitate domestic regulation in defining how such obligations are to be

---

[17] Brazilian Constitution, Art. 178: *"The law shall provide for the regulation of air, water and ground transportation, and it shall, in respect to the regulation of international transportation, comply with the agreements entered into by the Union, with due regard to the principle of reciprocity."* For a case discussing the application of tax exemptions based on international treaties on air transportation, see STF, Ação Direta de Inconstitucionalidade 1600, Relator para o acórdão: Ministro Nelson Jobim, 26.11.2011, D.J.U. 20.6.2003.

[18] French Constitution, Article 55 reads: *Les traités ou accords régulièrement ratifiés ou approuvés ont, dès leur publication, une autorité supérieure à celle des lois, sous réserve, pour chaque accord ou traité, de son application par l'autre partie.*

[19] Brand (1997), p. 607.

discharged. In fact, the right of access to courts does not entail a favorable judgment according to the parties' expectations and arguments, and cannot overlook the existence of programmatic rules. Non-self-executing rules exist at the domestic constitutional law level, and are not a feature that is exclusive to international treaties. Therefore, the potential lack of direct effect of international trade agreements—which would preclude private companies from challenging domestic public policy to obtain a better bargain or profit out of international trade agreements on market access—does not qualify as an impediment to the right of access to courts. After all, in principle, international trade agreements do not provide for individual rights and accordingly, private companies or individuals may not argue for legal protection under state-to-state rules and obligations on market access.

At the international level, the argument that the denial of private invocability of international rules before domestic courts would consubstantiate a violation of the right of access to courts has already been refuted by the European Court of Human Rights in the *Markovic and others v. Italy* case,[20] discussed in Chap. 2. Therefore, the reason why traditionalism has not been challenged in Brazilian courts seems to be more linked to legal culture aspects as well as political and economic incentives than a constitutional impediment. Indeed, back in 1977 the Brazilian Supreme Court had already considered the judicial enforcement of the GATT national treatment rule as a settled question,[21] an interpretation that has not changed to this date. As Guzman and Pauwelyn note, *"the direct effect of WTO treaty in Brazil's legal system is illustrated by consolidated judicial understandings (called "Súmulas") of the two highest courts in Brazil."*[22]

To analyze Brazilian judiciary's decisions, it is important to first briefly mention the most important domestic courts and their jurisdiction: the Supreme Federal Court of Brazil [hereinafter also referred to as *Brazilian Supreme Court*], and the Superior Court of Justice. Being the highest court of the domestic judiciary, the Brazilian Supreme Court is responsible for safeguarding the Constitution, and has extraordinary appellate jurisdiction regarding constitutional challenges against international treaties.[23] With national jurisdiction, the Brazilian Supreme Court may receive appeals against both federal and state courts decisions. Furthermore, the Brazilian Supreme Court has abstract judicial review over international treaties incorporated into domestic law when challenged against the Brazilian Constitution.[24]

The Brazilian Supreme Court has therefore an important role in defining the relationship between international law and domestic law by setting the standards of judicial enforcement of international rules within the Brazilian territory. It is well-known that, in most democratic countries, national supreme courts may set

---

[20] *Markovic and Others v. Italy* [GC], n. 1398/03, Eur. Ct. H.R. (2006).

[21] *Súmula* 575 of the Brazilian Supreme Court was first published on 3 January 1977.

[22] Guzman and Pauwelyn (2009), p. 77.

[23] Brazilian Constitution, Art. 102, III, b.

[24] Brazilian Constitution, Art. 103.

3.2 The Traditionalist Role of Brazilian Courts in WTO Agreements

guidance or precedent to lower courts on the application of judicial construction doctrines, such as direct effect or consistent interpretation, although in common law jurisdictions precedent usually has a different weight. [25]

In Brazil, in broad terms, cases filed against the local customs authorities on the implementation of international trade measures, or based on violation of WTO agreements are to be filed before the federal courts of general jurisdiction, as there is no specialized court for trade matters. The Brazilian Constitution allows plaintiffs to file cases against the federal government or agencies before the federal courts where the plaintiff is domiciled, where the facts of the case occurred, or at the Brazilian capital.[26] It is the plaintiff's choice.

Yet, another important national court is the Superior Court of Justice [*Superior Tribunal de Justiça*], the court of last resort for federal non-constitutional matters. As in most jurisdictions, the Brazilian Constitution invests high courts with original jurisdiction *ratione personae* of suits affecting certain government authorities like ambassadors, ministers of state, and the head of the state. In this vein, if a plaintiff seeks the nullification of an act of the Brazilian foreign trade chamber [*Câmara de Comércio Exterior—CAMEX*],[27] the Superior Court of Justice has original

---

[25] Civil law and common law legal communities have different perceptions on precedent. The diverse stances on the role of precedent in civil law and common law is derived from the fact that, in general, common law considers the citation of previous cases as a source of law, whereas civil law countries mostly do not consider the citation of previous cases as controlling legal authority. Oliveira and Garoupa (2012) noted that:

> [c]ase law is a primary source of law in the common law while in the civil law world, codes provide the fundamental law, statutes further develop the codes, and courts merely provide interpretation. In such context, it is traditionally said there is no precedent in civil law. It is true that there is no absolute precedent in the common law sense. It would be unthinkable and inconsistent in a civil law system that precedents could be used to undermine the code law. However, legal precedents are reasonable because it is argued that the courts have arrived at the correct interpretation of a particular aspect of code law. Other courts should be expected to follow such precedent not because the precedent is case law but rather it declares the adequate interpretation of code law. Hence precedents cannot exist without a clear code source. Furthermore, they are declaratory in the sense that they do not create law, but clarify the correct interpretation of the law.

[26] Brazilian Constitution, Art. 109, paragraph 2.

[27] Trade policy in Brazil is coordinated by the *Câmara de Comércio Exterior—CAMEX* [Foreign Trade Chamber]. The CAMEX aims to formulate, adopt, implement and coordinate policies of international trade of goods and services in Brazil, and has a deliberative organ named "Council of Ministers" composed by: (1) the Minister of Development, Industry and Foreign Commerce; (2) the Chief of Staff of the President of the Republic; (3) the Minister of Foreign Relations; (4) the Minister of Finance; (5) the Minister of Agriculture, Livestock and Food Supply; (6) the Minister of Planning, Budget and Management; and (7) the Minister of Agrarian Development. The CAMEX is composed by the Administration Executive Committee, the Executive-Secretariat, the Consultation Council of the Private Sector, and the Committee of Financing and Guarantee of Exports. The Executive Committee of Administration encompasses more than 26 government officials from diverse sectors including, besides the above mentioned Ministries, representatives from the Central Bank of Brazil, the National Bank of Economic and Social Development, the Ministry of Labor and Employment, the Ministry of Science and Technology, the Ministry of the

jurisdiction to hear the case, with the right of appeal to the Supreme Court. If the request for a *writ* of mandamus is filed against the President of Brazil, then it is the Brazilian Supreme Court that has original jurisdiction to hear the case.

To sum up, private individuals or companies willing to challenge a trade measure need to file a case before the federal courts of first instance, or the Superior Court of Justice, or even the Supreme Court, depending on the status of the respondent authority against which their claim is addressed. The next section turns attention to key cases where Brazilian courts have considered issues involving WTO agreements.

3.3 Brazilian Cases

With the brief explanation of the traditionalist role of Brazilian courts, this section presents actual cases litigated before domestic courts in Brazil and assesses how the judiciary applies and interprets the WTO agreements. This study demonstrates that the long Brazilian tradition of domestic application of international treaties reveals that several disadvantages of traditionalism regarding WTO agreements, described in the trade scholarly debate,[28] have taken place in Brazil. In a general overview, traditionalism regarding WTO agreements in Brazil has generated (1) a flood of individual cases, (2) diverse and inconsistent rulings among domestic courts within Brazil, (3) domestic courts' interpretation of WTO rules different from the international and foreign interpretation of trade rules, and finally (4) disequilibrium in international trade's concessions and rights. In addition, traditionalism in WTO agreements has allowed the impairment of important public policy goals aiming at the protection of higher societal values such as environment protection and food supply, disregarding therefore the principle of popular sovereignty and democratic self-government, as well as the function and objective of international trade agreements.

It is relevant to note that the WTO rules that have been often invoked before Brazilian courts are mostly the GATT provisions, as it is the oldest and most well-known agreement under the WTO umbrella. As for the Antidumping Agreement,[29] cases have been brought before Brazilian lower courts as the CAMEX has used this commercial defense mechanism starting the beginning of the 1990s. According to Department of Trade Defense [*Departamento de Defesa Comercial*, hereinafter

---

Environment and the Ministry of Tourism. Because trade policy is a federal attribution, in case state authorities in Brazil are interested in any particular international trade action, they have to negotiate it along with the federal government through the Minister of Foreign Relations. Brazilian local authorities have no official participation in setting international trade policies.

[28] *See* Table 2.1 at Sect. 2.3.1.

[29] Although the Antidumping Agreement was accorded in 1979, it was only incorporated in the Brazilian domestic legal order in 1987. *See* Decreto n. 93941, de 16 de janeiro de 1987, D.O.U. de 19.1.1987.

3.3 Brazilian Cases

DECOM][30] statistics, Brazil started 500 dumping investigation processes from 1998 until 2013.[31] From the dumping investigations, 51 % recommended the imposition of definitive antidumping duties, 34 % terminated without the adoption of a definitive measure, 3 % undertook commitments, and 11 % are under analysis.[32] Consequently, the imposition of antidumping duties by the government, either provisional or definitive, may be a cause of litigation involving the antidumping regulations before Brazilian courts. In these cases, private companies importing the products subject to antidumping duties may challenge such imposition, but it is not usual that these cases reach the Supreme Court. As of date, one very important issue with regards to antidumping duties is under consideration before the Supreme Court, and it encompasses several different lawsuits from all over the country questioning the application of antidumping duties to imports when the corresponding sales contract was concluded before the date of inception of the antidumping duties.[33]

All the cases selected are representative of numerous similar cases dealing with the same controversy on the merits. To avoid charges of selection bias among which cases were picked as descriptive of the Brazilian courts' behavior in the application and enforcement of WTO rules, this study selected the leading cases decided by the Brazilian Supreme Court that settled numerous similar cases dealing with the same controversy on the merits starting of 1988, and one case of the Superior Court of Justice. This research chose to select judicial decisions rendered from 1988 because it is the year the current Brazilian Constitution entered into force, after democracy was reinstated. Yet, historical references will be made for understanding the background of the issue and, if applicable, older cases will also be alluded to, for the sake of historical accuracy.

Finally, this study will describe in detail all the arguments and votes in each case Brazilian case for two main reasons. First, there is not much published about Brazilian courts' decisions in the international legal scholarship and no version in English of such decisions[34]; a comprehensive description of the selected Brazilian cases will contribute to fill this gap by providing all the main arguments and counterarguments presented, as well as a thorough rationale of the decisions. Second, the detailed explanation of Brazilian cases is necessary for accuracy purposes because there is not only one single unified opinion written by only one justice in the Brazilian courts' decisions, unless the justices choose to concur with the rapporteur of the case without any further consideration. In highly controversial

---

[30] The DECOM is the Brazilian authority responsible for trade remedies investigations, working under the Secretariat of Foreign Trade [*Secretaria de Comércio Exterior*, hereinafter SECEX] of the Ministry of Development, Industry and Foreign Trade.

[31] Departamento de Defesa Comercial (2013), pp. 18–39.

[32] Ibid., p. 46.

[33] *See* Sect. 3.3.3.

[34] All Brazilian judicial decisions are available in Portuguese only; therefore any excerpts of Brazilian courts' decisions were translated into English by the author.

issues, it is common that justices present their individual votes orally or in written to express their views when deciding a leading case, rather than simply concurring with the rationale of the rapporteur. Indeed, the debates and votes during the courts' decision-making process in Brazil are part of the decision, regardless whether they consist of oral or written votes given by the Justices during the deliberation process. Consequently, all individual votes are important on their own to identify the reasoning behind the decision reached.

Based on this qualitative research, this study selected four cases to be studied. The first case examines the liberal application of the GATT national treatment rule on imports of codfish, different from the international and foreign interpretation. The second case discusses the notorious imports of retreaded tires which, besides generating numerous domestic courts injunctions, have also produced contradictory rulings from MERCOSUL and WTO dispute settlement systems. The third case assesses the anomalous mix between trade rules and constitutional guarantees in domestic litigation over the application of antidumping duties to existing contracts at the time of the imposition of such duties—a "*hybrid*" that Knop has already anticipated. Lastly, the fourth case illustrates how Conforti's perception of judicial deference to the executive may not be necessarily a nationalist perspective, but in fact be compliant with international trade rules.

3.3.1 The Imports of Codfish Case: Extraordinary Appeal n. 229096[35]

Being one of the most vivid discussion topics in international trade, the application of national treatment principle prescribed in GATT Article III[36] was object of a recurring issue in international trade rules litigation before Brazilian courts. The national treatment rule aims at ensuring that imported products are treated equally to local products after they enter the domestic market—meaning after the imposition of customs duty on imports. Along with the most-favored nation principle, the national treatment rule is considered a major pillar of the international trade system, and permeates the WTO agreements. It is also present in GATS Article 16 and TRIPS agreement Article 3. The purpose of the national treatment principle is to

---

[35] STF, Recurso Extraordinário 229096, Relatora para o acórdão: Ministra Cármen Lúcia, 16.8.2007, D.J.U. 11.4.2008.

[36] GATT, Article III—National Treatment on Internal Taxation and Regulation

> 1. The contracting parties recognize that internal taxes and other internal charges, and laws, regulations and requirements affecting the internal sale, offering for sale, purchase, transportation, distribution or use of products, and internal quantitative regulations requiring the mixture, processing or use of products in specified amounts or proportions, should not be applied to imported or domestic products so as to afford protection to domestic production.

avoid protectionism in the application of domestic measures, as explained by the WTO Appellate Body in *Japan—Alcoholic Beverages*[37] case:

> The broad and fundamental purpose of Article III is to avoid protectionism in the application of internal tax and regulatory measures. More specifically, the purpose of Article III "is to ensure that internal measures 'not be applied to imported or domestic products so as to afford protection to domestic production'". Toward this end, Article III obliges Members of the WTO to provide equality of competitive conditions for imported products in relation to domestic products. "[T]he intention of the drafters of the Agreement was clearly to treat the imported products in the same way as the like domestic products once they had been cleared through customs. Otherwise indirect protection could be given". Moreover, it is irrelevant that "the trade effects" of the tax differential between imported and domestic products, as reflected in the volumes of imports, are insignificant or even non-existent; Article III protects expectations not of any particular trade volume but rather of the equal competitive relationship between imported and domestic products. Members of the WTO are free to pursue their own domestic goals through internal taxation or regulation so long as they do not do so in a way that violates Article III or any of the other commitments they have made in the WTO Agreement.[38]

3.3.1.1 The Historical Background on the National Treatment Rule in Brazilian Domestic Litigation

The case law of the Brazilian Federal Supreme Court on the GATT national treatment rule has been consistent for several decades and has confirmed the direct effect of WTO law in Brazil. Back in 1976, the Supreme Court enacted *Súmula* 575, which states that that imported goods from GATT member states are exempted from ICM[39]—a state tax on the circulation of goods and provision of certain services—if the similar national product is exempted (a Supreme Court's *súmula* is a one-sentence pronouncement which states succinctly the reasoning of the Supreme Court on reiterated matters).[40] In one of the eight leading cases that originated the *Súmula* 575 in 1976, the Office of the Prosecutor General's opinion stated that the national treatment rule should be applied to imported products

---

[37] WTO, *Japan—Taxes on Alcoholic Beverages*, WT/DS8/AB/R, WT/DS10/AB/R, WT/DS11/AB/R, adopted Nov. 1, 1996.

[38] WTO, *Japan—Taxes on Alcoholic Beverages*, WT/DS8/AB/R, WT/DS10/AB/R, WT/DS11/AB/R adopted Nov. 1, 1996, p. 16.

[39] ICMS is the acronym for the state tax *Imposto sobre Circulação de Mercadorias e Serviços*, established by Article 155, II, of the Brazilian Constitution Article 155, which reads:

> Article 155 – The states and the Federal District shall have the competence to institute taxes on: (...)
> II – transactions relating to the circulation of goods and to the rendering of interstate and intermunicipal transportation services and services of communication, even when such transactions and renderings begin abroad.

[40] On the definition, origins and objectives of the *súmula*, *see* Oliveira (2006), pp. 110–111. For more details on the differentiation between the ordinary *súmula* and the new *súmula vinculante*, *see* Oliveira and Garoupa (2012).

independently of proof of reciprocity from the exporting country.[41] The Rapporteur of the case, Justice Moreira Alves, considered that the GATT, as a contract-treaty, was in force in Brazil and therefore prohibited even indirect discrimination of the imported goods vis-à-vis the national product.[42] Consequently, per the Supreme Court's jurisprudence since the 1970s, tax benefits must be extended to imported goods if granted to similar products in Brazil. The issuance of a *Súmula* is an emblematic pointer to the large number of cases that have reached Brazilian courts with the consequent demand of a clear guideline from the Brazilian Supreme Court to solve the controversy. The objective of the *Súmula* is to guide lower courts to apply the court's rulings on identical cases on the same issue and, at the same time, to expedite the disposition of a profusion of cases brought before the Supreme Court with the same underlying issue. In fact, the Supreme Court of Brazil has consistently given direct effect to GATT Article III, and provided guidance to lower courts on this issue.

A major concern, however, is the definition of what are like products for the application of the national treatment rule on concrete cases. This topic is usually framed under a matter of fact by lower courts, rather than as matter of right that can be reviewed at the Supreme Court level.

3.3.1.2 The National Treatment Rule on Imports of Codfish Prior to the Constitution of 1988

From the private invocability of the GATT national treatment rule before the Brazilian judiciary, this study next demonstrates that the self-executing character of WTO law has generated (1) a flood of individual cases, (2) diverse and inconsistent rulings among domestic courts within Brazil, (3) domestic courts' interpretation of WTO rules different from the foreign and international interpretation, and (4) disequilibrium in international trade's concessions and rights.

A paradigmatic issue that acted as a major catalyst for a flood of cases before Brazilian courts on GATT Article III was whether the exemption of state taxes (ICM) on salted and dried fish would encompass imported codfish. Originally created in 1968 as an exemption of state taxes regarding fish generically,[43] new regulations of this measure included dried and salted fish in 1971,[44] and prohibited

---

[41] STF, Recurso Extraordinário 83531, Relator Ministro Moreira Alves, 10.2.1976, D.J.U. 7.4.1976, pp. 5–6.

[42] Ibid., p. 9.

[43] Rebouças (1998). The author explains that the origin of the exemption of state taxes on fish, in a general way, was the "Convênio de Porto Alegre" enacted in 1968.

[44] Protocolo AE 09/71, de 15 de dezembro de 1971, D.O.U de 31.12.1971.

the application of the tax exemption to crustacean and mollusk, as well as to haddock, codfish, hake and salmon in 1980.[45] Revoked in 1987,[46] new and successive regulations reinstated the exemption in 1989[47] up to 1999.[48] The state tax exemption was said to be designed to encourage the consumption of dried and salted national fish by the local population aiming at avoiding waste of fresh fish harvested in Brazilian waters, which rots when not speedily sold, and facilitating food stocking. Local importers went to courts requesting the state tax exemption to apply to imports of codfish based on GATT Article III. A northern Atlantic fish that is not found in Brazilian waters, codfish is mostly harvested in Norwegian waters and is considered a delicacy in Brazil, usually consumed in festive occasions like Easter and Christmas.

Numerous cases were brought before Brazilian courts and conflicting rulings were rendered throughout the country in both first and appellate instances, even between the two chambers of the Supreme Court. The First Chamber of the Supreme Court had considered valid the distinction between codfish and the dried and salted national fish and had sustained the imposition of state tax on codfish.[49] Conversely, the Supreme Court's Second Chamber was deciding in favor of the application of GATT national treatment to codfish as a like product to dried salted national fish.[50]

The internal divergence within the Supreme Court was later harmonized.[51] When solving the divergence, Justice Raphael Mayer, rapporteur of the case, acknowledged the conflicting rulings and pondered that the Norwegian codfish, as a species belonging to the genus dried and salted fish, could be categorized as a like product to national dried and salted fish.[52] Consequently, Brazilian states could not tax dried and salted codfish while exempting national dried and salted fish due to GATT national treatment rule. Justice Sydney Sanches, in his concurring vote, cited the definition of codfish made by several dictionaries, and taking as a matter of fact that there is no codfish in Brazilian waters with no like Brazilian fish species, affirmed that the exclusion of codfish from state tax exemption was nevertheless innocuous because codfish was included in the tax exemption under the bigger umbrella of dried and salted fish in Brazil.[53]

---

[45] Convênio ICM 07/80, de 13 de junho de 1980, D.O.U de 17.6.1980.

[46] Convênio ICM 29/87, de 18 de agosto de 1987, D.O.U de 20.8.1987.

[47] Convênio ICMS 117/89, de 7 de dezembro de 1989, D.O.U. de 12.12.1989.

[48] The last regulation providing for a ICMS exemption on dried and salted fish was Convênio ICMS 23/98, de 20 de março de 1998, D.O.U de 26.3.1998, which expired on 30 April 1999.

[49] STF, Recurso Extraordinário 101966, Relator Ministro Soares Muñoz, 24.4.1984, D.J.U 25.5.1984.

[50] STF, Recurso Extraordinário 99860, Relator Ministro Aldir Passarinho, 12.4.1983, D.J.U 20.5.1983.

[51] STF, Recurso Extraordinário 105606, Relator Ministro Rafael Mayer, 26.11.1985, R.T.J. 116/794.

[52] Ibid., p. 798.

[53] Ibid., pp. 802–805.

The prevailing position in the Brazilian judiciary on the national treatment principle differs from the international and foreign interpretation of trade rules. Although very disputed, the liberal interpretation of the meaning of like products prevailed before Brazilian courts, and presents itself as a "liberal account of likeness" because, being one of the most disputed issues of international trade, the definition of likeness at the WTO jurisprudence seems to be much more stricter, as well at the European perspective.

At the WTO dispute settlement system, the national treatment rule has received a very restrict interpretation. To decide cases of alleged discrimination based on origin, panels and the Appellate Body have focused on whether domestic products and imports are alike, and "*once they find likeness, discrimination almost follows naturally, as an afterthought.*"[54] The comparison between the domestic product and the imported one is fundamental to determine likeness, and the WTO jurisprudence has decided on this issue in a case-by-case basis using the following criteria: the product's end-uses, consumer tastes, the product's physical characteristics, and tariff classifications.[55] Although never recurring to tariff classifications, Brazilian courts seem to understand that the broad category of dried and salted fish encompasses any fish, national or foreign, in a manner that setting aside a foreign fish would qualify as indirect discrimination. Indeed, the Harmonized System of tariff nomenclature for imports provides a classification for "*Fish, dried, salted or in brine*" under heading 0305, but also has specific tariff lines for different types of fish, such as codfish 0305.49.0100, and salmon 0305.41.0000.

On the other hand, a market analysis of consumer preferences could have shown that Brazilian consumers make a difference between Norwegian codfish as opposed to other kinds of dried and salted fish, indicating that consumers would not take a national fish for codfish. Moreover, the exclusion of codfish from state tax benefits could have been considered as fulfilling a legitimate tax objective of charging luxury food higher than food eaten on a daily needs.[56] In any event, there are no easy answers when it comes to define likeness. Yet, the need to liberally interpret international trade rules seems to be a major benefit than the costs of having a strict interpretation of likeness to favor a state tax collection. After all, as Justice Rezek noted, strict interpretations of likeness can backfire in relation to future complaints against major trading partners that could harm Brazilian products abroad, and risk the Brazilian much cherished reputation of compliance with international law.[57]

In addition to the WTO interpretation on the meaning of likeness, the Brazilian perspective on the application of the national treatment principle also seems to

---

[54] Pauwelyn (2006), p. 5.

[55] Ibid., p. 2.

[56] According to Van Der Veen, luxury food can be understood as "*foods that are unusual or desirable because of their foreign origin*" and usually consumed on special occasions. *See* Van der Veen (2003), p. 406.

[57] STF, Recurso Extraordinário 114379, Relator Ministro Francisco Rezek, 17.12.1987, D.J.U. 8.4.1988, p. 9.

3.3 Brazilian Cases   83

differ from the European interpretation. We can consider, for example, that stricter views on national treatment are argued, such as the in the *EC—Sardines*[58] case, where the European authorities considered that two species of sardines found in different waters—one around Europe, and the other in the Pacific coast—were not like products. This perspective, which was disputed before the WTO dispute settlement system and not before domestic judiciaries, vividly contrast with the more flexible views of the Brazilian judiciary on what like products may be. As seen above, dried and salted codfish found in Norwegian waters was considered a like product to dried and salted fish found in Brazil, a country where codfish is not found in its waters. It seems very unlikely that any contracting party to the WTO system, particularly the European Union, would choose to advance such liberal account of likeness even when the resulting decision would favor their exports in a specific case, because in the future such interpretation will be used against them.[59]

The codfish case demonstrates that when domestic courts consider the application of national treatment rule in domestic litigation and decides unilaterally what constitutes a like product, it brings about disequilibrium in international trade's concessions and rights and inconsistencies in meaning of international trade rules. The judicial interpretation of likeness in the codfish case has broadened Brazilian obligations before the WTO by providing imports with a flexible meaning of likeness which is not similarly ensured by other major WTO contracting parties, where private claims of national treatment violations are not even allowed.

3.3.1.3 The National Treatment Rule on Imports of Codfish After the Constitution of 1988

When a new democratic Constitution was enacted in 1988, considerations about Brazil's international responsibility and the need to abide to the GATT national treatment rule over imports of codfish were confirmed again by the Supreme Court. Faced with a constitutional change, the Brazilian Supreme Court reaffirmed its previous jurisprudence on the GATT national treatment. This case is a relevant one because it is a prime illustration of the implicit application of the consistent interpretation doctrine. This case is a reaffirmation of the liberal interpretation of the national treatment rule which, as already explained above, is different from the international and foreign interpretation of trade rules, and causes disequilibrium in international trade concessions.

Following the end of the military dictatorship period in Brazil (1964–1984), the application of the GATT national treatment rule to imports of codfish was greatly challenged throughout the country, and a flood of individual cases followed. The Supreme Court was again seized to have the ultimate say on the issue. In regulating taxation among the different levels of government, the Brazilian Constitution of

---

[58] WTO, *European Communities—Trade Description of Sardines*, WT/DS231.
[59] Sykes (2005), p. 651.

1988 prescribed that the Federal Union may not exempt the payment of taxes from the states, the federal district, or the municipalities.[60] Faced with this new constitutional provision, the Superior Court of Justice and several appellate courts decided that international treaties contracted by the Federal Union could no longer impose restrictions on taxes imposed by the other levels of government. According to this reasoning, the Brazilian Constitution of 1988 had revoked the possibility that the GATT Article III be applied to state taxes.

As a result, diverse and inconsistent decisions were rendered in rulings among lower courts in Brazil; most of them were validating the imposition of state taxes (ICMS) on imported products when the like national products were exempted. This constitutional controversy eventually reached the Brazilian Supreme Court to decide whether the GATT was in accordance with the Brazilian Constitution of 1988.[61]

In interpreting Article 151, III of the Federal Constitution of 1988, the Supreme Court made a distinction between the role of the Federal Union as subject of domestic law, and the functions of the Brazilian State as subject of public international law at the international level. The Supreme Court concluded that Article 151, III applies to the Federal Union in its domestic role, because such provision regulates the internal division of powers between the federal and states taxation. The Supreme Court considered that only the Federative Republic of Brazil, as subject of international law, has the power to make international treaties, not the Federal Union at the domestic level, the states or municipalities. Consequently, the Court clarified, the President's powers to make international treaties represent his functions as a head of the Brazilian State at the international level, and therefore the President has the power to sign international treaties that affects state taxes.[62]

The Supreme Court's rationale derives from Kelsen's concept of the state as a *"total legal order"* that can regulate human behavior in all directions. According to Kelsen, the state as total legal order is connected domestically in *"partial legal orders."* Such partial legal orders not only include member states, but the federation itself, which is different from the *"federal state."* As Kelsen (1967) notes:

> The concept of a material sphere of validity is applied, for example, when a total legal order—such as that of a federal state comprising several member states—is articulated into several partial legal orders, whose spheres of validity are delimited with respect to the objects to be regulated by these partial orders: For example, if the legal orders of the

---

[60] Brazilian Constitution, Article 151 reads:

It is forbidden for the Union: (. . .)
III – to institute exemptions from taxes within the powers of the states, of the Federal District or of the municipalities.

[61] STF, Recurso Extraordinário 229096, Relatora para o acórdão: Ministra Cármen Lúcia, 16.8.2007, D.J.U. 11.4.2008.

[62] Ibid.

member states are competent to regulate only those objects which are specifically enumerated by the constitution; if—in other words—the regulating of these objects falls within the competence of the member states, whereas the regulation of all other objects is reserved for the legal order of the federation, which, in itself is also a partial legal order. The material sphere of validity of a total legal order is always unlimited, in the sense that such an order, by its very nature, can regulate the behavior of the individuals subjected to it in all directions.[63]

The Supreme Court's decision conveys the understanding that the Brazilian State, as subject of public international law, may comparably act as a unitary state (or "total legal order") at the international arena, with treaty-making power over state taxes. For the sake of accuracy with the content of the Supreme Court decision, it is necessary to note that a side issue was also debated. In this judgment, Justice Ilmar Galvão expressed his views on the scope of application of the controverted Article 98 of the National Tax Code. Enacted in 1966 during the military dictatorship, this article prescribes that "[*t*]*reaties and international conventions revoke or modify the domestic legislation on taxation, and will be observed by supervening domestic legislation.*" The application of Article 98 of the National Tax Code was highly contentious in the legal academia in Brazil. Some authors claimed that Article 98 provided a higher status of international treaties over domestic federal law, while others had argued that it was unconstitutional as the hierarchy of laws is domain of the Brazilian Constitution, passing through commentary considering Article 98 a useless clause, as international treaties would qualify as special law and the principle *lex posterior generalis non derogat priori speciali* never required this kind of provision to be applied.[64]

Justice Ilmar Galvão, in the lines of Kelsen's theory, asserted that Article 98 was compatible with the Brazilian Constitution of 1988 because Article 98 clarified the national character of international treaties on taxation, as they are a legal norm derived from the Federal Union as a total legal order, not as a partial legal order.[65] On the other hand, Justice Sepúlveda Pertence evaluated that it was not enough to characterize Article 98 as a national law to allow the Federal Union to enter into competences reserved to the states.[66] Justice Sepúlveda Pertence added that the state tax exemption based on an international treaty may be deemed valid because it is under the concept of an "*autonomous exemption*" derived from international law, as opposed to "*heteronomous exemption*," prohibited within the domestic legal order. In any case, the issue over the scope of application of Article 98 of the National Tax Code is not settled, as it was not a central for the Court to make its decision. Indeed, Article 98 is currently been challenged before the Supreme Court in another case involving the application of the Convention between Brazil and

---

[63] Kelsen (1967), p. 15.

[64] For a detailed explanation of the divergent positions on the academic debate in Brazil over Article 98 of the National Tax Code, *see* Moser (2007).

[65] STF, Recurso Extraordinário 229096, Relatora para o acórdão: Ministra Cármen Lúcia, 16.8.2007, D.J.U. 11.4.2008, p. 7.

[66] Ibid., pp. 5–6.

Sweden for the avoidance of double taxation in relation to income tax levied on dividends of Volvo to its shareholders in 1993.[67]

3.3.1.4 The Assessment of the Case

The Supreme Court decision to uphold the application of the national treatment rule on imports of codfish after the enactment of the Federal Constitution of 1988 is a relevant one because it is a paramount example of the reading that judges are not inclined to decide that a supervening domestic law trumps a previous international treaty, unless the legislator, including the constituent assembly, intentionally chooses to repeal such international obligations in a clear way. Indeed, without express legislative intent to revoke an international treaty—by means of a disposition in the newly-enacted legislation clearly stating that it revokes a given treaty—judges will most likely interpret the new legislation in a way that is consistent with the corresponding international treaty. In the Brazilian experience, a new constitutional order did not change the Brazilian Supreme Court openness towards a consistent interpretation to balance international law with domestic constitutional rules. The liberal account of meaning of the national treatment rule was reaffirmed and, as explained above, such interpretation is different from the international and foreign interpretation of trade rules, and causes disequilibrium in international trade concessions, as other WTO members would not concede the same liberality on the definition of likeness.

The underlying stakes of this case may also reveal a different perspective from the more familiar application of the separation of powers principle, whereby there is a struggle in the allocation of powers between the judiciary and the other branches of government on matters that affect foreign affairs. The issue here was not on the role of judicial review as if encroaching the legislative powers to revoke international treaties through enacting conflicting domestic law, mostly important, in this case, constitutional law. In fact, there was no fierce debate on whether the judiciary should have decided the case or not. The major issue was the extent of the role of the Federal executive in representing the country, as a unity, at the international level. In such conflict, it is the function of the judiciary to decide the extent of the President's powers when representing Brazil as a subject of international law. In addition to the Supreme Court's openness to international law and enforcement of Brazilian international obligations, this case reflects the differences between the contexts where constitution-making occurs. As Jackson (2004) explains

> Federal constitution making may occur in many historic settings, including: (1) devolutionary federalism, where, as in Belgium, an existing unitary state devolves constitutional

---

[67] STF, Recurso Extraordinário 460320, Relator Ministro Gilmar Mendes. Although a very interesting case, this dispute does not refer to WTO obligations and therefore will not be object of this study. The judgment session started on 31 August 2011, when the Rapporteur read his vote, but it was then adjourned due to the request of Justice Dias Toffoli (pending at the time of writing).

powers to its subnational units; (2) as a centralizing move from confederation to federation, as was the case for the United States in 1789 and Switzerland; or (3) as a gradual consolidation of former colonies into a single national state, as was arguably the case for both Australia and Canada.[68]

More like a devolutionary federalism, as opposed to the widely known U.S. transfer of powers to a central government, the Brazilian federalism was originated from a historically centralized government—the former Empire of Brazil—which transferred some of its powers to the states, in a decentralization movement to give powers to subnational units, in the Brazilian case, the states and, since 1988, the municipalities. Therefore, the conflicts of allocation of powers are more inclined to focus on the vertical separation of powers, that is, the federal government, the states and the citizens, rather than generate conflicts horizontally between the roles of the judiciary in foreign affairs vis-à-vis the other branches of government.

In summary, this study demonstrates that the Brazilian Supreme Court confirmed its previous case law on the national treatment rule through implicitly applying the doctrine of consistent interpretation when faced with a constitutional change. By privileging the application of a multilateral treaty, the Brazilian Supreme Court deferred to international trade obligations and reassured the private invocability of WTO agreements before domestic courts, while reaffirming the strong Presidential powers to negotiate international treaties on behalf of the country including state taxes matters. Traditionalism in international trade law has allowed the private invocability of the WTO national treatment rule to consider codfish and other species of Brazilian fish as like products. Traditionalism has also generated a multitude of individual cases before Brazilian domestic courts, inconsistent rulings among domestic courts within Brazil, a diverse application of WTO rules vis-à-vis foreign and international interpretation of trade rules in favor of imported products, with the consequent disequilibrium in international trade concessions and rights.

Therefore, this case confirms that the Brazilian Supreme Court followed the traditional approach in the international legal scholarship in acknowledging the WTO rules. Indeed, the Supreme Court did not consider the specific function and objective of international trade agreements, or the principle of self-government in international trade relations. However, these arguments were never raised in the domestic litigation, which precludes any clear positioning of the Court about them. After all, under the strict procedures of the extraordinary appellate review, the Supreme Court did not have any possibility of considering reasoning that were not previously brought up by the parties in litigation.

---

[68] Jackson (2004), p. 133.

3.3.2 The Retreaded Tires Case: ADPF 101[69]

Known in the international trade scholarly debate as the Brazilian retreated tires case, the Brazilian Supreme Court case ADPF 101[70] is a paradigm for studying domestic litigation involving rulings issued by the WTO dispute settlement mechanism and by regional trade agreements dispute settlement system. The Brazilian government banned the import of used goods, including used tires and retreaded tires. MERCOSUL countries were later freed from the import ban due to a ruling from the MERCOSUL dispute settlement system.[71] At the domestic level, Brazilian retreaders obtained multiple provisional injunctions before federal courts in Brazil authorizing the import of used tires. Meanwhile, the European Union successfully challenged the import ban on retreated tires before the WTO dispute settlement mechanism.[72]

---

[69] STF, Argüição de Descumprimento de Preceito Fundamental 101-DF, Relatora: Ministra Carmem Lúcia, 24.6.2009, D.J.U. 4.6.2012.

[70] ADPF is the acronym for *Argüição de Descumprimento de Preceito Fundamental* [Claim of Non-Compliance with a Fundamental Precept]. This claim is under the competence of the Supreme Court for abstract control of constitutionality, and aims at avoiding or repairing damages to a fundamental precept of the Constitution, caused by acts of the Public Power. One of ADPF's requirements is the existence of a relevant constitutional question; the relevancy of the issue may be proven through the indication of multiple and conflicting judicial decisions on the same question.

[71] MERCOSUR, Ad hoc Arbitral Tribunal Award, Import Prohibition of Remoulded Tyres from Uruguay, 9 January 2002.

[72] WTO, *Brazil—Measures Affecting Imports of Retreaded Tires*, WT/DS332/R, WT/DS332/AB/R, adopted 3 December 2007. The Panel report defined the products at issue in the following way:

> 2.1 This dispute concerns retreaded tyres which are produced by reconditioning used tyres by stripping the worn tread from a used tyre's skeleton (casing) and replacing it with new material in the form of a new tread and, sometimes, new material covering also parts or all of the sidewalls.
> 2.2 Retreaded tyres can be produced through a number of different methods all encompassed by the generic term "retreading." These methods are: (i) top-capping, which consists in replacing only the tread; (ii) re-capping, which entails replacing the tread and part of the sidewall; and (iii) remoulding or "bead to bead" method, which consists of replacing the tread and the sidewall including all or part of the lower area of the tyre.
> 2.3 There are different types of retreaded tyres which correspond to the different types of casings used to produce them, namely: passenger car retreaded tyres, commercial vehicle retreaded tyres, aircraft retreaded tyres and other. Under international standards, passenger car tyres may be retreaded only once. By contrast, commercial vehicle and aircraft tyres may be retreaded more than once.
> 2.4 Under the Harmonized System nomenclature, retreaded tyres are classified under HS heading 4012 "Retreaded or used pneumatic tyres of rubber; solid or cushion tyres, tyre treads and tyre flaps, of rubber", and in particular under four sub-headings: 4012.11, which refers to retreaded tyres of a kind used on motor cars, including station wagons and racing cars; 4012.12, which includes the kind of retreaded tyres used on buses or lorries; 4012.13, which refers to the kind used on aircraft; and 4012.19, which comprises all other types of retreaded tyres. Consequently, for international trade purposes, retreaded tyres are to be distinguished from both used tyres and new tyres. Used tyres are classified under the HS sub-heading 4012.20, whereas new tyres are classified under HS heading 4011.

3.3 Brazilian Cases

The dispute over the Brazilian ban on imports of retreaded tires is relevant because it provides a practical example on how traditionalism in international trade rules precipitate (1) a flood of individual cases, and even when not in absolute numbers, the impact of these cases on a specific trade measure end up by impairing the trade policy choice in its entirety (2) diverse and inconsistent rulings among domestic courts, (3) domestic courts' interpretation of WTO rules differ from the international interpretation of trade rules, with the aggravation that, by applying WTO rules, it precipitated (4) a violation of Brazilian international obligations derived from the MERCOSUR trade dispute settlement system.

Because this case is complex and involves several international treaties as well as divergent rulings from different trade dispute settlement mechanisms, this section will first describe the arguments in domestic litigation, followed by the rationale of the individual votes of the Brazilian Supreme Court Justices identifying the reasoning for upholding the import ban.[73] Then, this section will proceed to make an assessment of the case in general terms. Finally, it will consider specifically the way the Brazilian Supreme Court responded to the complexity of existing duplicate proceedings with contradictory rulings from WTO and MERCOSUL trade dispute settlement mechanisms.

3.3.2.1 The Domestic Litigation

This case has specifically produced a flood of cases before domestic courts and involved decisions of four federal appellate courts (out of five existing courts), and 25 federal courts of first instance. For instance, at the Federal Appellate Court of the fourth Region alone, there were 45 different cases involving the imports of retreaded tires.[74] The amount of domestic litigation and court injunctions were so significant for the trade measure at issue as the amount of injunctions practically neutralized the governmental ban, and were object of core arguments at the WTO dispute settlement system.[75]

Several constitutional arguments were used as grounds for Brazilian courts' decisions, being the most relevant for the purpose of this study: (1) violation of the constitutional freedom of commerce and free competition, as the retreaded tires

---

[73] The decision of the Brazilian Supreme Court on the ADPF 101 is particularly long, amounting to 278 pages.

[74] STF, Argüição de Descumprimento de Preceito Fundamental 101-DF, Relatora: Ministra Carmem Lúcia, 24.6.2009, D.J.U. 4.6.2012, pp. 167–169.

[75] *See* all reports on the dispute WTO, *Brazil—Measures Affecting Imports of Retreaded Tires*, WT/DS332/R, WT/DS332/AB/R, WT/DS332/16.

industry had its production diminished or even terminated, and therefore would unfairly benefit competition from new tires industry; and (2) violation of the equality principle, as used tires from MERCOSUL were permitted, while other countries' products, mainly originated from the European Union, were not allowed. According to the arguments presented by the parties, the core of the litigation revealed an apparent clash between two constitutional norms: on one hand, the fundamental right to health and to an ecologically balanced environment (Articles 6 and 225 of the Constitution), and on the other hand, the promotion for a sustainable economic development that would include used tires imports because it generated jobs and cheaper retreaded tires for the least-advantaged parts of the Brazilian population.

In addition to the flood of cases, the diverse and inconsistent rulings among domestic courts, the General-Advocacy of the Union filed before the Supreme Court a claim of non-compliance with fundamental precept (ADPF)[76] to defend the import ban against Brazilian courts' injunctions. The ADPF is a kind of judicial action that allows direct access to the Supreme Court to settle, under the Court's abstract control of constitutionality, when there is a manifest judicial controversy over the application of a fundamental norm. In this case, the General-Advocacy argued that the judicial controversy over the import ban concerned the meaning and extent of Article 225 of the Federal Constitution, which states that "*[a]ll have the right to an ecologically balanced environment, which is an asset of common use and essential to a healthy quality of life, and both the Government and the community shall have the duty to defend and preserve it for present and future generations.*"

The General-Advocacy also based its arguments on the Preamble of the Basel Convention on the Control of Transboundary Movements of Hazardous Wastes and their Disposal, in force in Brazil since 1993, which fully recognizes that "*any State has the sovereign right to ban the entry or disposal of foreign hazardous wastes and other wastes in its territory.*"[77] The Brazilian government also brought up in the case the information that the import ban exception to MERCOSUL countries was enacted to comply with the arbitral award in favor of Uruguay before the MERCOSUL dispute settlement system. The government also informed the Court that it was then facing a case against the European Union before the WTO dispute settlement system on the same matter, and reproduced the public health arguments Brazil presented to support the import ban in its WTO's first submission. Therefore, based on health concerns originated from the flood of used tires imports in the Brazilian market, along with the possibility of losing the case before the WTO

---

[76] The "claim of non-compliance with fundamental precept" is the English translation of the *ação de descumprimento de preceito fundamental* (ADPF).

[77] Basel Convention on the Control of Transboundary Movements of Hazardous Wastes and their Disposal, Mar. 23, 1989 (entry into force 5 May 1992), incorporated in Brazilian domestic legislation by Decreto n. 875, de 19 de julho de 1993, D.O.U. de 20.03.1993.

3.3 Brazilian Cases

dispute settlement, the Brazilian government asked the Federal Supreme Court to revoke the provisional measures granted by lower courts.

Due to the relevance and implications of the case, the Rapporteur, Justice Carmém Lúcia, called a two-day *amicus curiae* public session [*audiência pública*] whereby previously admitted third parties, NGOs, and interest groups were granted permission to present oral statements and expose their views as *amicus curiae* on the case.[78] As in the Court's practice, this public session was held during the initial phase of the proceedings so that the Rapporteur could hear and gather all relevant arguments and evidence to enhance democratic access to the Court's decision-making process.[79]

Questioning the import ban, importers of retreaded tires presented formal and substantial challenges against the government prohibition grounded mainly on the principle of legality and free competition. They claimed that such import restrictions could only be imposed through statutory law enacted by the Brazilian Congress, and not by executive regulations. They also argued that the industry was addressing the environmental concerns by destroying ten used tires for every retreaded tire imported, and accused the import ban to be a protectionist measure lobbied by multinational tire producers located in Brazil aiming at hindering competition from the cheaper retreaded tires industry. Importers also contended that retreaded tires should be distinguished from used tires, and fostered the interpretation that the executive measures only aimed at banning imports of used tires for direct consumer use, allowing the import of retreaded tires as feedstock. Finally, they demonstrated that, due to the import ban, numerous plants would be out of business and consequently lay off their employees, all of which would violate the principle of free exercise of any economic activity and the pursuit of full employment (Article 170, VIII, and sole paragraph).[80]

---

[78] For more information on the role of *amici curiae* before the Brazilian Supreme Court, *see* Gontijo and Peter da Silva (2010).

[79] Calling for an *Amicus curiae* session is a discretionary choice of the Rapporteur, who presides the session. Some other justices occasionally attend parts of these sessions, at will. The *audiência pública* are open to the public and are broadcasted by radio and television (Radio and TV Justiça).

[80] Brazilian Constitution, Article 170, I, VI reads:

> Art. 170. The economic order, founded on the appreciation of the value of human work and on free enterprise, is intended to ensure everyone a life with dignity, in accordance with the dictates of social justice, with due regard for the following principles: (...)
> VIII – pursuit of full employment; (...)
> Sole paragraph – Free exercise of any economic activity is ensured to everyone, regardless of authorization from government agencies, except in the cases set forth by law.

3.3.2.2 The Decision of the Brazilian Supreme Court

With five concurring written opinions, the Court, by majority, declared that all interpretations, including the judicial ones, which allow the import of retreaded tires, were unconstitutional for violating the right to health and the right to an ecologically balanced environment.[81] In what concerns the substantial arguments, the Court considered that, according to the Brazilian Constitution, it is the duty of the government to guarantee the right to health through social and economic policies (Article 196)[82] and to defend the environment and preserve it for the present and future generations (Article 225).[83] In addition, the Court pondered that the constitutional principles of the Brazilian economic order ensure national sovereignty and permit differentiated treatment to products according to their impact on the environment (Article 170, I and VI).[84] As a result, the Court found that the import ban on retreaded tires was a legitimate governmental policy on waste management to protect health and the environment for present and future generations. In relation to the formal breach allegation, the Court rejected the importers' argument based on the principle of legality. The Court considered that, under the Brazilian political-administrative structure, the Ministry of Development, Industry and Foreign Trade may impose trade restrictions through administrative regulations, because it has the attribution to develop foreign trade policies and enforce trade measures in Brazil. Therefore, it was not required that the import ban was enacted by Congress legislation.

---

[81] STF, Argüição de Descumprimento de Preceito Fundamental 101-DF, Relatora: Ministra Carmem Lúcia, 24.6.2009, D.J.U. 4.6.2012.

[82] Brazilian Constitution, Article 196 reads:

> Art. 196. Health is a right of all and a duty of the State and shall be guaranteed by means of social and economic policies aimed at reducing the risk of illness and other hazards and at the universal and equal access to actions and services for its promotion, protection and recovery.

[83] Brazilian Constitution, Article 225 reads:

> Art. 225. All have the right to an ecologically balanced environment, which is an asset of common use and essential to a healthy quality of life, and both the Government and the community shall have the duty to defend and preserve it for present and future generations.

[84] Brazilian Constitution, Article 170, I, VI reads:

> Art. 170. The economic order, founded on the appreciation of the value of human work and on free enterprise, is intended to ensure everyone a life with dignity, in accordance with the dictates of social justice, with due regard for the following principles:
> I – national sovereignty; (...)
> VI – defense of the environment, including through differentiated treatment according to the environmental impact of products and services and their processes of production and rendition.

3.3 Brazilian Cases

In addition to the opinion of the Rapporteur, the final decision however was construed by diverse rationales from each of the five individually written concurring votes. In her opinion, Justice Carmém Lúcia presented a historical evolution of the environment legislation in Brazil, including international environmental treaties that Brazil is a signatory party. Among the international rules, she noted that the Rotterdam Convention on the Prior Informed Consent Procedure for Certain Hazardous Chemicals and Pesticides in International Trade allows the signatory parties to deliberate which dangerous chemical products may be imported in their territory, and which ones are banned for harming human health and the environment. Such Convention together with the Basel Convention on the Control of Transboundary Movements of Hazardous Wastes and their Disposal, in her views, constitute the framework of international rules that regulate the international trade of chemicals that are considered toxic or harmful to health and the environment. She also summarized the proceedings and findings of both the MERCOSUL[85] and WTO[86] dispute settlement cases, and reproduced several paragraphs from their respective reports. On the alleged incoherence on the Brazilian legislation in allowing imports of retreaded tires from MERCOSUL, she noted that such exception was only conceded in compliance with a MERCOSUL Arbitral decision, and was afterwards revoked by the Brazilian executive.

She noted that conflicting judicial decisions within the Brazilian judiciary on the import of retreaded tires needed special attention from the Supreme Court in light of Brazil's international obligations, but mainly in light of the competence of the Supreme Court as the final interpreter of constitutional principles. She considered that the question on the imports of retreaded or used tires required balancing constitutional principles to find the correct equilibrium and remarked that the guarantee of full employment cannot authorize non-compliance with the right to health and to an ecologically-balanced environment.

Even though concurring with the conclusion of the Rapporteur, Justice Eros Grau did not agree with the use of the ponderation of principles interpretation to decide the question; instead, he interpreted the question based on the totality of the constitutional rules. According to his views, the technique of pondering principles—through which the constitutional interpreter allocates more or less weight to one principle as opposed to another principle—reflects a subjective choice unprovided with legality. He continued that, once judges could discretionarily pick one out of many principles according to their own preferences, such choices would be very dangerous because legal rationale vanishes and legal uncertainty predominates.

Justice Ayres Britto considered that tires were anti-ecological products that contributed to the environmental deficit due the hazardous character of waste

---

[85] MERCOSUR, *Ad hoc* Arbitral Tribunal Award, *Import Prohibition of Remoulded Tyres from Uruguay*, 9 January 2002.
[86] WTO, *Brazil—Measures Affecting Imports of Retreaded Tires*, WT/DS332/R, WT/DS332/AB/R, adopted 3 December 2007.

tires. In his vote, he concurred with the Rapporteur and expressed that the preservation of the environment became extremely important to all legal orders, as a condition of sustainability of the planet that imposes itself on the freedom of trade based on the precautionary principle. He continued that remoulded tires have half of the life span of new tires and, for their countries of origin, retreaded tires are environmental waste then exported to Brazil, bringing about serious damage to constitutionally protected values.

Justice Ellen Gracie found that the import ban was in accordance with the Constitution and reflected the government's effort to implement economic policies to protect the environment for present and future generations. She explained that the import ban did not impede the free exercise of the economic activities of the remoulded tires' industry. Instead, she underlined that the remoulded tires industry was an important ally to reuse waste, but the Court could not grant the request of importing a most economically advantageous foreign feedstock that was extremely harmful to the environment. Justice Ellen Gracie also annexed to her vote the reasoning she adopted when suspending provisional measures issued by lower courts against the import ban while she was the president of the Court.[87]

Justice Celso de Mello stated that all have the right to an ecologically balanced environment, a third generation right, and it is the duty of all collectivity to preserve the environment. He mentioned that the application of the precautionary principle in this case results from Article 225 of the Constitution, while also referring to the Principles 15 and 17 of the 1992 Rio Declaration,[88] the Basel Convention, and the Stockholm Convention on sustainable development. In his views, the core of the dispute between Brazil and the European Union at the WTO was the sustainable development through public policies of health and environmental protection, specifically waste management. Justice Celso de Mello considered that the fundamental issue at stake before the Brazilian Supreme Court was the management of toxic waste and human health that should be made in light of the international obligations and Brazilian legislation. Citing the Supreme Court ruling on ADI 3540,[89] Justice

---

[87] STF, Agravo Regimental na Suspensão de Tutela Antecipada 171-PR, Relatora: Ministra Ellen Gracie, 12.12.2007, D.J.U. 29.2.2008.

[88] Rio Declaration on Environment and Development, adopted in Rio de Janeiro 1992 during the United Nations Conference on Environment and Development:

Principle 15 – In order to protect the environment, the precautionary approach shall be widely applied by States according to their capabilities. Where there are threats of serious or irreversible damage, lack of full scientific certainty shall not be used as a reason for postponing cost-effective measures to prevent environmental degradation.
Principle 17 – Environmental impact assessment, as a national instrument, shall be undertaken for proposed activities that are likely to have a significant adverse impact on the environment and are subject to a decision of a competent national authority.

[89] STF, Medida Cautelar na Ação Direta de Inconstitucionalidade 3540, Relator: Ministro Celso de Mello, 1.9.2005, D.J.U. 3.2.2006.

Celso de Mello stated that the freedom of exercise of economic activity under the principles of the economic order in the Brazilian Constitution could not compromise the protection of the environment by purely economic reasons that could damage health, safety, and well-being of the population.

Lastly, Justice Gilmar Mendes refuted the alleged violation of the principle of legality as the Basel Convention is incorporated in the Brazilian domestic legal order, and therefore has the status of federal law authorizing the executive measures imposing the import ban on retreaded tires.

The Court concluded by granting its decision retroactive effects (*ex tunc*), which meant that the Court's ruling was to be enforced against all previously granted injunctions that have not been carried out yet, including those based on final judicial decisions rendered by lower courts. For obvious reasons, the Court excluded the judicial orders that had already been implemented, as it would be practically unfeasible to reverse the effects of these orders by seizing imports within Brazilian territory and returning them to their country of origin.

The only dissenting vote, Justice Marco Aurélio stated that the principle of free exercise of economic activity, on which the Brazilian economic order is founded, cannot be restricted by the duty of the State to protect the environment without compliance with the principle of legality. According to his opinion, as the Brazilian Constitution establishes that "*no one shall be obliged to do or refrain from doing something except by virtue of law*,"[90] the import restriction on retreaded tires could only be created by a law issued by the Brazilian Congress, in observance of the principle of separation of powers, not by executive regulation. Justice Marco Aurélio also found that the government measures were violating the principle of free competition and free enterprise, because the retreaded tires industry could not be held responsible for tire waste when in fact they were importing tires to add value to remoulding tires to compete with multinational tire industries by offering tires with better prices to the least-advantaged population. According to his opinion, the principle of free competition and free enterprise could not be forgotten by the executive, which was encroaching on Congress' power to prohibit the importation of products for the use of the Brazilian population.

3.3.2.3 The Assessment of the Case

This case has distinctive features to be considered in the analysis of multilevel trade litigation. There is a concurrence between multilateral and regional trade proceedings with contradictory judgments over the same measure, along with domestic courts being seized to adjudicate on the same matters. It shows a profound challenge on how to provide judicial adjudication on constitutional norms while preserving the multilateral and regional trade systems. For advocates of multilevel judicial governance in international trade literature, this case in particular triggers

---

[90] Brazilian Constitution, Article 5, II.

several questions such as whether GATT Article XXIV is still sufficient to address the increasingly complex relationship between regional and multilateral trade systems, and adds controversy to the existing debate on the application of GATT Article XX to balance trade and non-trade disputes.[91]

From the analysis of ADPF 101, it could be said that the Brazilian Supreme Court in adjudicating on international trade matters gave prevalence to fundamental and social rights guaranteed by the Constitution. Indeed, business interests might go against fundamental and social rights like, in the present case, the right to health and to a balanced environment. Therefore, market liberalization and free enterprise cannot forgo public health and environment protection by corporate interests of profit efficiency. In this case, the fact that imports of retreaded tires from Europe were considered as better feedstock than their Brazilian counterparts does not surpass higher societal values of public health and environmental concerns on toxic waste.

Nevertheless, the Court also found relevant the impact of its ruling on the Brazilian stance at the international level. At the time of the judgment, the Court seemingly gave high consideration to the consequences of potential international responsibility of Brazil for not complying with the WTO report on the case *Brazil—Measures Affecting Imports of Retreaded Tires*.[92] Although not explicitly, the Supreme Court's final decision backed the international obligations of Brazil derived from the WTO dispute settlement system, and enabled Brazil to comply fully with the recommendations of the WTO Dispute Settlement Body on September 2009. It can therefore be considered that the Court implicitly applied the doctrine of consistent interpretation with the WTO agreements, although this doctrine was never mentioned in the Court's ruling. Moreover, the Supreme Court's decision demonstrated the direct effect of international treaties once incorporated within Brazilian legal order, and showed an overt attitude towards the enforcement of international law at the domestic level.

As mentioned above, before reaching the Supreme Court, the controversy on the import ban on retreaded tires brought about many lawsuits before almost 30 different first instance and appellate courts. Although the involvement of these courts may not be considered as a flood of cases in absolute terms, it should be noted that this issue involved a very specific industry segment. The amount of litigation domestic courts faced on the import ban was very comprehensive of the industry sector, and included even the retreaded tires industry' union. More importantly, however, is the fact that the European Union considered that the amount of courts' injunctions were enough to incur Brazil into non-compliance with WTO rules. After all, the amount of litigation and parties involved basically hindered the governmental measure in a way that impaired the objective and goals of the governmental policy and threatened Brazil with retaliation from the EU before the WTO dispute settlement mechanism.

---

[91] Marimon et al. (2009).
[92] WTO, *Brazil—Measures Affecting Imports of Retreaded Tires*, WT/DS332/AB/R, adopted 3 December 2007.

3.3.2.4 Brazilian Domestic Courts Faced with Divergent Rulings from Different Trade Dispute Settlement Mechanisms

An additional complexity to be analyzed in relation to the way Brazilian courts adjudicate on WTO rules derives from the existence of conflicting dispute settlement rulings from WTO and MERCOSUL in the retreated tires case. Due to fragmentation of international law, other than the WTO, states have formed regional free trade areas to increase freedom of trade and promote closer integration among countries parties to such agreements.[93] Because regional and international trade agreements carry their own dispute settlement mechanisms, a concurrence between multilateral and regional trade rulings arises, which may sometimes result in conflicting judgments over the same dispute. This concurrence may produce substantive overlaps and procedural overlaps. Pauwelyn explains that substantive overlaps *"arises, for example, where the WTO permits a safeguard or health measure but a regional agreement prohibits such measure within the region."*[94] As for procedural overlaps, they occur when *"a country challenges another country first under a regional agreement (such as MERCOSUR or NAFTA) and, thereafter, the dispute is sent a second time before the WTO."*[95]

However, this scenario has occurred in very rare occasions so far because, most of the times, a diplomatic solution or a negotiable compromise is reached. De Cara shows that *"(1) there is always a possibility to negotiate in international trade relations and (2) it is through international trade measures that at the end of the day, states are made to enforce the rules."*[96] In some other cases, an economic shift changes the business's framework and therefore starting domestic litigation is no longer necessary, or the litigation before an international trade dispute settlement mechanism may be more efficient in terms of time-frame results as opposed to other alternatives.

The consequent proliferation of international trade agreements has raised a scholarly debate on the question of overlapping jurisdictions and rules from diverse international trade systems.[97] The International Law Commission advances the idea that states should apply conflict clauses when entering new international treaties: *"When States enter into a treaty that might conflict with other treaties, they should aim to settle the relationship between such treaties by adopting appropriate conflict clauses."*[98]

---

[93] GATT, Article XXIV, paragraph 4.

[94] Pauwelyn (2009), p. 5.

[95] Ibid.

[96] de Cara (2007), p. 1376.

[97] See Marceau and Wyatt (2010), Pauwelyn and Salles (2009), and Bartels and Ortino (2006).

[98] International Law Commission (2006), paragraph 251, conclusion 30.

However, creating conflict clauses does not suffice to solve the question in what concerns multilateral and regional trade agreements. Such provisions do not prevent duplicate proceedings with potential conflicting rulings from different dispute settlement systems when countries from different regions are the complainants, as the dispute on the Brazilian import ban on retreaded tires demonstrated. In this case, Uruguay was the complainant in the MERCOSUL dispute, whereas at the WTO DSS the complainant was the European Union. As a matter of fact, MERCOSUL has choice of forum clauses and therefore seems to conform to the International Law Commission Study Group suggestion. Therefore, the potential for duplicate proceedings with contradictory rulings is an immediate concern[99] that will most likely increase in the long run with the expansion of regional trade agreements and complexity of their interactions with the WTO system.

In the Brazilian experience at the ADPF 101, the Supreme Court faced a complex domestic litigation on the governmental import ban on retreaded tires that had also triggered conflicting dispute settlement rulings from the MERCOSUL and WTO trading systems. At the international level, the dichotomy between regionalism and multilaterism has created tensions and potential for conflict. The Brazilian import ban on retreaded tires gives a good illustration of what such overlaps may produce. At the national level, multiple provisional measures given by different lower courts made the final decision more complex, with several different parties, courts, and involvement of organized civil society.

With the functions of a constitutional court, the Brazilian Supreme Court mainly considered the constitutional principles of right to health and environmental protection, as well as the constitutional principles of the economic order, to decide whether to sustain or invalidate the governmental ban on import of retreaded tires. The Supreme Court concluded that, under Brazilian Constitution, the economic activity could not trump the right to health and environmental protection.

In addition to constitutional rules, the Supreme Court also considered Brazil's international obligations while deciding the case. The Rapporteur of the case not only mentioned the rulings from both MERCOSUL and WTO dispute settlement systems; she expounded the developments of both disputes and their final findings. In what refers to the domestic legal status of dispute settlement rulings, the Brazilian Supreme Court implicitly reaffirmed the dualist rationale that such rulings are not legally binding in the Brazilian territory, as such question was not even discussed. Although it is true that international rulings of international trade dispute settlement systems cannot be directly enforced before domestic courts,[100] they are nevertheless considered part of Brazil's international obligations. Accordingly, the

---

[99] Hillman (2009), p. 202.

[100] Other countries' judiciaries have clearly stated that the rulings of GATT/WTO dispute settlement system are not binding domestically. *See* Matsushita et al. (2006), p. 102: the authors explain that "*it is the responsibility of Congress and the President to ensure conformity between U.S. and WTO law,*" and therefore imply that courts are not supposed to be in charge of implementing WTO law.

3.3 Brazilian Cases

Rapporteur mentioned the MERCOSUL and WTO rulings as they composed part of the arguments presented before the Supreme Court. In her vote, Justice Carmém Lúcia also expressly mentioned other international obligations Brazil have arising from environmental protection treaties.

From the Supreme Court's final decision, one can conclude that the Court interpreted both MERCOSUL and WTO rulings in a dualist perspective that decisions from trade dispute settlement systems are external sources to Brazilian domestic legal order. At the same time, however, in terms of substance, the Supreme Court disregarded the MERCOSUL ruling, and concurred in substance with the WTO findings. It can be extract from this finding that the Supreme Court implicitly applied the doctrine of consistent interpretation with WTO agreements, though such expression was never used in the judgment. In the operative part of the decision, the Rapporteur declared unconstitutional, with retroactive effect (*ex tunc*), all interpretations, including the judicial ones, that allowed the importation of retreaded tires of any kind, included the remolded ones. If one reads between the lines, "all interpretations" implicitly stated that the content of the MERCOSUL ruling could not be implemented within Brazilian territory, including through governmental agencies. Although international dispute settlement systems decisions do not have domestic legal value, the Court apparently found important to state, although implicitly, that it would not allow trade considerations supplant environment protection and the right to health, even regarding the MERCOSUL integration process.

Another point worthy of note is that the Supreme Court did not directly address the question of whether MERCOSUL or WTO rules would prevail. The Supreme Court went beyond the dichotomy of multilateralism and regionalism, and brought to the debate other international treaties on sustainable development and environmental protection to which Brazil is also a member. The international treaties mentioned during the judgment were: (1) the Rotterdam Convention on the Prior Informed Consent Procedure for Certain Hazardous Chemicals and Pesticides in International Trade, (2) the Basel Convention on the Control of Transboundary Movements of Hazardous Wastes and their Disposal, and (3) 1992 Rio Declaration on Environment and Development.

Accordingly, one can conclude from the ADPF 101 decision that the Supreme Court, in analyzing Brazil's international obligations, did not restrict itself to the directly involved international trade rulings, or rules, be it the WTO, or the MERCOSUL. Instead, the Supreme Court reached for other international treaties on environmental protection. The Supreme Court considered that the governmental import ban and other environment protection measures were regulating Brazil's international obligations derived from the Basel Convention. Therefore, the Supreme Court did not isolate the international trade agreements, as self-contained regimes, from other areas of international law. To illustrate, Justice Gilmar Mendes refuted the alleged violation of the principle of legality by considering the Basel Convention as the federal law that had permitted the enactment of the import ban by the executive.

From the analysis of this case, the scholarly debate on the relationship, or lack of it, between the WTO agreements and other rules of international law, like environmental protection and human rights[101] was not addressed at the domestic level. At the domestic level, the Supreme Court seemed to have corroborated in this specific case the understanding that when there is a conflict between trade agreements and other areas of international law, the latter ones will prevail.

For these reasons, it can be concluded that the Brazilian Supreme Court, when faced with rules, or rulings, from different international trade dispute settlement systems has implicitly agreed in substance with the WTO ruling, but not in form, as the latter is not legally binding in the Brazilian domestic order and was based on the GATT Article XX exceptions. The Brazilian Supreme Court, instead of GATT Article XX exceptions, considered international obligations undertaken by Brazil outside WTO agreements. Here, environmental protection agreements prevailed. Lastly, the Supreme Court implicitly stated that the MERCOSUL interpretation on the matter was unconstitutional and the WTO interpretation on the merits prevailed, what can be interpreted as an implicit application of the doctrine of consistent interpretation in relation to WTO agreements.

3.3.3 The Radial Tires Case: Extraordinary Appeal n. 632250[102]

This case is an important one because it displays the struggle in the application of international trade rules while considering constitutional principles at the domestic level. Being conceived and written by economists to enhance market access towards free trade, the design of the WTO agreements was not directed to deal with individual rights as granted by domestic law. Furthermore, this case shows that the perspective advocated by traditionalism may provoke unintended consequences that do not foster international trade rules as envisioned at the international level, as broad trade policy goals are impaired by judicial decisions that, although well-intentioned, disregarded commercial defense rights to avoid predatory practices in international trade.

In addition, this case is illustrative of a perceived common pattern in first instance courts when faced with international trade issues. It seems that the first instance courts, usually closer to the individual dramas of the litigants, are more inclined to concede to the plaintiffs' predicaments and not to the broad goals of national trade policy and commercial defense actions by government agencies. Here, direct effect of WTO agreements generated a domestic court' interpretation different from the international and foreign interpretation of trade rules, with a potential disequilibrium in international trade's concessions and rights.

---

[101] *See* Pauwelyn (2003), Petersmann (2002), and Alston (2002).

[102] STF, Recurso Extraordinário n. 632250, Relator: Ministro Joaquim Barbosa (pending).

3.3.3.1 The Domestic Litigation

According to WTO rules, dumping is characterized when *"products of one country are introduced into the commerce of another country at less than the normal value of the products."*[103] If dumping causes or threats material injury to the local industry, WTO law recognizes the right of member countries to apply antidumping measures with the goal of offsetting dumping. In Brazil, the application of the Antidumping Agreement was defined by Law 9019,[104] of 1995, and the corresponding dumping proceedings regulated by presidential Decree 1602,[105] of 1995, later superseded by presidential Decree 8058,[106] of 2013. Dumping duties are set by the interministerial body CAMEX, based on a report issued by the Department of Commercial Defense (DECOM) under the Secretariat of Foreign Trade (SECEX) of the Ministry of Development, Industry and Foreign Trade.

The application of the Antidumping Agreement by Brazilian courts raised an interesting question in the relations between international trade rules and domestic constitutional law, what Knop called "hybrid" interpretation because it is not wholly domestic, not wholly international.[107] A most prominent issue before the Brazilian judiciary is whether antidumping duties can be collected from imports purchased before the imposition of antidumping duties is publicized. Commentary has noted that in Brazil *"courts have reaffirmed the rule according to which antidumping duties are not applicable to products shipped from the exporting country before the publication of the administrative order imposing the measures in the official gazette."*[108]

In the present case study, a Brazilian importer of new radial tires for buses and trucks from China filed a preventive writ of *mandamus*[109] before the first instance federal court in Itajaí, state of Santa Catarina, aiming at avoiding the collection of antidumping duties by the Brazilian customs authority[110] in relation to its import operations. The plaintiff alleged that the contract to buy the radial tires from China was concluded on 4 November 2008, that is, before the enactment of CAMEX Resolution n. 79[111] of 18 December 2008, which imposed provisional antidumping duties on those products from China. According to his views, the customs authority could not collect antidumping duties on those imports because their purchase contract was made before the date of the determination of provisional antidumping

---

[103] GATT, Article VI.
[104] Lei n. 9019, de 30 de março de 1995, D.O.U. de 31.03.1995.
[105] Decreto n. 1602, de 23 de agosto de 1995, D.O.U. de 24.8.1995.
[106] Decreto n. 8058, de 26 de julho de 2013, D.O.U. de 29.7.2013.
[107] Knop (2000), p. 506.
[108] Peixoto (2010), p. 38.
[109] JF/SC, Mandado de Segurança n. 2009.72.08.001594-1, Itajaí, Juiz Antonio Fernando Schenkel do Amaral e Silva.
[110] Delegacia da Receita Federal do Brasil em Itajaí, Santa Catarina.
[111] Resolução n. 79, de 18 de dezembro de 2008, D.O.U. de 19.12.2008.

duties by CAMEX Resolution 79. The plaintiff basically argued that applying antidumping duties to a commercial contract concluded before the entry into force of Resolution 79 would violate the constitutional principles of due process, legal certainty, vested right and perfect juridical act. As a counter-argument, the Federal Union stated that antidumping duties were collected in accordance with GATT/WTO rules, and aimed at providing standards of competition without which perverse commerce would to take place and destroy the national producers of like products.

There was a controversy on whether the import license was granted before or after Resolution CAMEX was in force. The plaintiff argued that it requested the import license in November 2008, which later expired, and a new one substituted it. The customs authority considered that the import license issued in November 2008 actually expired on 27 January 2009, without a previous timely request for renewal, which therefore would constitute a cancellation. According to the customs authority, a new import license request was made more than thirty days later of the expire date, that is on 27 February 2009, when Resolution 79 was already in force and, in consequence, this last request should be considered as the original import license request. In any case, the customs authority demonstrated that the goods in question were shipped from China to Brazil on 19 March 2009, clearly after the issuance of CAMEX Resolution in December 2008. The Federal Union argued that the date of the sales contract is not relevant for the application of antidumping duties, which are collected based on the import declaration for customs clearance.

The federal judge of first instance found that the date of the import license request was not pertinent to decide the case; instead, he considered that the date of the sales contract performed abroad was the relevant fact. He also considered the fact that CAMEX Resolution became effective at the date of its official publication, without any intervening period. According to his views, importers should have been warned about the imposition of antidumping duties in time so that they could adapt to these new rules. In light of these findings, the first-instance judge ruled that the CAMEX Resolution, as applied, was in violation of the principle of legal certainty and vested rights of companies and consumers. Therefore, the first-instance judge ruled that contracts made before the entry into force of CAMEX Resolution 79 were excluded from collection of antidumping duties. Accordingly, the judge granted the writ to allow customs clearance of the radial tires imported from China by the plaintiff without the collection of antidumping duties.[112]

The Federal Union appealed. The Federal Appellate Court of the fourth Region[113] reversed the order of the first instance court. The Federal Appellate Court considered that the date of the sale transaction was not a relevant factor to

---

[112] The goods had already been released from customs because the importer secured the payment of the antidumping duties by making a deposit in a bank account under judicial control.

[113] TRF-4, Apelação/Reexame Necessário n. 2009.72.08.001594-1, Relatora: Des. Federal Luciane Amaral Corrêa Munch, 25.5.2010, D.J.U. 17.6.2010. TRF-4 stands for *Tribunal Regional Federal da 4ª Região*—the Federal Appellate Court of the fourth Region.

3.3 Brazilian Cases 103

be considered in the application of antidumping duties. Instead, the Federal Appellate Court affirmed that the date of the import declaration was the correct reference that should be considered in the case. The Federal Appellate Court explained that antidumping duties are applied on the importation of goods, which happens in a different moment in time than the sales contract, and that the importation of goods initiates when the importer registers its import declaration.

The importer then appealed to the Supreme Court,[114] arguing that importation proceedings have several stages and that antidumping duties could not be imposed in relation to its imports in this case. The Supreme Court found that this case passed the general relevance-test, as required in Brazilian legislation on the admissibility of extraordinary appeals to the Supreme Court in force since 2007. In other words, the Supreme Court decided to hear the case because it had a general importance for Brazilian legal order that transcends the isolated interest of the parties in litigation. According to Justice Joaquim Barbosa, Rapporteur of the case, the alleged offense to the constitutional principle of non-retroactivity of laws in the application of antidumping duties requires a uniform response from the judiciary.[115] Justice Joaquim Barbosa stated that *"the relevance of this discussion is reinforced by the present social and economic context, in which international trade relations are subject to disequilibrium caused by concessions of benefits and incentives, not always endorsed by collegiate groups in charge of free competition."*[116]

Acting in its capacity as custodian of the law (*custos legis*), the Office of the Prosecutor General expressed its opinion that the CAMEX Resolution derived from Law 9019, of 1995 (Article 7, 2 and Article 8), which authorized the imposition of antidumping duties starting from the date of its publication, and at the time the importer registers its import declaration. In this line of thought, the Office of the Prosecutor General considered that the CAMEX Resolution is an act under the category of secondary law, which enforced the existing antidumping legislation. Accordingly, the Office of the Prosecutor General suggested the Court to affirm the decision of the Federal Appellate Court of the fourth Region.

At the time of writing, the Supreme Court has not decided the appeal.

3.3.3.2 The Assessment of the Case

This case brings into question Conforti's assumption that domestic judges be a better venue for enforcing international law vis-à-vis the executive. This case provides an example of the unintended consequences of traditionalism in international trade law when trade rules designed for regulating international relations among the executive powers are interpreted by the domestic judiciary in an anomalous mix between trade rules and domestic law. Designed to regulate inter-

---

[114] STF, Recurso Extraordinário n. 632250, Relator: Ministro Joaquim Barbosa (pending).
[115] STF Press Release (2011).
[116] Ibid.

state relations, the GATT/WTO agreements have guaranteed commercial defense in case imports may cause, or threaten, serious injury to domestic industry. However, based on the interpretation of domestic constitutional rights, domestic courts have not considered WTO rights of imposition of antidumping duties. Here, the domestic lower courts' interpretation of international trade rules has in fact restricted WTO rules by not allowing the imposition of antidumping rights on imports found to be dumped in the Brazilian territory.

The domestic application of trade remedies is certainly interpreted in a different way by other WTO members. To protect their local industry based on the WTO rules, other WTO members such as the United States authorize the levy of antidumping duties after the import transactions were concluded. The Antidumping Agreement allows under certain circumstances the application of retroactive duties on products that entered the domestic territory up to 90 days before the entry into force of the provisional antidumping duties.[117]

In addition, this case is illustrative of a perceived common pattern in first instance courts when faced with international trade issues. It seems that the first instance courts, usually closer to the individual dramas of the litigants, are more inclined to concede to the plaintiffs' predicaments and not to the broad goals of national trade policy and commercial defense actions by government agencies. Here, a domestic court' interpretation on antidumping duties is different from the international and foreign interpretation of trade rules, with a potential disequilibrium in international trade's concessions and rights.

The Supreme Court will still give the ultimate say on this issue, and its future decision will be applied to all cases with similar questions in the country. Yet, regardless of the outcome at the Supreme Court level, unintended consequences of traditionalism are already visible, as commercial defense may be impaired in favor of predatory trade practices out of an anomalous mix between trade rules and domestic constitutional law. In fact, the potential for increased litigation on the time validity of the antidumping duties is heightened as the newly-enacted

---

[117] Antidumping Agreement, Article 10.6 reads:

Article 10 – Retroactivity (...)
10.6 A definitive anti-dumping duty may be levied on products which were entered for consumption not more than 90 days prior to the date of application of provisional measures, when the authorities determine for the dumped product in question that:
(i) there is a history of dumping which caused injury or that the importer was, or should have been, aware that the exporter practises dumping and that such dumping would cause injury, and
(ii) the injury is caused by massive dumped imports of a product in a relatively short time which in light of the timing and the volume of the dumped imports and other circumstances (such as a rapid build-up of inventories of the imported product) is likely to seriously undermine the remedial effect of the definitive anti-dumping duty to be applied, provided that the importers concerned have been given an opportunity to comment.

legislation—presidential Decree 8058, of 2013—has provided for the possibility that antidumping duties be levied retroactively after a final determination that dumped imports have caused material injury to the domestic industry.[118]

3.3.4 The Thermo Bottles Case: Special Appeal n. 1105993[119]

Although this case is not representative of a multitude of similar individual cases, the issue involved qualifies as relevant because it shows how domestic courts' interpretation of WTO rules may be different from the international and foreign interpretation of trade rules, and how traditionalism interferes with public policy choices in a way that shifts the domestic balance of powers that violates the principle of popular sovereignty and democratic self-government by impairing the choice of how international trade obligations are discharged.

3.3.4.1 The Domestic Litigation

An import and export company filed an action to avoid the applicability of antidumping duties on the imports of vacuum flasks (thermo bottles) from China, challenging the interministerial ordinance n. 28, of 1998, which imposed antidumping duties of 44 % *ad valorem* on thermo bottles and 65 % on glass ampoules from China. Because of the particular situation of China—which is not predominantly a market economic and their domestic market do not permit a proper comparison, not to mention its currency artificial devaluation making exports unfairly cheaper[120]— the Brazilian authorities in charge of the dumping investigation determined the margin of dumping by the comparable prices of like products in Belgium and the United Kingdom. In assessing the dumping margins, the products were not distinguished in relation to their quality and finishing, but only by quantity.

The plaintiff alleged that the antidumping duties were not applicable on its imports of thermo bottles because their import price was higher than the "normal price" considered in the dumping investigation proceedings. The Federal Appellate Court of the fourth Region,[121] confirming the first instance court decision, granted the plaintiff's request. This Federal Appellate Court found that there was no reason

---

[118] Article 85, Decreto n. 8058, de 26 de julho de 2013, D.O.U. de 29.7.2013.

[119] STJ, Recurso Especial 1105993, Relatora: Ministra Eliana Calmon, 4.2.2010, D.J.U. 18.2.2010.

[120] Davis and Back (2010).

[121] TRF-4, Apelação Cível n. 2003.04.01.023436-7/PR, Relator: Des. Federal Joel Ilan Paciornik, 7.11.2007, D.J.U. 28.11.2007. TRF-4 stands for *Tribunal Regional Federal da 4ª Região*—the Federal Appellate Court of the fourth Region.

for the application of antidumping duties on the plaintiff's imports of thermo bottles from China, because the price paid by the plaintiff was higher than the "normal price" considered in the dumping investigation.

The Federal Union appealed to the court of last resort for non-constitutional federal law matters, the Superior Court of Justice.[122] The Superior Court reversed the ruling, stating that the judiciary could not substitute the specialized governmental agency—the Secretariat of Foreign Trade (SECEX)—in the dumping investigation. It concluded that the judiciary encroached in the executive' prerogatives when the appealed decision compared the weighted average of "normal value" with individual prices of imports in an isolated way, which is an exception method of calculation not applicable to the case at hand. It stated that the dumping margin is the measure of the actual or potential damage to the national industry in a certain period of time, and the antidumping duties aims at offsetting these effects.

According to the Superior Court of Justice's ruling, judicial review on dumping investigations are restricted to the application of rules of procedure, and the judiciary cannot replace the technical analysis of SECEX in assessing markets and weighed averages during different timeframes. The Superior Court highlighted that the presidential Decree 1602,[123] of 1995, which at that time regulated the application of the rights recognized in the WTO Antidumping Agreement, established in Article 3 that the SECEX had the attribution to conduct the dumping investigation as well as all requests of non-application of antidumping rights. It added that the plaintiff should request to SECEX the review of the antidumping duties, because such assessment required technical knowledge due to the complexity and nature of calculation and technical reports about the national industry.

The Superior Court of Justice stated further that, besides the rule of Article 3, SECEX is the correct authority to analyze the plaintiff's request even to avoid errors of calculation as happened in the present case. In addition, the Court noted that Article 59 of Decree 1602 guaranteed the right of a summary review to exporters subject to antidumping duties that were not doing business during the period of the dumping investigation.

3.3.4.2 The Assessment of the Case

Although not explicitly mentioned, the noteworthy issue in this decision is the principle of separation of powers and the proper role of courts in trade defense matters. The power and independence of the judiciary in Brazil enabled lower courts to disregard the need for complex models for calculating the "normal value" of imports from China, which does not have a market economy, and substitute the specialized governmental agency in assessing calculations. Conversely, at the

---

[122] STJ, Recurso Especial 1105993, Relatora: Ministra Eliana Calmon, 4.2.2010, D.J.U. 18.2.2010.

[123] Decreto n. 1602, de 23 de agosto de 1995, D.O.U. de 24.8.1995.

Superior Court, judicial deference was given to the specialized governmental agency to evaluate the impact of certain imports from China in the domestic industry. In this case, lower courts activism in supplanting foreign trade defense was replaced by deference to the executive at the Superior Court level. This case also brings into question Conforti's assumption that deference to the executive is a hindrance to the application of international law, because the government in this case was in fact following trade rules and a domestic court decided to intervene and accept the importer's perception and allegations of normal value to achieve a better price to its imports.

This case is also exemplificative of the perceived patterns of first instance courts in being closer to specific dramas of companies litigating against governmental trade policies aiming at getting a better margin of profit or bargain in their commercial activities. Here, it can be seen that higher courts may review such cases and provide lower courts with guidance in international trade issues. In the political aspect of the role of domestic courts, higher courts turn out to be more effective than lower courts, that are closer to litigants' particular dramas and do not have the broad picture of international trade issues, and that may neutralize a legitimate governmental trade policy when there are multiple private claims against it.

Nevertheless, the question that remains is the time-length it takes for higher courts to review appeals and the impairment of commercial defense rights in international trade until the final decision is rendered.

This case concludes the Brazilian case studies where the GATT or the Antidumping Agreement was discussed before domestic courts. The next section will conclude this chapter by drawing general findings of the impact of traditionalism in the meaning of international trade rules in the Brazilian example.

3.4 Conclusion

This chapter has provided a panorama of the effects of traditionalism with regards to international trade agreements through the experience of the Brazilian courts. This chapter demonstrated, through empirical studies on actual litigation in Brazilian courts, concrete examples how traditionalism in the GATT/WTO agreements has affected the function and objective of international trade agreements, and impaired the principle of popular sovereignty and democratic self-government in choosing how international trade obligations are discharged. In the cases studied, several consequences of direct effect of WTO agreements found in the international scholarly debate were identified. Private companies have guaranteed access to courts when public policy goals affect their private interests, usually for maintaining or achieving a better commercial bargain for profit. While guaranteeing the possibility of discussing commercial bargains by private companies before Brazilian courts, the cases presented occasions where traditionalism brought on the disequilibrium in the reciprocal and mutual concessions regarding market access envisioned in the function and objective of WTO agreements, as well as the imbalance in the principle of popular sovereignty and democratic self-government.

In a general perspective, there were several unintended outcomes found in traditionalism in the Brazilian case studies. First, a flood of individual claims throughout the country reached the judiciary against the governmental ban on imports of used tires, on the application of national treatment to imports of codfish, and on the inapplicability of antidumping duties to products purchased before the enactment of the trade defense measure.

Naturally, these multiple individual claims have brought divergent judicial decisions within the judiciary. Accordingly, many of these claims against governmental trade policies resulted in the impairment of the executive's trade policy choices. At a first look, a flood of cases arisen under international trade rules may not be much different from any other domestic controversial issue where there may be lots of individual complaints. It can be argued, therefore, that there is not a flood of cases in the specific case of trade and that the numbers of cases against governmental trade measures are not relevant in absolute terms. However, the domestic litigation against a trade measure in a specific industry, although in absolute terms may amount to only hundreds of cases, in relative terms it may in practice annul a trade measure in its entirety. Other than impairing the governmental policy choice, the complicating factor in these cases, however, is the impact of such decisions may have in the international responsibility of Brazil. When the amount of cases in relative terms turns out to impair the trade measure, such impairment may be considered by another WTO member as enough to incur Brazil into international responsibility. Accordingly, as earlier mentioned, the EU filed a complaint against Brazil at the WTO dispute settlement system and even jeopardized Brazilian international stance on the WTO and Brazilian economy with serious and imminent retaliation, as seen in the *Brazil—Retreated Tires* case, where the import ban on retreaded tires was challenged in almost 30 different domestic courts in Brazil.

Second, the trade scholarly debate raises discussions on whether different and inconsistent interpretations at the domestic level bring about more uncertainty on the application of international trade rules. Uncertainty in meaning of international trade rules is particularly relevant when it comes to the controversial and always intricate definition of like products in light of the principle of national treatment. In fact, the application of GATT Article III to concrete disputes, just like in the WTO dispute settlement system, raises a lot questions as for the meaning of likeness, and the level of scrutiny that should be applied to define what like-products are. What would be the parameters or circumstances to define likeness? In principle, first instance courts and appellate courts are the instances where matters of fact are to be discussed and, accordingly, where the key question of whether products are alike shall be addressed. In regard to the application of national treatment in the *Imports of Codfish case*, the Brazilian judiciary applied GATT Article III, which implicitly showed that this rule was considered as sufficiently precise to be given direct effect. At the Supreme Court level, however, the meaning of "likeness" was not reviewed because, after the enactment of the Federal Constitution of 1988, this kind of assessment is made by lower courts and is interpreted as a matter of fact, not a matter of law to be reviewed by the Supreme Court. Accordingly, the Supreme Court does not assess the application of likeness to the products in question by lower courts. As there are no fixed parameters to establish likeness in a uniform way, if different appellate courts decide differently whether products are alike, it can bring instability and different applications of the national treatment.

In what concerns the Brazilian experience, the occurrence of diverse judicial decisions interpreting trade rules grounded on the application of WTO agreements is intensified by two particular factors: the distinct mixed configuration of the judiciary in Brazil, where judicial selection process encompasses both career and reputation judges, as well as the lack of judicial self-restraint based on an expansive interpretation of the constitutional right of access to courts.

The distinctive feature of the Brazilian judiciary comes from its particular institutional configuration, derived from a mixed system of judicial selection.[124] "Career judges,"[125] who can be selected early in their careers and, although without much working experience, are insulated from political pressures, compose the entire first instance courts in Brazil. "Recognition judges,"[126] who are appointed by the President of Brazil subject to Senate approval and are much more senior in the legal profession, sometimes with political experience, compose the Supreme Court of Brazil. Generally speaking, the appellate courts are composed by 4/5 of career judges and 1/5 of recognition judges. As a result, the hybridism of the judicial career structure in Brazil reflects the independence of lower courts in deciding on policy issues against the government that sometimes can be understood in other countries as falling under the political question doctrine.

On the other hand, at the Supreme Court level, the rapporteur of the case, when faced with a relevant constitutional issue of general interest—governmental trade policy measures included—may admit third parties, such as interest groups and non-governmental organizations, to submit written briefs on their views about the case, as spontaneous *amicus curiae* submissions. The rapporteur of the case may also allow such spontaneous *amicus curiae* to present oral statements to expound their viewpoint in the controversy in a public session [*audiência pública*] broadcasted on television. As a matter of fact, the Brazilian judiciary's structure provides

---

[124] For more detailed information on judicial selection in Brazil, *see* Garoupa and Oliveira (2011).

[125] For legal scholarship on the distinction between career judges and reputation judges, *see* Georgakopoulos (2000) and Garoupa and Ginsburg (2010). Garoupa and Ginsburg explain such distinction as follows:

Comparative lawyers have contrasted the "career" and "recognition" models of judicial organization. The career judiciary, in which judges join the judiciary at a young age and remain there for their entire careers, refers to the system prevalent in most though not all civil law jurisdictions. The recognition judiciary, in which judges are appointed later in life in recognition of other career achievements, is frequently associated with the U.S. and most common law jurisdictions.

[126] Garoupa and Ginsburg (2010).

an environment of independence at the lower courts' level and democratic access to the Supreme Court litigation involving governmental policies.

While the Brazilian judiciary has a mixed composition and is very institutionally independent which generate different and inconsistent rulings, conflicting and inconsistent interpretation at the lower domestic courts' level may be naturally overcome through guidance from the Supreme Court. The Supreme Court may set precedents and guidance to lower courts on relevant trade issues, although the definition of likeness may be trickier to be reviewed, as it is usually understood as a question of fact, not as a matter of right. Whenever there are multiple private claims challenging governmental trade policies, guidance from the Supreme Court is crucial in the political dimension of domestic adjudication of international trade rules. Nevertheless, the length of proceedings and time-consuming litigation has provoked, at least in the Brazilian case, serious threat of retaliation from other WTO members at the international level.

Of course, proponents of traditionalism could also argue that domestic courts should follow the WTO Appellate Body rulings. And therefore there would not be any possibility of non-compliance with WTO rules and the potential threat of retaliation would be non-existing. This argument however would not survive closer examination. To expect that the WTO Appellate Body rulings have already decided on the multiple issues that can arise at the domestic level from the application of trade rules to real facts in the real world seems overly auspicious. The outcome of WTO disputes, like domestic litigation in general, is not beforehand undoubtedly foreseeable and predictable in matters of fact and of law, and therefore it would be not possible for domestic courts to anticipate what would be the ruling of the WTO dispute settlement body in domestic litigation which, as argued, becomes a hybrid that is not domestic nor international law. In any case, even if there would be a clear and straightforward WTO Appellate Body ruling on the issue to be decided by a domestic court, constitutional pluralism theorists have let very clear that both domestic and international courts are not willing to submit to another court's decisions—a topic that will be further elaborate in Sect. 4.4.

Third, traditionalism regarding WTO agreements in Brazil has produced a more flexible interpretation from the way other WTO members interpret the application of national treatment. In what concerns the definition of "like products," if the judiciaries of diverse countries decide differently if two products are alike or not, this also brings imbalance in trade relations, rather than the desired objective of the Marrakech Agreement to bring about greater global coherence in trade. Therefore, traditionalism regarding WTO agreements may bring more inconsistency and incoherence as different WTO members will most likely have different ways of interpreting trade rules, provoking more imbalance and legal uncertainty.

By shifting to domestic judges the application of the national treatment rule instead of the executive, trade remedies may lose their function as judges can be more liberal at the domestic level, than what the international practice suggests. Governments therefore have their capability of reacting to predatory practices on international trade diminished by its own judiciary, which was never the objective of the WTO agreements.

3.4 Conclusion

Lastly, the international scholarly debate draws attention that foreign policy, including trade policy, is not the domain of the judiciary, and reflects the principle of popular sovereignty and democratic self-government. Adjudicating on matters involving international trade rules interferes with public policy choices and seems to violate the principle of popular sovereignty and democratic self-government in choosing how international trade obligations are discharged. Moreover, the mix between international trade law and domestic constitutional law seems to create imbalance in the international trade rights and obligations, as the Brazilian judiciary has been denying commercial defense rights against imports that are dumped in the Brazilian territory out of an alleged violation of the perfect juridical act that would guard contract of sales from being changed by supervening antidumping duties. WTO agreements provide for the right to impose antidumping duties which obviously can only be levied when the product being dumped enters the domestic territory. To allow that products being dumped may have a free pass in the territory cannot be considered as "enforcement" of international trade rules, and seems to fall under what Knops calls a hybrid of international and domestic law that surely does not promote fair international trade. In demonstrating the consequences of domestic courts' interpretation and application of international trade rules, the question now turns to why Brazilian domestic courts would intervene in trade public policy.

There are several reasons why Brazilian courts are intervening in public policy choices. First, Brazilian domestic judges seems to feel compelled to adjudicate cases when seized even though their decisions may impact and bring imbalance in Brazil's international trade concessions, because of the broad interpretation of the Constitution rule that *"the law shall not exclude any injury or threat to a right from the consideration of the Judicial Power."*[127]

Second, and most importantly, first instance courts are usually adjudicating individual claims that, in principle, on their own, will not cause any great impact in Brazil's public policy major goals, and first instance courts often do not know or anticipate whether there are multiple cases on the same subject in other first instance courts around the country. However, when there are multiple individual claims throughout the country, all individual injunctions together, as seen in the cases researched, may provoke serious consequences for Brazil at the WTO level.

Third, even if domestic judges may happen to be aware that other first instance courts are being seized on the same controversy, there is no way to predict if their own individual decisions will be joined by other similar decisions in a way that would threaten Brazil' international trade broad policy goals and relations. Of course, in cases of multiple individual claims, there is the possibility, at the Supreme Court level, to have *amicus curiae* intervention and public hearings where all interested parties can discuss the impact of decision on governmental trade policies and mutual concessions. However, until the Supreme Court ultimately have the chance to settle the issue, a long time will have passed, usually

---

[127] Brazilian Constitution, Article 5, XXXV.

several years, maybe even a decade. In the meantime, multiple courts' injunctions will hinder the effects of legitimate domestic trade measures, such as antidumping duties, thus impacting and causing imbalance on Brazilian trade relations and commercial defense rights. Indeed, under Sykes' theory on the function and objective of international trade agreements, governments should be the political filters for trade rules enforcement, as they are aware of the mutual gains and commitments made on market access, and the impact of their decisions in the domestic legal order and their consequences at the international level.

Of course, judicial review may eventually invalidate WTO-inconsistent action[128] and interpret domestic law in a way that fosters international trade rules in Brazil under the consistent interpretation doctrine. To illustrate how Brazilian courts can interpret domestic and constitutional law to promote trade rules, in addition to the analyzed cases, there is a recent case decided by the Supreme Court of Brazil where an exporting company sought to avoid paying a social security contribution based on the constitutional tax immunity on export revenues.[129] With a decisive reasoning on a 6-5 vote, Justice Ellen Gracie stated that Article 195 of the Federal Constitutional prescribes that "*social welfare shall be financed by all of society*" and, in addition to other constitutional grounds and a thorough analysis of Brazilian tax law, considered that the purported exemption on social security taxes could constitute a violation of the Agreement on Subsidies and Countervailing Measures. Indeed, the prohibited subsidies on Article 3 of the Subsidies Agreement comprise subsidies contingent upon export performance, including exemption of "direct taxes" which, according to endnote 56, are taxes on profits. Justice Ellen Gracie concluded that it was not reasonable to interpret the Constitution as if it had the intention to violate Brazilian international obligations before the WTO, more so if there were a more adequate interpretation that could be used. This opinion demonstrated that potential violations of WTO agreements and the consequent concerns on Brazilian international responsibility can also be used to reinforce constitutional arguments at the Supreme Court level, favoring a consistent interpretation of constitutional norms with international treaties.

Indeed, the international state responsibility for judicial decisions that are incompatible with the international obligations of a state has been recognized since the past century.[130] Nevertheless, whenever the domestic judiciary's interpretation of trade agreements restrains trade remedies, or unilaterally expands the concessions made at the international level, the function and objective of international trade agreements are distorted.

---

[128] Guzman and Pauwelyn (2009), p. 77.

[129] STF, Recurso Extraordinário 564413, Relator: Ministro Marco Aurélio, 12.8.2010, D.J.U. 6.12.2010. In this case, the Supreme Court established that the tax immunity of export revenues granted by Constitutional Amendment 33 did not include the social security contribution on net profits of exporting companies.

[130] Jiménez de Aréchaga and Tanzi (2001), pp. 364–365.

3.4 Conclusion

From the cases analyzed in this study, the reasons why Brazilian courts adopted traditionalism regarding WTO agreements have also become apparent. Actual examples of arguments favoring traditionalism regarding WTO agreements were found in the cases studies: (1) the long Brazilian tradition of domestic application of international treaties; and (2) the economic interest in maintaining Brazil's reputation of compliance with international law.

In what concerns the Brazilian internal legal order, traditionalism however have not produced all desired effects anticipated in the scholarly debate. A general argument in favor of traditionalism is that granting private actors the right to sue the government based on trade rules empowers individuals *"to balance protectionist producer interests predominant in national regulations."* However, the controversy before Brazilian courts over the non-retroactivity of antidumping duties displays a puzzling result from the interaction between international trade rules and domestic law. The Antidumping Agreement not only grants WTO members the possibility of levying provisional antidumping duties as of the date of a preliminary affirmative determination of dumping has been made,[131] but also establishes that antidumping duties are to apply to products which *enter* for consumption after the decision enters into force.[132] Moreover, the Antidumping Agreement even provides for the possibility of imposing retroactive duties in certain circumstances.[133] Notwithstanding such rules, Brazilian courts have impeded the application of antidumping duties as of the date of entry into force of the governmental measure to products previously purchased. Therefore, this case demonstrates that, on one hand, private actors can question trade policies before the judiciary, and, on the other hand, liberality towards granting court injunctions against governmental commercial defense goals can in fact restrict the government in accomplishing such goals to ensure fair trade. Nevertheless, the question that arises is whether economic interests of private actors should supersede governmental policy set by democratically elected governments in compliance with international rules aiming at broader goals of protecting the national economy. Indeed, the interactions between domestic law and international trade rules can hinder international trade rules, instead of enforcing them according to the WTO agreements.

Another general reason for the adoption of traditionalism regarding WTO agreements by Brazilian courts is that it shows the firm commitment of Brazil in abiding to international trade obligations. As Jackson and Sykes note, the greater commitment to following international rules may increase the mutual gains from international agreements.[134] Nevertheless, the absence of reciprocity regarding traditionalism in WTO agreements by the major trading countries' of the world instead seems to turn the Brazilian stance on WTO agreements as a disadvantage,

---

[131] Raslam (2009), p. 50.

[132] Antidumping Agreement, Article 10.

[133] Ibid.

[134] Jackson and Sykes (1997), p. 462.

because it allows more room for strategic behavior[135] to the biggest economies, while Brazil ties its own hands. In fact, as the scholarly debate shows, traditionalism in WTO agreements should not be granted while there is no reciprocity from other countries. In any case, regardless the lack of reciprocity from major world trading partners regarding the domestic effects of WTO agreements, traditionalism in Brazil sure has the advantage of keeping the Brazilian reputation of compliance with international law which in principle may serve this country's economic interests. On the other hand, such reputation can also be impaired by domestic courts' decisions, such as in the *Retreated Tires* case.

In summary, the cases studied showed several situations that occur when private parties are granted the right to invoke international trade rules before the Brazilian domestic judiciary, and the challenges and benefits derived from this possibility. In Brazil, traditionalism regarding the GATT and the Antidumping Agreement has brought up multiple and inconsistent decisions, which, in some cases have jeopardized legitimate governmental policy goals and Brazil's stance on the international trade arena. So far, traditionalism regarding WTO rules does not seem to have encouraged broad trade policy goals that benefit the WTO Member State as a whole according to internationally agreed rules, but certainly have ensured private individuals a way of discussing public policies on trade judicially, another aspect of the current trend on judicialization of politics whereby Brazilian courts have been most activist in assessing highly politically controverted matters.[136] Above all, it can be concluded therefore that traditionalism has caused imbalance on internationally agreed reciprocal and mutual trade concessions in detriment of rights and commitments in market access as envisioned by the WTO agreements. Consequently, the transfer of power from the executive to the judiciary as a way to enhance the enforceability of international law does not reveal itself as a more efficient venue for compliance with international trade rules.

Surely, traditionalism regarding the GATT and the Antidumping Agreement in the Brazilian example has not corresponded to its primary purpose of constraining recalcitrant governments that violate international law, as the Brazilian government has been fairly following international trade commitments and obligations. Therefore, Conforti's assumption that the domestic courts, as domestic legal actors, are a proper venue to enforce international trade law does not seem to be valid for the Brazilian reality on the behavior of judges. Traditionalism in Brazil is only aggravated by the fact that, instead of having prevented the state from violating international law, Brazilian lower courts have granted injunctions inducing Brazil into non-compliance with international trade rules or restraining Brazil's commercial defense rights recognized in international law.

---

[135] Ibid.

[136] Since democracy was reinstated, the Brazilian judiciary has been seized to decide cases ranging from governmental economic policies to affirmative action in public universities, including stem cells research and, of course, the import ban on used tires, just to name a few hot topics. For more detailed information on how Brazilian courts have been provoked to decide on political issues, *see* Taylor (2004) and Rodrigues (2009).

3.4 Conclusion

The approach adopted by Brazilian courts on international trade rules bring into question the validity of the premises of traditionalism and therefore reconsideration of the matter in relation to international trade rules may prove necessary. The analysis of the way Brazilian courts have adjudicated on the GATT and Antidumping Agreement reveals certain patterns that question the prevailing ideas in traditionalism regarding international trade law. The validity and universalism of traditionalism's premise—that governments violate international law, and due to lack of enforcement mechanisms at the international level, domestic courts can act effectively to restrain their executive and comply with international law—seem to be designed to cope with major developed countries' behavior at the international level, and do not apparently apply in a generalized way. In this line of thought, if traditionalism's premise may seem true in relation to the behavior of developed economies, like the United States and the European Union, it does not seem accurate in relation to an emerging economy such as Brazil.

Even in relation to rich economies, traditionalism regarding WTO agreements overlooks the principle of popular sovereignty and democratic self-government by circumventing elected officials in charge of preserving higher societal values. After all, economic interests for profits and businesses' growth may not supplant higher values of a state's society. Commentary has noted that Brazilian lower courts have been activists by prioritizing local social or individual rights over federal public policy, and have impaired the implementation of federal and state legislation, as well as administrative actions.[137] Accordingly, tax regulations have been regularly challenged before the Brazilian judiciary, where lower courts often have granted provisional injunctions against the collection of taxes they found unconstitutional or illegal, *"thwarting the myriad purposes for new tax measures."*[138] The creativity of domestic lawyers to challenge international trade policy before the domestic judiciary can be adamant for exploiting legal loopholes without consideration of whether such sought benefits were in accordance with the interpretation the international community accorded to international rules. Consequently, Brazilian courts indeed have the power and independence to constrain governmental bodies when interpreting international treaties even if such interpretation disregards the meaning of WTO rights of commercial defense, as accorded at the international level.

Then, the question turns to whether the function and objective of WTO agreements are achieving their full efficacy through Brazilian domestic courts adjudication. The power and independence of the Brazilian lower courts in interpreting WTO law seems to produce more instability when intervening in questions of GATT's international concessions, rights and obligations. After all, the Brazilian government has historically followed international law and, in case of potential violation of international obligations, the WTO provides a mechanism for solving conflicts derived from international trade rules. International rulings and negotiations have historically sufficed to make the executive conform to Brazil's

---

[137] Ballard (1999), p. 252.
[138] Ibid.

international obligations. In any case, the recurring pattern that Brazilian lower courts prioritize economic bargains of individual importers over broader national goals of trade policy will most likely continue in the future, causing imbalance in Brazil's international trade rights and concessions, with potential to incur Brazil in international responsibility over non-compliance with WTO rules. In this comparative work, the extent to which this assessment on Brazil may be expanded to other countries will be discussed on Chap. 5, as it is necessary to first analyze the European Union perspective on international trade agreements, which this study will now turn attention to.

References

Alston P (2002) Resisting the merger and acquisition of human rights by trade law: a reply to Petersmann. Eur J Int Law 13(4):815–844
Ballard M (1999) The clash between local courts and global economics: the politics of judicial reform in Brazil. Berkeley J Int Law 17:230–276
Bartels L, Ortino F (eds) (2006) Regional trade agreements and the WTO legal system. Oxford University Press, Oxford
Brand R (1997) Direct effect of international economic law in the United States and the European Union. Nw J Int Law Bus 17:556–608
Cassese A (1985) Modern constitutions and international law. Collected courses of the Hague academy of international law, vol 192. Martinus Nijhoff, Dordrecht
Conforti B, Francioni F (eds) (1997) Enforcing international human rights in domestic courts. Martinus Nijhoff, Dordrecht
Crawford J (2012) Brownlie's principles of public international law. Oxford University Press, Oxford
Davis B, Back A (2010) IMF sees Yuan as undervalued. Wall Street Journal, 27 July 2010. http://online.wsj.com/article/SB10001424052748703700904575390410108751210.html#. Accessed 4 Sept 2014
De Búrca G, Scott J (eds) (2003) The EU and the WTO: legal and constitutional issues. Hart, Oxford
de Cara JY (2007) International trade and the rule of law. Mercer Law Rev 58:1357–1380
Departamento de Defesa Comercial. Relatório DECOM (2013) http://www.desenvolvimento.gov.br//arquivos/dwnl_1389971877.pdf. Accessed 4 Sept 2014
Dillon S (2002) International trade and economic law and the European Union. Hart, Oxford
Faro de Castro M (1997) The courts, law and democracy in Brazil. Int Soc Sci J 49:241–252
Garoupa N, Ginsburg T (2010) Hybrid judicial career structures: reputation v. legal tradition. Paper presented at Faculty Forum, University of Illinois & Chicago-Kent College of Law, 12 November 2010. http://www.cunef.edu/libreria/Garoupa_pape.pdf. Accessed 4 Sept 2014
Garoupa N, Oliveira MAJSC (2011) Choosing judges in Brazil: reassessing legal transplants from the United States. Am J Comparative Law 59:529–561
Georgakopoulos N (2000) Independence in the career and recognition judiciary. Univ Chic Law School Roundtable 7:205–225
Gontijo A, Peter da Silva CO (2010) O papel do amicus curiae no Estado constitucional: mecanismo de acesso da transdisciplinaridade no processo de tomada de decisão constitucional [The role of amicus curiae on the constitutional state: mechanism of transdisciplinary access on constitutional decision-making process]. http://www.conpedi.org.br/manaus/arquivos/anais/fortaleza/3299.pdf. Accessed 4 Sept 2014
Guzman A, Pauwelyn J (2009) International trade law. Aspen, New York

Hillman J (2009) Conflicts between dispute settlement mechanisms in regional trade agreements and the WTO – What should the WTO do? Cornell Int Law J 42:193–208

International Law Commission (2006) Report of the study group on the fragmentation of international law: difficulties arising from the diversification and expansion of international law. A/61/10, Paragraph 251 Conclusion 30. http://legal.un.org/ilc/reports/2006/2006report.htm. Accessed 4 Sept 2014

Jackson V (2004) Comparative constitutional federalism and transnational judicial discourse. Int J Const Law 2:91–138

Jackson J, Sykes A (1997) Questions and comparisons. In: Jackson J, Sykes A (eds) Implementing the Uruguay round. Clarendon, Oxford

Jiménez de Aréchaga E, Tanzi A (2001) International state responsibility. In: Bedjaoui M (ed) International law: achievements and prospects. Martinus Nijhoff, Dordrecht

Kelsen H (1967) Pure theory of law. University of California Press, California

Knop K (2000) Here and there: international law in domestic courts. N Y Univ J Int Law Polit 32:501–535

Marceau G, Wyatt J (2010) Dispute settlement regimes intermingled: regional trade agreements and the WTO. J Int Disp Settlement 1:67–95

Marimon R et al (2009) Multilevel judicial governance between global and regional economic integration systems: institutional and substantive aspects. Eur U Inst Max Weber Programme Working Paper 2009/41. Accessed 4 Sept 2014

Matsushita M, Schoenbaum T, Mavroidis P (2006) The world trade organization: law, practice and policy. Oxford University Press, Oxford

Moser C (2007) Isenção heterônoma por via de tratado internacional: uma análise da jurisprudência do Supremo Tribunal Federal [Heteronomous exemption by virtue of an international treaty: an analysis of the jurisprudence of the Supreme Federal Court]. Rev EMARF 2ª Região 9:83–283

Oliveira MAJSC (2006) Reforming the Brazilian Supreme Court: a comparative approach. Wash Univ Glob Stud Law Rev 5:99–150

Oliveira MAJSC, Garoupa N (2012) Stare Decisis and Certiorari Arrive to Brazil: a comparative law and economics approach. Emory Int Law Rev 26(2):555–598

Ortino F (2004) Basic legal instruments for the liberalisation of trade: a comparative analysis of EC and WTO law. Hart, Oxford

Pauwelyn J (2003) Conflict of norms in public international law: how WTO law relates to other rules of international law. Cambridge University Press, New York

Pauwelyn J (2006) The unbearable lightness of likeness. http://ssrn.com/abstract=2030940. Accessed 4 Sept 2014

Pauwelyn J (2009) Legal avenues to "multilateralising regionalism": beyond Article XXIV. In: Baldwin R, Low P (eds) Multilateralising regionalism, challenges for the global trading system. Cambridge University Press, New York

Pauwelyn J, Salles LE (2009) Forum shopping before international tribunals: (real) concerns, (im) possible solutions. Cornell Int Law J 42:77–118

Peixoto BL (2010) Brazil. In: The handbook of trade enforcement. Global Competition Review, London

Petersmann EU (2002) Time for a United Nations "Global Compact" for integrating human rights into the law of world-wide organizations: lessons from European integration. Eur J Int Law 13(4):621–650

Raslam RAA (2009) Antidumping: a developing country perspective. Kluwer Law International, The Netherlands

Rebouças MCA (1998) A Súmula 71 do Superior Tribunal de Justiça e o nefasto perigo da generalização [The Súmula 71 of the Superior Court of Justice and the harmful danger of generalization]. Rev Jur Procuradoria Geral da Fazenda Estadual 31:53–62

Rodrigues I (2009) Judicialization of politics: constitutional review and intrastate litigiousness in contemporary Brazil. Paper presented at the annual meeting of the Southern Political Science Association, 7 January 2009. http://www.allacademic.com/meta/p275709_index.html. Accessed 4 Sept 2014

STF Press Release (2011) Reconhecida repercussão geral de recursos que questionam normas antidumping [General repercussion recognized in appeals questioning antidumping rules], 7 January 2011. http://www.stf.jus.br/portal/cms/verNoticiaDetalhe.asp?idConteudo=169149. Accessed 4 Sept 2014

Sykes A (2005) Public versus private enforcement of international economic law: standing and remedy. J Legal Stud 34:631–666

Taylor MM (2004) Working the courts: the worker's party and the judicialization of politics in Brazil. Paper presented at the annual meeting of the American Political Science Association, 2 September 2004. http://www.allacademic.com/meta/p61115_index.html. Accessed 4 Sept 2014

Van der Veen M (2003) When is food a luxury? World Archaeol 34:405–427

Weiler JHH (ed) (2005) The EU, the WTO and the NAFTA: towards a common law of international trade? Oxford University Press, Oxford

Chapter 4
The Relations Between International Trade Agreements and Domestic Courts in the European Union

This chapter examines the relations between WTO agreements and domestic courts in the European Union context. To understand the relationship between WTO agreements and domestic courts in the region, this chapter first apprehends the domestic status of the WTO agreements in the European Union. Then, this chapter expounds the rational choice theory approach of the ECJ regarding such agreements. This study next explores the cases on which the ECJ built the distinctive nature of WTO Agreements. Subsequently, as both the European Union and the European Member States in their own capacity are parties to the WTO agreements, this chapter also assesses the degree of cooperation of national courts of the European Union Member States with the ECJ case law in relation to the WTO Agreements. This book explores the degree of cooperation of national courts through the lens of constitutional pluralism, as the main doctrine explaining the European legal order and its relationship with domestic courts, mainly constitutional courts of the European Union member countries. However, the study of the national constitutional courts of the 27 European Member States would be beyond the scope and objectives of this research. This study accordingly focuses on German and Italian courts to exemplify how national domestic courts have responded to the GATT obligations and the ECJ jurisprudence, because both Germany and Italy were founding member states of the Community that possessed constitutional courts in their domestic legal systems at the time of entry into force of the GATT 1947.

4.1 The Domestic Status of International Treaties in the European Union

To examine the European Union courts' perspective on international trade agreements, it is useful to briefly mention that the current framework establishing the European Union core provisions and operations is the Treaty on European Union (TEU) and the Treaty on the Functioning of the European Union (TFEU), as consolidated by the Treaty of Lisbon, which entered into force in December 2009.[1] Although the Treaty of Lisbon integrated the European Communities under the European Union, the ECJ cases mentioned in this study will make reference to the then existing European Communities (EC), or the European Economic Community (EEC). For this reason, and for the sake of historical accuracy with the opinions of the ECJ, this study will keep the references to "EC" and "Community" whenever they are referred to in scholarly commentary or cases' citations, and will elaborate on the cases using the same terminology.

As a unique structure, the European Union has legal personality,[2] and has three main categories of competences. Besides the EU exclusive competences that its Member States have delegated to it,[3] it has also shared competences with its

---

[1] Treaty of Lisbon.

[2] Consolidated version of the Treaty on European Union, Article 47.

[3] Consolidated version of the Treaty on the Functioning of the European Union, Article 3:

1. The Union shall have exclusive competence in the following areas:
   (a) customs union;
   (b) the establishing of the competition rules necessary for the functioning of the internal market;
   (c) monetary policy for the Member States whose currency is the euro;
   (d) the conservation of marine biological resources under the common fisheries policy;
   (e) common commercial policy.
2. The Union shall also have exclusive competence for the conclusion of an international agreement when its conclusion is provided for in a legislative act of the Union or is necessary to enable the Union to exercise its internal competence, or in so far as its conclusion may affect common rules or alter their scope.

4.1 The Domestic Status of International Treaties in the European Union

Member States,[4] as well as supporting competences.[5] This study however does not aim to give a full account of all the EU competences. Instead, this study focuses on international trade agreements, which fall under the exclusive competence of the EU in what concerns common commercial policy. The European Union is exclusively responsible for establishing the common commercial policy of the region *"with regard to change in tariff rates, the conclusion of tariff and trade agreements relating to trade in goods and services, and the commercial aspects of intellectual property, foreign direct investment, the achievement of uniformity in measures of liberalization, export policy and measures to protect trade such as those to be taken*

---

[4] Consolidated version of the Treaty on the Functioning of the European Union, Article 4:

1. The Union shall share competence with the Member States where the Treaties confer on it a competence which does not relate to the areas referred to in Articles 3 and 6.
2. Shared competence between the Union and the Member States applies in the following principal areas:
(a) internal market;
(b) social policy, for the aspects defined in this Treaty;
(c) economic, social and territorial cohesion;
(d) agriculture and fisheries, excluding the conservation of marine biological resources;
(e) environment;
(f) consumer protection;
(g) transport;
(h) trans-European networks;
(i) energy;
(j) area of freedom, security and justice;
(k) common safety concerns in public health matters, for the aspects defined in this Treaty.
3. In the areas of research, technological development and space, the Union shall have competence to carry out activities, in particular to define and implement programmes; however, the exercise of that competence shall not result in Member States being prevented from exercising theirs.
4. In the areas of development cooperation and humanitarian aid, the Union shall have competence to carry out activities and conduct a common policy; however, the exercise of that competence shall not result in Member States being prevented from exercising theirs.

[5] Consolidated version of the Treaty on the Functioning of the European Union, Article 6:

The Union shall have competence to carry out actions to support, coordinate or supplement the actions of the Member States. The areas of such action shall, at European level, be:
(a) protection and improvement of human health;
(b) industry;
(c) culture;
(d) tourism;
(e) education, vocational training, youth and sport;
(f) civil protection;
(g) administrative cooperation.

in the event of dumping of subsidies."⁶ In addition to external commercial policy, the European Union has also competence to conclude association agreements with third countries or international organizations.⁷ For being exclusively in charge of the external commercial policy of EU region, the EU courts is the proper setting to analyze international trade agreements, particularly considering the EU treaty-making powers and the fact that EU Member States may no longer unilaterally conclude international trade agreements.

Because of its exclusive competence on common commercial policy, the EU may enter into international trade agreements with countries of the world as well as with international organizations, being subject to rights and obligations under international law. Under EU law, international trade agreements have primacy over community secondary law,⁸ and are binding on the Union institutions and on the Union Member States.⁹

The European legal order is predominantly understood as having a monistic approach towards international law, as the reception of international agreements does not require any internal incorporation process. In the *Haegeman v. Belgium* case,¹⁰ the ECJ decided that from the entry into force of the Agreement of Association between the European Economic Community and Greece, such agreement would become part of the Community legal order. As a result, it was established that there was no need for an incorporation process of this international agreement into the Community law.¹¹ It could be concluded from this case that the ECJ took a monist approach regarding the relationship between international law and EU law. This case is of paramount significance for the jurisdiction of the ECJ because it introduced the automatic treaty incorporation. Such ruling impacted the external relations of EU Member States with non-automatic treaty incorporation, because "*it was no longer the domestic legislature which determines the role of domestic courts in treaty enforcement*"¹²; instead, it was the EC to take such a role in relation to Community agreements.¹³ As for the EU Member States with automatic treaty incorporation, this case also had a significant effect because the decision on the direct effect of a Community agreement would not be in their national courts' prerogative, but a competence of the ECJ.¹⁴

Similarly to Brazil, the European Union legal order does not have a general rule that clearly defines the relationship between European Union law and international law. The Treaty on European Union has provisions fostering international law that

---

[6] Consolidated version of the Treaty on the Functioning of the European Union, Article 207.
[7] Ibid., Article 217.
[8] Consolidated version of the Treaty on the Functioning of the European Union, Article 216 (1).
[9] Ibid., Article 216 (2).
[10] Case C-181/73, *R. & V. Haegeman v. the Belgian State*, 1974 E.C.R. 449, paragraph 5.
[11] Eeckhout (2004), p. 277.
[12] Mendez (2010), p. 88.
[13] Ibid.
[14] Ibid.

mandates the Union to contribute to the strict observance and development of international law[15] and determines the Union to seek to advance respect for international law in the wider world.[16] Because the European Union treaties are silent about the status of international agreements within the European Union competences, it is for the case law of the European Court of Justice (ECJ) to decide on the status of these international agreements in the European Union context.

The ECJ has jurisdiction to adjudicate on cases brought by a Member State, an institution or a natural or legal person, and on other cases provided for in the Treaties.[17] In addition, the ECJ may also give preliminary rulings, at the request of courts or tribunals of the Member States, on the interpretation of Union law or the validity of acts adopted by the institutions.[18] In this case, if a private party invokes any provision of the WTO agreements as a basis for litigation before the national judiciary of a EU Member State against any European authority or legislation, the national court should refer the legal issue to the ECJ, which should interpret the EU law or the validity of its acts through the preliminary ruling mechanism.

In what concerns the main doctrines courts use to refer to international law, the ECJ established the doctrine of direct effect for the first time in *Van Gend en Loos v. Netherlands Inland Revenue Administration*.[19] The European Union, after the *Van Gend en Loos* ruling, embraced the doctrine of direct effect of Community law whereby rules of Community law have legal effects in the Community member states by conferring rights and imposing obligations which can be enforceable before national courts. In fact, the ECJ entitled private parties to legal standing to sue if their governments did not comply with international obligations of the European Union.

In considering the relationship between domestic and international law, the ECJ however does not concede a single and uniform approach for all international trade agreements in the European legal order. Instead, the doctrine developed by the ECJ on the external competence of the EU is very complex.[20] The ECJ has adopted different positions depending on the international agreement involved. Although the ECJ considers that international agreements may in principle have direct effect,[21] the Court has made distinctions on the implementation of international rights and obligations within the European legal system in relation to WTO agreements, a position that Sect. 4.2 will further develop. As Craig and De Búrca (2008) notes,

> When it comes to international agreements, the question whether they can have direct effect concerns the capacity of such agreements to be directly invoked and enforced not only

---

[15] Consolidated version of the Treaty on European Union, Article 3(5).

[16] Ibid., Article 21 (1).

[17] Ibid., Article 19 (3) (a) (c).

[18] Ibid., Article 19 (3) (b).

[19] Case 26/62, *Van Gend en Loos v. Netherlands Inland Revenue Administration*, 1963 E.C.R. 1.

[20] Craig and De Búrca (2008), p. 167.

[21] Ibid., p. 168.

within the legal orders and before the courts of the Member States, but also within the EC legal order and before the ECJ. Arguments may be made both for and against the direct effect of international agreements. On the one hand, as treaties concluded with other States or international organizations, they can be viewed as traditional international agreements biding only the States or organizations which signed them, and having no specific effect on individuals and no automatic 'self-executing' quality. On the other hand, as agreements entered into by the Community, they can be viewed as sharing some of the key characteristics of EC law, and in particular could be capable of direct effect and enforcement by individuals whenever sufficiently precise and unconditional.[22]

In other words, depending on the circumstances, the ECJ considers that international agreements may have direct effect or not, taking into consideration not only legal criteria provided for in the *Van Gend en Loos* case, but also other considerations such as the spirit, general scheme and terms of the agreement,[23] as in the case of the GATT/WTO agreements, which will be specifically analyzed in Sect. 4.2. For now, it suffices to review the ECJ Advocate General Kokott's explanation on the ECJ case law regarding the status of international agreements in the EU legal order:

> 71. Furthermore it is generally the case that an international agreement cannot normally serve as a benchmark against which the validity of acts of EU institutions can be reviewed in legal proceedings brought by individuals (that is by natural or legal persons) unless, by the nature and broad logic of that agreement, it is capable of conferring rights which an individual can invoke before the courts. In other words, therefore, the international agreement in question must affect the legal status of the individual.
> 72. The legal status of individuals is affected, in particular, where they are granted independent rights and freedoms under an international agreement, as is the case, for instance, with many association, cooperation and partnership agreements concluded by the European Union. Environmental agreements can also contain provisions on which any interested party is entitled to rely before the courts.
> 73. The only limited ability of individuals to invoke international agreements as a benchmark for validity before the courts can be explained by reference to the objective of affording the individual legal protection: under EU law – as in the majority of domestic legal systems – individuals generally enjoy legal protection in so far as it is necessary to safeguard their guaranteed rights or freedoms (see also the first paragraph of Article 47 of the Charter of Fundamental Rights of the European Union).[24]

Like the GATT/WTO agreements, the ECJ has also considered that the United Nations Convention on the Law of the Sea (UNCLOS) did not have direct effect in the European legal order due to its nature and structure, as it did not have rules intended to apply immediately and directly to individuals and did not confer individuals rights or freedoms.[25]

---

[22] Ibid., p. 207.

[23] Case C-469/93, *Amministrazione delle Finanze dello Stato v Chiquita Italia SpA*, 1995 E.C.R. I-04533, paragraph 25.

[24] Opinion of the Advocate General Kokott delivered in the case C-366/10, The Air Transport Association of America and Others v. Secretary of State for Energy and Climate Change, 2011 E.C.R. 00.

[25] Case C-308/06, *International Association of Independent Tanker Owner (Intertanko) and Others v. Secretary of State for Transport*, 2008 E.C.R. I-4057.

Yet, the classic paradigm on the direct effect of international treaties in the European Union[26] is the *Hauptzollamt Mainz v. Kupferberg* case,[27] discussing the legal effects of the non-discrimination rule prescribed in the 1972 bilateral treaty between the European Economic Community and Portugal, that is, before such country was member of the Community. In Germany, certain spirits made from wine benefited from a reduction on the domestic duty on spirits. A German importer requested the release of imports of port wine from Portugal in German territory with such reduction on the domestic duty on spirits, based on treatment accorded to domestic liqueur wines which had additional spirits from fruit farm cooperative distilleries. The German customs office claimed that port wine produced in Portugal could not enjoy the duty reduction because such benefit was directed to fermented wines only. Facing questions of Community law, the German Federal Finance Court therefore requested a preliminary ruling to the ECJ. In this case, ECJ asserted monism as the applicable theory in the European context, and discussed whether a private party could invoke the rules of an agreement concluded by the European Communities before European courts. The ECJ found that *"international agreements are binding on the institutions of the community and on member states*,"[28] both of which have an incumbency to ensure compliance with the international agreements obligations. However, the ECJ stated that, although a free-trade agreement provision *"is in principle capable of having direct effect in the member states of the Community*,"[29] it is for the Court to ensure uniform application of such a provision within the Community by deciding its effects. To decide whether a certain provision in an international agreement have direct application or not, the ECJ established that it is necessary to analyze such provision in light of the object and purpose of the agreement, as well as of its context. In this case, the ECJ decided that, while the provision in cause was *"directly applicable and capable of conferring on individual traders rights which the courts must protect*,"[30] there was no violation of the prohibition of discrimination. The ECJ considered that the products at issue, that is, port wine or *"liqueur wines fortified with spirits*," and *"wines resulting from natural fermentation"* were not like products.

There are more examples on the ECJ fluctuations on the direct effect—or self-executing character—of international trade agreements in the EU legal order. There have been instances where the ECJ has considered that international trade rules

---

[26] Due to the entry in force of the Treaty of Lisbon on December 2009, what was known before as the "European Communities" is now referred to as "European Union."

[27] Case C-104/81, *Hauptzollamt Mainz v C.A. Kupferberg & Cie KG a.A.*, 1982 E.C.R. 3644.

[28] Ibid.

[29] Ibid.

[30] Ibid.

derived from association agreements, or free trade agreements with neighboring states, have direct effect in the European legal order, regardless of whether there is reciprocity or not in obligations and commitments from the other signatory parties.[31]

Association agreements are prescribed in Article 217 of the TFEU.[32] In the European legal order, association agreements usually establish a close cooperation in political and economic terms. Association agreements may therefore involve a privileged relationship with the EU and even as a preparation for EU membership in the future, providing for trade liberalization.[33] To illustrate how an association agreement may be accorded direct effect by the ECJ, one may look at the 4th ACP-EEC Lomé Convention with the African, Caribbean and Pacific Group of States (ACP countries), which provided for a system of preferential trade to promote economic and social development of these countries by broadening the access of their products to the European market. The ECJ distinguished the special nature of the Lomé Convention from the legal nature of the GATT, and considered that the 4th ACP-EEC Convention contained provisions that conferred rights that individuals could invoke before national courts.[34]

Another example of an association agreement the ECJ has granted direct effect is the agreement between the EEC and Turkey concluded in 1963, which aimed at strengthening trade and economic relations as a preparation towards the accession of Turkey to the then EEC. While interpreting the Association Agreement between the EEC and Turkey, the ECJ considered that provisions that set out a program to implement the freedom of movement of workers had direct effect in the Member States of the Community. The ECJ stated that

> Like the provisions of agreements concluded by the Community with non-member countries, provisions adopted by an Association Council created by an association agreement in order to ensure the implementation of its provisions must be regarded as being directly applicable when, regard being had to their wording and their purpose and nature, as well as to those of the association agreement, they contain a clear and precise obligation which is not subject, in its implementation or effects, to the adoption of any subsequent measure.[35]

In summary, association agreements concluded with European neighboring states and Turkey, as well as agreements concluded with former colonies in the

---

[31] Craig and De Búrca (2008), p. 168.

[32] Consolidated version of the Treaty on the Functioning of the European Union, Article 217:
The Union may conclude with one or more third countries or international organizations agreements establishing an association involving reciprocal rights and obligations, common action and special procedure.

[33] European Union—European External Action Service (2014).

[34] Case C-469/93, *Amministrazione delle Finanze dello Stato v Chiquita Italia SpA*, 1995 E.C.R. I-4533, Grounds of Judgment, paragraph 35.

[35] Case C-192/89, *S. Z. Sevince v Staatssecretaris van Justitie*, 1990 E.C.R. I-03461, Summary of Judgment, paragraph 2.

4.1 The Domestic Status of International Treaties in the European Union

case of Lomé Conventions have been considered as ensuring private invocability of international obligations, or direct effect in the European legal order.

However, the direct effect of association agreements raise the same problems as the WTO agreements but, interestingly enough, the result is different. A possible explanation for the association agreements exception in the European Union context seems linked to the EU trying to maintain their dominant position in their former colonies, and to increase their participation at the domestic level of future EU members. Cottier points out that the content of these association agreements are similar to the rules of the EU domestic law and therefore the potential for conflict is irrelevant.[36] This way, the EU is actually exporting their internal rules to other countries.[37]

From Cottier's observation, it can be concluded that granting direct effect to association agreements would most likely not cause any interference in the EU's right to self-government, because such agreements are in line with EU domestic law. In asserting that association agreements "belong to the realm of Community law,"[38] Cottier calls such agreements as "hegemonial" agreements.[39] However, while such hegemonial agreements in principle do not provoke a shift of power within the domestic bodies of the EU, this may not be true in relation to the other signatory parties. It is possible that non-EU states and former colonies may have their right to self-government impaired with the direct effect of association agreements in their internal legal orders, but, as noted, reciprocity is not required by the ECJ in association agreements.

In any event, the direct effect of association agreements presents an unequal power relationship between the EU and its former colonies and potential EU members. The direct effect of association agreements therefore is not related to the function and objective of trade agreements in providing market access in an equal state-to-state perspective. It is a power relation where the other side of the balance is either a former colony or an aspiring EU member. In such positions, it is unlikely that these countries would be a threat at all for the EU domestic legal order and its right to self-government, particularly considering that, as earlier mentioned, the content of such agreements corresponds to EU domestic law.

When there is a competing power with rules that interfere with domestic public policy choices—like the United States dispute based on the WTO agreements in the *Hormones* case[40]—the ECJ case law closes the door for direct effect. As Cottier acknowledges, direct effect of relevant WTO rules would inevitably put the EU courts "*in a dominant position and in conflict with domestic policies adopted by the*

---

[36] Cottier (2009), p. 314.

[37] Ibid.

[38] Ibid.

[39] Ibid.

[40] *European Communities—Measures Concerning Meat and Meat Products (Hormones)*, WT/DS26/AB/R, adopted 13 February 1998.

political branches of the Union."[41] The lack of direct effect of WTO law in the European context is a topic that this study will now address.

4.2 The Rational Choice Theory Perspective of the European Court of Justice Regarding WTO Agreements

As noted, the ECJ did not automatically grant direct effect to all international trade agreements. In the European Union context, the question of direct effect of WTO agreements, or the absence of it, is a much debated matter because of the supremacy of international treaties in relation to EU legislation.[42] The European Court of Justice does not grant direct effect to WTO agreements *"when it comes to forcing the legislative institutions of the Union to comply with WTO law."*[43] While adopting traditionalism in other areas of international law, the ECJ has exceptionally embraced the rational choice theory in relation to WTO Agreements. The ECJ has considered that WTO Agreements do not have direct effect, and do not provide private rights that can be directly invoked in domestic litigation. Although having generally admitted the private invocability of association agreements in domestic litigation, the ECJ has firmly adopted the rational choice theory with regards to the GATT which falls under the EU exclusive competence on common commercial policy.

The European Union courts have shown a steady position in deferring to the executive on issues regarding GATT/WTO rules. As per Conforti's typology, the European Court of Justice, as a domestic legal operator in the application of international law to the common commercial policy of the region, has presented a mixed level of enforcement of international trade agreements at the domestic level. On one hand, the ECJ (1) has adopted the direct effect of association agreements with neighboring states and former colonies; (2) has implicitly interpreted domestic law in a consistent way with international law, and (3) has not used the political question doctrine to avoid deciding on highly controversial issues. On the other hand, the ECJ (1) has denied direct effect to the GATT/WTO agreements; and (2) has granted judicial deference towards the executive. The ECJ's position was heavily criticized by Conforti.[44]

To understand the role of the ECJ in the interpretation of WTO rules, it is first necessary to explain that the European Union and its 27 Member States are all parties to the WTO Agreements in their own right.[45] Notwithstanding the fact that

---

[41] Cottier (2009), p. 314.
[42] Von Bogdandy (2008), p. 404.
[43] Ibid.
[44] Conforti (1993).
[45] WTO Member Information (2014).

4.2 The Rational Choice Theory Perspective of the European Court of Justice...   129

EU Member States are also present at WTO meetings, the EU speaks for all its member countries most of the times.[46] The double membership is based on the ECJ understanding that the WTO is a mixed agreement, that is, an agreement where both the European Union and its Member States are signatory parties, with third countries. This decision stemmed from a conflict at the moment of the signature of the Final Act and the WTO agreement in Marrakech in 1994.[47] At that occasion, the Commission was convinced that the signature of these acts was part of the exclusive competence of the European Community. On the other hand, representatives of the European Member States also considered that such acts were within their national competence.

To solve this lack of concordance, the Commission consulted the ECJ, as the Court has advisory competence to clarify questions on the division of competence between the European Union and the Member States to conclude an agreement with third countries. The Commission specifically requested the ECJ in the Advisory Opinion n. 1/94[48] whether the European Community had the competence to conclude alone the all parts of the WTO agreements concerning goods, services, and the trade-related aspects of intellectual property rights. In relation to the WTO agreements, the ECJ stated that, according to Article 113 of the EC Treaty, the Community has sole competence to conclude the multilateral agreements on trade in goods, while the Community and its member states are jointly competent to conclude GATS and TRIPs. Therefore, both the European Union and its Member States are signatory parties to the WTO agreements.

The European Union has substituted European member states in relation to GATT since 1968, and has therefore the ECJ has exclusive jurisdiction to decide how GATT applies within the European Union.[49] In other words, if a domestic court of a European Member State is seized to decide whether a trade measure is compatible with the GATT, the domestic judge would need to refer the question to the ECJ under the preliminary ruling procedure.[50] However, the ECJ case law has long established that GATT/WTO agreements do not have direct effect. Indeed, if an international treaty does not have direct effect within the European Union, *"neither an individual party, nor a Member State may invoke before the Court of Justice the incompatibility of a Community rule with such a treaty."*[51] As a result, in what concerns trade in goods prescribed by the GATT, national courts of the European Union in principle would not have jurisdiction to interpret GATT provisions, due to the lack of direct effect of the GATT in the national legal orders. In Sect. 4.4 below, the degree of cooperation of national courts with the European Court of Justice in relation to its case law on WTO Agreements will be examined.

---

[46] Ibid.
[47] Advisory Opinion n. 1/94, 1994 E.C.R. I-5389, paragraph 5.
[48] Ibid., paragraph 6.
[49] Holdgaard (2008), p. 188.
[50] Ruttley (1998), p. 147.
[51] Schermers and Waelbroeck (2001), p. 192.

In any case, the application of GATT in the Member States of the European Union increasingly derives from EU law rather than domestic principles in the application of international agreements at the national level.[52]

Because the ECJ distinguished the GATT from other international treaties, much criticism was drawn by legal scholars and practitioners, which generated an extensive literature on the question of the direct effect of GATT/WTO agreements. Advocates for the reinforcement of WTO rules in domestic legal orders assert that the strengthening of their effects would prevent governmental power abuse and promote equality between producers and consumers.[53] Petersmann defends that "*the purpose of WTO provisions may go beyond intergovernmental rights and obligations by protecting also democratic decision-making, private transactions, other private interests and legitimate expectations of private rights holders.*"[54] Along Petersmann's line of thought, Kuilwijk sustained that the reiterated denial of direct effect to GATT provisions, in his views, would show that the ECJ was protectionist and was not concerned with individual rights.[55]

Conversely, other commentators applaud that WTO Agreements do not have direct effect in the European Union. Bogdandy sustains that the lack of direct effect of WTO Agreements under the European Union "constitutional law" is beneficial because one should limit the enforcement of international law at the domestic level if it clashes with European constitutional principles, such as democratic government, legal certainty and legal equality.[56] According to Bogdandy, giving direct effect to the WTO Agreements would require harmonization of different national regulatory schemes with the consequent increase of transnational legislation at the global level, which would be critical for two reasons: first, it is unlikely that a global lawmaking mechanism can be created and, second, if created, such mechanism would impair democratic self-government and subsidiarity to a greater level than within the European Union.[57] Bogdandy also defends that legal certainty would be impaired because industries make heavy investments according to specific regulatory legal frameworks and schemes and, in case direct effect is given to WTO Agreements, "*a national producer would be uncertain to what extent the law that it must follow applies equally to foreign producers.*"[58] Lastly, according to Bogdandy's view, legal equality would also be compromised, as there are no instruments that can "*guarantee legal equality in applying WTO law to competitors from different jurisdictions.*"[59]

---

[52] Sacerdoti and Venturini (1992), p. 346.

[53] Cass (2005), pp. 21–22.

[54] Petersmann (2006), p. 9.

[55] Berkey (1998), p. 626.

[56] Von Bogdandy (2008), p. 398.

[57] Ibid., pp. 405–407.

[58] Ibid., p. 406.

[59] Ibid.

4.2 The Rational Choice Theory Perspective of the European Court of Justice... 131

Indeed, there are relevant reasons why the ECJ took this position, particularly in light of the underlying stakes involved in the European context. The fundamental issue was the scope and legitimacy of judicial review vis-à-vis the executive prerogatives in foreign policy-making. Bronckers (2008a) also added a silent stake in regard to the ECJ autonomy over the ultimate say on European trade regulation as opposed to WTO arbiters[60]:

> Another consideration militating against direct effect, attributed to the Court but not made explicit in its judgments, is that the scope of the WTO agreements is so pervasive that by granting direct effect the European courts would endanger the autonomy of the EC and assign the role of final arbiter over EC regulation to the WTO.[61]

Such conflicts in the European context are coupled with the need of ensuring the supremacy of European Union secondary legislation and the uniform application of WTO obligations in the European Union territory. Cottier and Schefer however argued that the ECJ position would be dangerous because, on one hand, it protects EU legislation inconsistent with WTO law but, on the other hand, brings about potential turmoil within the EU, as domestic courts in EU Member States can find EU legislation inapplicable based on constitutional grounds, therefore eroding the primacy of EU law over national law.[62]

Conversely, Bronckers remarks that the ECJ decision to deny private parties the right to challenge Community measures grounded on WTO agreements aimed at ensuring that Community legislature or executive had *"opportunity to find an alternative solution, even temporarily, in order to bring their legal position in conformity with their WTO obligation,"*[63] although the goal of the WTO dispute settlement system is to bring members into compliance with their WTO obligations. Bronckers continues that the rationale given by the ECJ—in the sense that the WTO relies on reciprocity and concessions, and the main trading countries of the world do not grant WTO Agreements with direct effect—corroborates the support the ECJ

---

[60] Bronckers (2008a), p. 887.

[61] Ibid.

[62] Cottier and Schefer (1998), p. 105. The authors state:
The dual membership of the EU and the Member States to the WTO is perhaps the most important policy argument in the EU. The effects of protecting instruments inconsistent with WTO obligations are interesting to observe. While the issue of direct effect of GATT rules (and the relationship of GATT and EU law under Article 234 para. 1 EC Treaty) has been controversial among lower German administrative courts, defense strategies against GATT inconsistent instruments have shifted towards constitutional arguments. The cost of denying direct effect to GATT rules is potential turmoil within the EU's legal order. Following the German Bundesverfassungsgericht in its decisions on the Maastricht treaty, the Verwaltungsgericht Frankfurt am Main has held EU regulation 404/93 partly inapplicable on grounds of German constitutional law. This correlation is of great importance. The policy of the ECJ of ignoring the GATT for the sake of securing secondary EU law may undermine EU law from a different angle and lead to an erosion of the primacy of EU law over national law and to *Rechtszersplitterung*: serious fragmentation, disruption and weakening of the emerging international federal structure of EU law.

[63] Bronckers (2008a), p. 886.

gives to the European Union bodies to control the application of international treaties in member states. Kuijper and Bronckers also note that the ECJ rulings interpreting WTO law in "*a modicum of dualism*" were primarily generated by the legislature itself, which considered WTO agreements in a dualist manner not only in the European Union, but also in the United States.[64] According to Kuijper and Bronckers (2005), the need of a legislative transposition to render direct effect to the agreements can also be drawn from the WTO agreements themselves:

> Such transposition incidentally, would seem to be completely in accordance with the legal policy behind the WTO Agreement and many of its Annex I agreements, which contain provisions obliging the Member States to take the necessary measures to carry out the agreement in question or to take all the necessary measures of a general or a special character to ensure the conformity of its laws with the agreement concerned. Such provisions are often accompanied by a provision requiring notification of any change in the laws concerned. All these provisions can be seen as indications that *the treaty drafters implicitly considered the WTO Agreement and its annexes as non-self-executing*. This is corroborated by the WTO secretariat's policy, insisting *inter alia* that countries, in particular in Latin America, that relied on direct effect in order not to adopt implementing legislation for anti-dumping, should pass such legislation nonetheless.[65] (Emphasis added)

In what concerns WTO recommendations and rulings, Bronckers notes that the EU courts are more inclined to refer to other European courts, such as the European Court of Human Rights and the European Free Trade Association Court, even though the European Communities are members of diverse multilateral agreements with their own dispute settlement mechanisms.[66] For instance, in *Kadi v. Council of the European Union*,[67] the ECJ annulled the European regulation implementing a United Nations Security Council Resolution to impose anti-terrorism sanctions because it violated fundamental rights. The ECJ considered that the Community judiciary must fully review the lawfulness of all Community acts *in the light of the fundamental rights forming an integral part of the general principles of Community law*.[68] Such decision brought a lot of scholars to debate over the implications and consequences of the ECJ position on international institutions. De Búrca pointed out the risk for the European Union image as a "virtuous international actor,"[69] while Nollkaemper suggested that international law should accommodate challenges to the supremacy of international law based on the protection of fundamental rules of domestic law that have an international nature of fundamental rights.[70]

---

[64] Kuijper and Bronckers (2005), p. 1315.
[65] Ibid.
[66] Bronckers (2007), p. 604.
[67] Joined Cases C-402/05 P and C-415/05 P, *Yassin Abdullah Kadi and Al Barakaat International Foundation v. Council of the European Union and Commission of the European Communities*, 2008 E.C.R. I-6351.
[68] Ibid., paragraph 326.
[69] De Búrca (2010).
[70] Nollkaemper (2009).

With this academic debate, the following section will turn to the specific cases through which the ECJ has built the rational choice theory approach with regards to WTO rules in domestic courts. This study will focus on the GATT and the Antidumping Agreement, both of which fall under the EU exclusive competence.

4.3 ECJ Cases

This section will examine significant cases through which the ECJ has construed the adoption of the rational choice theory with regards to WTO rules in domestic courts and, as earlier explained, focusing on the GATT and the Antidumping Agreement. Created in 1951, the ECJ needed to build its case law throughout the years, and had a paramount role in the European integration process while establishing its exclusive jurisdiction to adjudicate on EU law. For this reason, the GATT/WTO becomes a particularly interesting subject matter in the ECJ case law, as the GATT pre-existed the Court and was object of litigation several times, where the ECJ was seized to settle the dispute. The ECJ case law is firm in denying direct effect to GATT/WTO agreements, as the analysis of the cases below will demonstrate.

Differently from the Brazilian legal order, where individual votes of the Brazilian Supreme Court Justices are publicized, whether dissenting or concurring with the majority, the ECJ opinions do not have dissenting votes, and are presented as a sole and uniform opinion. This feature of the ECJ turns the analysis of the cases more conclusive, as it does not allow for possible minority votes to be expounded and therefore the possible degree of internal divergence among members of the Court are unknown for the public. At the same time, because the opinions of the ECJ are published in several languages, such opinions are widely accessible to international law comparativists from different countries, as opposed to Brazilian courts decisions, which are only available in Portuguese and therefore have a very limited accessibility for the international scholarly debate due to language constraints. For these reasons, the ECJ cases in this study will not need much detailed description as the Brazilian cases required.

4.3.1 *International Fruit Company Case*

Before the *International Fruit Company* case, the existing judicial opinion on the status of international trade agreements was the above mentioned *Kupferberg* case. However, the first specific decision the ECJ rendered regarding the legal status of the GATT is the *International Fruit Company* case,[71] in 1972. This decision is

---

[71] Joined Cases 21–24/72 *International Fruit Company NV and Others v Produktschap voor Groenten en Fruit*, 1972 E.C.R. 1219.

important because it is the leading case where the ECJ found that the GATT did not have direct effect.

4.3.1.1 The Domestic Litigation

The Community Regulations 459/70, 565/70 and 686/70 provided for protective measures applicable to the importation of apples into the Community by demanding an import license and imposing a maximum of 80 % of a reference quantity the applicant had imported in during the same month of the previous year. In the Netherlands, the plaintiff's firms requested such import licenses for importing eating apples from third countries, which were denied by the Dutch agency responsible for issuing import certificates. The case was sent to the ECJ under the preliminary ruling procedure to decide whether the Community Regulations 459/70, 565/70 and 686/70 were incompatible with Article XI of the GATT, which prescribes the general elimination of quantitative restrictions.

4.3.1.2 The Decision of the European Court of Justice

In deciding this case, the ECJ held that the Community had substituted the European member countries in relation to the GATT obligations starting from 1 July 1968, when the Common Customs Tariff entered into force.[72] Consequently, in the Court's reasoning, since that date, the GATT became binding on the Community and therefore the ECJ had exclusive jurisdiction to adjudicate on GATT's application within the Community.[73]

In addition to being the first case the Court decided on the status of the GATT, the ECJ laid down the requirements for analyzing whether an international agreement may constitute grounds for challenging the validity of acts of the Community institutions. In this case, the ECJ stated that all acts of the European Union (then European Communities) should respect the commitments made in international treaties when two conditions are met: (1) that the Community is bound by the international treaty and (2) the international treaty provision may have a direct effect, that is, be capable of conferring rights on citizens of the Community which they can invoke before national courts. In analyzing whether the GATT would meet these two conditions, the ECJ decided that the GATT did not have direct effect in the European legal order. The ECJ acknowledged that the first condition was met because the EC Member States were bound by the GATT when the European Economic Community was established and, therefore, the rights and obligations arising from the GATT could not be affected. However, the ECJ considered that the spirit, the general scheme and the terms of the GATT could not confer rights to the

---

[72] Holdgaard (2008), p. 188.
[73] Ibid.

4.3 ECJ Cases

citizens of the Community because of the principle of negotiations on the GATT's preamble and the great flexibility in GATT provisions. In examining whether the GATT Article XI was capable of conferring to citizens rights they can invoke before courts, the ECJ concluded that there were enough factors that did not allow Article XI of the GATT to have direct effect. In analyzing the terms of the GATT, the ECJ explained that:

> 21. This agreement which, according to its preamble, is based on the principle of negotiations undertaken on the basis of 'reciprocal and mutually advantageous arrangements' is characterized by the great flexibility of its provisions, in particular those conferring the possibility of derogation, the measures to be taken when confronted with exceptional difficulties and the settlement of conflicts between the contracting parties.
> 22. Consequently, according to the first paragraph of Article XXII 'Each contracting party shall accord sympathetic consideration to, and shall afford adequate opportunity for consultation regarding, such representations as may be made by any other contracting party with respect to ... all matters affecting the operation of this Agreement'.
> 23. According to the second paragraph of the same article, 'the contracting parties'—this name designating 'the contracting parties acting jointly' as is stated in the first paragraph of Article XXV—'may consult with one or more contracting parties on any question to which a satisfactory solution cannot be found through the consultations provided under paragraph (1)'.
> 24. If any contracting party should consider 'that any benefit accruing to it directly or indirectly under this Agreement is being nullified or impaired or that the attainment of any objective of the Agreement is being impeded as a result of', *inter alia*, 'the failure of another contracting party to carry out its obligations under this Agreement', Article XXIII lays down in detail the measures which the parties concerned, or the contracting parties acting jointly, may or must take in regard to such a situation.
> 25. Those measures include, for the settlement of conflicts, written recommendations or proposals which are to be 'given sympathetic consideration', investigations possibly followed by recommendations, consultations between or decisions of the contracting parties, including that of authorizing certain contracting parties to suspend the application to any others of any obligations or concessions under the General Agreement and, finally, in the event of such suspension, the power of the party concerned to withdraw from that agreement.
> 26. Finally, where by reason of an obligation assumed under the General Agreement or of a concession relating to a benefit, some producers suffer or are threatened with serious damage, Article XIX gives a contracting party power unilaterally to suspend the obligation and to withdraw or modify the concession, either after consulting the contracting parties jointly and failing agreement between the contracting parties concerned, or even, if the matter is urgent and on a temporary basis, without prior consultation.[74]

The rationale that the purpose, the spirit, the general scheme and the terms of the GATT qualifies such agreement as a non-self-executing treaty and therefore cannot have direct effect in the European internal legal order has been confirmed in the Court's case law ever since.[75]

---

[74] Joined Cases 21–24/72 *International Fruit Company NV and Others v Produktschap voor Groenten en Fruit*, 1972 E.C.R. 1219, paragraphs 21–26.

[75] Eeckhout (1997), p. 26.

4.3.1.3 The Assessment of the Case

This case is relevant because it builds on the concept of direct effect or non-self-executing international treaties. Most commonly understood as limited to a strict reading of the terms and words of the specific prevision at hand, the concept of direct effect or non-self-executing treaties was developed by the ECJ perspective to a broad interpretation of the international agreements as a whole in what concerns their purpose, spirit and general scheme, in addition to the terms of the agreements themselves. The ECJ ruling on the *International Fruit Company* case expanded the concept of the non-self-executing character of the GATT as not a question of whether the rule at stake, Article XI of the GATT, were clear and complete enough to be applied by courts. Instead, the ECJ considered the international agreement as a whole.

By not applying the doctrine of the direct effect, or the doctrine of consistent interpretation, the ECJ embraced the rational choice theory regarding the most proper role of domestic courts in relation to the GATT. The ECJ established that potential GATT violations cannot be grounds for judges to invalidate Community acts. According to the ECJ, the GATT is a diplomatic system in nature—based on negotiations with the possibility of reaching a mutually agreeable solution on potential disputes—not a legal one, and therefore does not allow judicial intervention.

Although a longtime proponent of Conforti's traditionalism to the point of creating itself the doctrine of direct effect of European Union law in national courts of European Member States, the ECJ ruling on the *International Fruit Company* was a significant innovation in the Court's case law. Considering that the benefits and concessions of the GATT are limited, that is, they can be suspended, modified in exchange of compensation agreed with the concerned parties, the ECJ position could be framed as in conformity with Sykes' theoretical perspective on the function and objective of international trade agreements.

4.3.2 Nakajima v. Council

The next relevant ECJ decision for this study is the *Nakajima v. Council* case.[76] Here, the plaintiff argued that EC Council regulations on antidumping duties breached the Agreement on Implementation of Article VI of the GATT (the Antidumping Agreement). This ECJ case is important because it established that, although the GATT Antidumping Agreement does not have direct effect in the European legal order, it is possible to challenge the validity of EC antidumping regulation grounded on the GATT Antidumping Agreement if such regulation

---

[76] Case C-69/89, *Nakajima All Precision Co. Ltd v. Council of European Communities*, 1991 ECR I-2169.

4.3.2.1 The Domestic Litigation

Nakajima was a Japanese company that exported certain printers to Europe that were not sold in the Japanese domestic market and were destined exclusively for exportation. During the antidumping investigation initiated at the request of the Committee of European Printer Manufacturers, the Council of the European Communities used the method of calculating the constructed value prescribed by supervening Council Regulation n. 2423/88 to determine the normal value of such products when they are not sold in the country of origin's domestic market. Along with other companies, Nakajima challenged the imposition of 12 % antidumping duties on their products as being unreasonable and discriminatory because of the method of calculation of the normal value of such products. Nakajima claimed that the Article 2 (3) (b) (ii)[78] of Council Regulation n. 2423/88 on

---

[77] The Nakajima case was preceded by the case C-70/87, *EEC Seed Crushers' and Oil Processors' Federation (Fediol) v. Commission*, 1989 E.C.R. 1781, which provided for the first glimpse of the distinction whereby the ECJ considered that GATT rules could be used to interpret Community regulations if such instruments expressly made reference to the GATT. The ECJ stated in *Fediol*, paragraph 22:

> 22. It follows that, since Regulation No 2641/84 entitles the economic agents concerned to rely on the GATT provisions in the complaint which they lodge with the Commission in order to establish the illicit nature of the commercial practices which they consider to have harmed them, those same economic agents are entitled to request the Court to exercise its powers of review over the legality of the Commission's decision applying those provisions.

The Nakajima case, however, is the paradigm ruling through which the ECJ established the interpretation on the exceptions to the GATT lack of direct effect. The Nakajima case provides clearer and more detailed reasoning as applied by the ECJ. For this reason, the Nakajima case will be the precedent used in this section to address the ECJ's exceptions to the lack of direct effect of GATT.

[78] Council Regulation n. 2423/88, Article 2 (3) (b) (ii):

Article 2 – Dumping (...)
2. A product shall be considered to have been dumped if its export price to the Community is less than the normal value of the like product.
B. NORMAL VALUE
3. For the purposes of this Regulation, the normal value shall be: (...)
(b) when there are no sales of the like product in the ordinary course of trade on the domestic market of the exporting country or country of origin, or when such sales do not permit a proper comparison: (...)
(ii) the constructed value, determined by adding cost of production and a reasonable margin of profit. The cost of production shall be computed on the basis of all costs, in the ordinary course of trade, both fixed and variable, in the country of origin, of materials and manufacture, plus a reasonable amount for selling, administrative and other general

protection against dumped imports from countries not members of the European Economic Community was not applicable to its products. It also claimed that the Council Regulation n. 3651/88 imposing a definitive antidumping duty on its products was void. Nakajima challenged Article 2 (3) (b) (ii) of the Council Regulation n. 2423/88, which established methods to calculate the constructed normal value of the product allegedly being dumped in the European market by making reference to the expenses and profits of other producers or exporters selling on the domestic market. To support its claims, Nakajima argued that Article 2 (3) (b) (ii) of the Council Regulation n. 2423/88 violated the Agreement on Implementation of Article VI of the GATT (the Antidumping Agreement), which requires a fair comparison to be made between the export price and the normal value in the determination of dumping.

4.3.2.2 The Decision of the European Court of Justice

While pointing out that Nakajima based its claims on the grounds for review of legality of the Council Regulation and not on the direct effect of the Antidumping Agreement, the ECJ cited the *International Fruit Company* case and considered that the Community was bound by the Antidumping Agreement, which aimed to provide rules to ensure uniformity and legal certainty in the application of Article VI of the GATT. Similarly following the precedent on the *International Fruit Company* case, the ECJ stated that the Antidumping Agreement did not have direct effect in the European legal order.

At the same time, however, the ECJ distinguished the case at hand from the *International Fruit* case because the Council Regulation 2423/88 was enacted for the express purpose of implementing the Antidumping Agreement. Therefore, in the Court's view, it was possible to review Community legislation vis-à-vis the Antidumping Agreement because the former aimed at implementing the latter. The ECJ concluded therefore that the Antidumping Agreement could be a parameter of interpretation of the Community Regulation in such circumstances.

After finding admissible to review whether the Council Regulation had overstepped the bounds of the Antidumping Agreement, the ECJ nevertheless

---

expenses. The amount for selling, general and administrative expenses and profit shall be calculated by reference to the expenses incurred and the profit realized by the producer or exporter on the profitable sales of like products on the domestic market. If such data is unavailable or unreliable or is not suitable for use they shall be calculated by reference to the expenses incurred and profit realized by other producers or exporters in the country of origin or export on profitable sales of the like product. If neither of these two methods can be applied the expenses incurred and the profit realized shall be calculated by reference to the sales made by the exporter or other producers or exporters in the same business sector in the country of origin or export or on any other reasonable basis.

concluded that the method of establishing the construed normal value of the product in question set out in the Council Regulation was reasonable and therefore in conformity with the Antidumping Agreement.

4.3.2.3 The Assessment of the Case

The *Nakajima* ruling is relevant because, while denying direct effect of the Antidumping Agreement, the ECJ opened the possibility of private parties to contest the validity of Community regulation by means of an objection of illegality because such regulation expressly aimed at implementing the Antidumping Agreement. Here, the ECJ decision is in coherence with the doctrine of non-self-executing treaties whereby once there is an implementing legislation, it is possible for private parties to confront such implementing regulation vis-à-vis the international treaty in question—namely, the Antidumping Agreement. When stating that the Antidumping Agreement does not have direct effect, the ECJ did not depart from its previous ruling on the *International Fruit Company* case and maintained that the GATT does not have direct effect in the European legal order.

Another important feature of the *Nakajima* case is that the ECJ used the doctrine of judicial deference towards the executive branch. Here, the ECJ deferred to the EC institutions a wide margin of discretion in the determination of the normal value of the printers in question by a method of calculating the constructed value:

> The basic anti-dumping regulation allows the Community institutions a margin of discretion, particularly in calculating the amount of the selling, general and administrative expenses to be included in the constructed normal value, and the fact that an institution exercises that discretion without explaining in detail and in advance the criteria which it intends to apply in every specific situation does not constitute a breach of the principle of legal certainty.[79]

In summary, the ECJ *Nakajima* ruling, by providing a possibility of relying on the GATT rules to challenge a Community measure, can be understood as reinforcing the rational choice theory perspective of the ECJ in what concerns the role of judges regarding the GATT/WTO agreements. Here, it is up to the executive to choose how to implement an international treaty, and not for the judiciary to decide the implementation of an international treaty. By finding that the provisions of the Community Resolution establishing the constructed normal value of the product in question were reasonable and therefore were in conformity with the GATT Antidumping Agreement, the Court ensured the executive's scope of maneuver to address complex economic situations according to the circumstances of the case. Equally, the rational choice theory perspective of the ECJ has been confirmed by deferring to the executive to adjust to intricate situations and avoiding superseding the executive's domain. Finally, the Court, while upholding the lack of

---

[79] Case C-69/89, *Nakajima All Precision Co. Ltd v. Council of European Communities*, 1991 ECR I-2169, Summary of the Judgment, paragraph 12.

direct effect GATT Antidumping Agreement, validated the Council Regulation and clearly endorsed the executive's discretion in choosing how to implement such Agreement within the European legal order.

4.3.3 Germany v. Council

The *Germany v. Council*[80] case is significant to the relations between the GATT/WTO agreements and national courts in the European Union. This case derives from a long-standing dispute over the imports of banana into the European internal market, which involved litigation at the national,[81] European[82] and international level.[83] This section will focus on the ECJ ruling, although the repercussion of this ECJ opinion on German courts will be addressed in Sect. 4.4.1 below.

The dispute over the tariff quotas on the imports of banana among different categories of traders before the ECJ is relevant because it is a case where two international trade agreements were invoked—the GATT and the Lomé Convention—and they were granted contrasting effects: the GATT, as the ECJ's previous case law established, was considered as not having direct effect, while the Lomé Convention was granted direct effect.

Another important feature of this case is that the non-invocability of the GATT before the EU courts, previously ruled in relation to individuals or private companies, was also extended to the EU Member States. Traditionally, there has been a distinction between two types of applicants before the ECJ, the "privileged" and the "non-privileged" applicants.[84] The privilege applicants is a group integrated by the

---

[80] Case C-280/93, *Federal Republic of Germany v. Council of the European Union*, 1994 E.C.R. I-5039.

[81] In Germany, the allocation of import quotas for bananas produced in non-traditional ACP countries was challenged by German importers of Banana—Atlanta Fruchthandelsgesellschaft mbH and others—before the Verwaltungsgericht Frankfurt am Main (Administrative Court). During the proceedings, the Administrative Court requested a preliminary ruling to the ECJ on the validity of the Council Regulation 404/93 on the common organization of the market in bananas. Here, the ECJ reaffirmed the decision on the *Germany v. Council* case and upheld the validity of Council Regulation 404/93 as it was not intended to ensure the implementation of a particular WTO obligation capable of setting aside the lack of direct effect of the WTO agreements. The litigation at the national level in Germany will be addressed at Sect. 4.4.1.

[82] Other than the present case *Federal Republic of Germany v. Council of the European Union*, 1994 E.C.R. I-5039, see *Atlanta Fruchthandelsgesellschaft mbH and others v. Bundesamt für Ernährung und Forstwirtschaft*, 1995 E.C.R. I-3799.

[83] WTO, *European Communities—Regime for the Importation, Sale and Distribution of Bananas*, WT/DS16, WT/DS27, WT/DS105, WT/DS158, WT/DS361, and WT/DS364. For a brief chronology of the bananas dispute before the GATT and the WTO, *see* WTO Press Releases (2009).

[84] Lang (2012).

4.3 ECJ Cases 141

EU Member States, the Council and the Commission, and has unrestricted standing to question Community acts.[85] The non-privilege applicants are private parties— that is, individuals or legal persons—and have more restrict requirements for standing.[86] This case is an important development of the European case law because, while reaffirming that the GATT cannot be invoked by individuals—or "non-privileged" applicants—the ECJ also extended the interpretation that GATT cannot be considered as ground to challenge Community law even by Member States. As privileged applicants, EC Member States in principle have a much broader standing before the Court. Yet, according to this *Germany v. Council* ruling, even Member States cannot challenge Community acts on grounds of GATT violations.

4.3.3.1 The Domestic Litigation

Known as the "*Banana case*," this dispute started with the introduction of a new banana import regime by Council Regulation 404/93. This Council Regulation gave preferential treatment to bananas originated from the African, Caribbean and Pacific countries (ACP countries), to the disadvantage of banana imports from Latin American countries which reached consumers with a lower price. The Council Regulation 404/93 aimed at implementing a common organization of the market in bananas, because Member States had different importation arrangements, some more flexible, others more restrict. The Council Regulation 404/93 provided for preferential treatment to ACP countries that were traditionally suppliers of the Community based on the 4th ACP-EEC Lomé Convention with the African, Caribbean and Pacific Group of States (ACP countries). Before the enactment of Council Regulation 404/93, Germany was allowed to import from an annual quota of bananas originated in third countries without customs duty under the framework of the Implementing Convention on the Association of the Overseas Countries and Territories (Banana Protocol).

Germany filed an action for the annulment of Council Regulation 404/93 before the ECJ under the then 1st paragraph of Article 173 of the EEC Treaty [now Article

---

[85] The then Article 173 (1) of the Treaty of Rome, now prescribed in the Consolidated version of the Treaty on the Functioning of the European Union, Article 263(1), provides Member States the possibility of challenging any Community act on "*grounds of lack of competence, infringement of an essential procedural requirement, infringement of the Treaties or of any rule of law relating to their application, or misuse of powers.*"

[86] The private parties standing before the ECJ was then prescribed in Article 173 (2) of the Treaty of Rome, and is now regulated in Article 263(4) of the Consolidated version of the Treaty on the Functioning of the European Union, which provides certain conditions of admissibility, which reads:

> Article 263 (4) – Any natural or legal person may, under the conditions laid down in the first and second paragraphs, institute proceedings against an act addressed to that person or which is of direct and individual concern to them, and against a regulatory act which is of direct concern to them and does not entail implementing measures.

263(4) TFEU]. In addition to alleging several procedural and substantial breaches of European law which are not object of this study, Germany argued that the Council Regulation 404/93 violated certain GATT rules, as well as the Lomé Convention.

4.3.3.2 The Decision of the European Court of Justice

The ECJ made reference to its previous case law confirming that while the Community is bound by the GATT, the Court must consider "the spirit, the general scheme and the terms of GATT." In its ruling, the ECJ reaffirmed that the GATT's flexibility and possibility of derogation of GATT's rights and obligations preclude the Court from taking such international agreements as grounds for assessing the validity of Community acts. The ECJ stated:

> 106. It is settled law that GATT, which according to its preamble is based on the principle of negotiations undertaken on the basis of 'reciprocal and mutually advantageous arrangements', is characterized by the great flexibility of its provisions, in particular those conferring the possibility of derogation, the measures to be taken when confronted with exceptional difficulties and the settlement of conflicts between the contracting parties.
> 107. The Court has recognized that those measures include, for the settlement of conflicts, depending on the case, written recommendations or proposals which are to be 'given sympathetic consideration', investigations possibly followed by recommendations, consultations between or decisions of the *contracting parties*, including that of authorizing certain contracting parties to suspend the application to any others of any obligations or concessions under GATT and, finally, in the event of such suspension, the power of the party concerned to withdraw from that agreement.[87]

The ECJ also mentioned the safeguards clause prescribed in Article XIX of the GATT—which allows states to impose emergency safeguard measures to suspend or modify or withdraw GATT obligations when imports increase as to cause serious injury or threat to domestic producers—to point out the flexibility that prevents GATT rules to be relied on as grounds to challenge the lawfulness of Community acts.

Although not examining GATT obligations of trade without discrimination, the ECJ addressed Germany's argument that the Council Regulation 404/93 violated the principle of non-discrimination derived from the Treaty on the Functioning of the European Union on the common organization of agricultural markets.[88] Germany argued that the subdivision of the tariff quota created an unjustified discrimination against more competitive traders operating in third countries. In relation to the alleged breach of the principle of non-discrimination, the ECJ considered such allegation as unfounded, because

---

[87] Case C-280/93, *Federal Republic of Germany v. Council of the European Union*, 1994 E.C.R. I-5039, paragraphs 106–107.

[88] Consolidated version of the Treaty on the Functioning of the European Union, Article 40 (3).

such a difference in treatment appears to be inherent in the objective of integrating previously compartmentalized markets [*open national markets and protected national markets*], bearing in mind the different situations of the various categories of economic operators before the establishment of the common organization of the market. The Regulation is intended to ensure the disposal of Community production and traditional ACP production, which entails the striking of a balance between the two categories of economic operators in question.[89]

With this rationale, the ECJ recognized that the Council Regulation affected differently the economic operators involved, but rejected the allegation of unjust discrimination. Moreover, the Court considered that there could have been other less onerous measures to ensure the disposal of Community and ACP production of bananas and integrate the various national markets. Nevertheless, the ECJ refused to substitute the Council's assessment on the appropriateness of the measures adopted as such policy choices were the Council's responsibility and they had not been proved to be manifestly inappropriate.[90]

4.3.3.3 The Assessment of the Case

This ruling illustrates the conflicting positions of the ECJ in relation to international trade agreements: a traditionalist perspective as well as a rational choice theory viewpoint. The ECJ, when faced with dispositions of both the Lomé Convention and the GATT, granted direct effect to the Lomé Convention as opposed to the GATT which, according to its settle law, has no direct effect in the European Union legal order. The ECJ considered the alleged infringement of Article 168 of the Lomé Convention to eventually reject Germany's claim, while the GATT violations were not addressed. This ruling is summarized as follows:

> 8. With respect to the establishment of a tariff quota, the import of bananas from ACP States into the Community falls under Article 168(2) (a)(ii) of the Fourth ACP-EEC Lomé Convention, Protocol 5 on bananas annexed to that Convention, and Annexes LXXIV and LXXV relating to that protocol. Under those provisions, the Community's only obligation is to maintain the advantages, with respect to access of ACP bananas to the Community market, which the ACP states had before that Convention, so that Regulation No 404/93 was able, without being in breach of Article 168(1) of the Convention, to impose a levy on imports of non-traditional ACP bananas exceeding a specified tonnage.
> 9. The special features of the General Agreement on Tariffs and Trade, which is characterized by the great flexibility of its provisions, in particular those conferring the possibility of derogation, the measures to be taken when confronted with exceptional difficulties and

---

[89] Case C-280/93, *Federal Republic of Germany v. Council of the European Union*, 1994 E.C.R. I-5039, paragraph 74.

[90] Ibid., paragraph 94:
> 94. While other means for achieving the desired result were indeed conceivable, the Court cannot substitute its assessment for that of the Council as to the appropriateness or otherwise of the measures adopted by the Community legislature if those measures have not been proved to be manifestly inappropriate for achieving the objective pursued.

the settlement of conflicts between the contracting parties, precludes the Court from taking provisions of GATT into consideration to assess the lawfulness of a regulation in an action brought by a Member State under the first paragraph of Article 173 of the Treaty. Those features show that the GATT rules are not unconditional and that an obligation to recognize them as rules of international law which are directly applicable in the domestic legal systems of the contracting parties cannot be based on the spirit, general scheme or terms of GATT. In the absence of such an obligation following from GATT itself, it is only if the Community intended to implement a particular obligation entered into within the framework of GATT, or if the Community act expressly refers to specific provisions of GATT, that the Court can review the lawfulness of the Community act in question from the point of view of the GATT rules.[91]

The opposing interpretations regarding different international trade agreements by the ECJ reflects a distinction based on power relations rather than on the subject matter of the treaty. The Lomé Convention aims to promote regional cooperation through for non-reciprocal trade preferences to favor former colonies of European countries, intending to assist such countries' development and growth while maintaining European influence in their businesses. With this rationale, the EU maintains their dominant position in its former colonies. On the other hand, the GATT provides for mutual and reciprocal benefits and obligations, although it has also addressed development concerns in providing an exception to the most favored nation treatment through the enabling clause,[92] but it does not allow picking which developing countries may benefit from it.

Here, the ECJ provided a great deference to Community's bodies by preventing even Member States from challenging Community law based on the GATT provisions. When the ECJ prevented even the privileged applicants from discussing potential GATT violations committed by Community acts, it therefore reinforced Community powers vis-à-vis Member States which are also members of the GATT/WTO system to preserve the scope of maneuver of the Community's executive bodies to implement trade policies. The ECJ's deference to the executive was also present when the Court exercised self-restraint in refusing to review policy choices of the Council to create a common organization of the market in bananas, unless such policy choices were manifestly inappropriate.

Besides the ECJ litigation, it is important to mention that the system of trade preferences given to ACP countries was brought before the GATT/WTO Settlement System in several disputes filed by Latin American countries and the United States. Although involving banana produced in Latin American countries, the main banana exporters were American-owned corporations. As a result, the United States was highly involved in the banana dispute at the GATT/WTO Dispute Settlement System. The United States' interests and participation in the banana dispute at the

---

[91] Case C-280/93, *Federal Republic of Germany v. Council of the European Union*, 1994 E.C.R. I-5039, Summary of Judgment, paragraphs 8–9.

[92] The enabling clause waives the most favored nation rule of GATT Article I by allowing differential and more favorable tariff treatment to products from developing countries. For an explanation on the origins of the enabling clause and its text, *see* Guzman and Pauwelyn (2009), pp. 631–632.

GATT/WTO—a country where the GATT/WTO agreements are non-self-executing by U.S. Congress legislation—seems to have also been a major influence in the rationale for the ECJ to ensure broad powers to Council regulations. The importance that ECJ has bestowed on the role of reciprocity with regards to the legal effects of GATT/WTO agreements among its most important trading players, particularly the United States, will be addressed in the next case.

4.3.4 Portugal v. Council

The *Portuguese Republic v. Council* case[93] is a significant one because the ECJ extended to the then recently-enacted WTO agreements the previous ECJ case law interpretation on the legal effects of the GATT 1947. Accordingly, in this case, the ECJ established that the WTO agreements had no direct effect in the European legal order.

This case is also of central importance to understand the core role of reciprocity in the ECJ opinions on the lack of direct effect of GATT/WTO agreements. The ECJ expressly relied on the principle of reciprocity to deny direct effect of WTO agreements at the domestic level to avoid uneven degrees of enforcement of WTO rules, which otherwise would occur as the major trading partners of the Community considered the WTO agreements as not having direct effect. Of course, the ECJ position aimed at the Community major trading partners, which were at that time the United States, Japan, China and Canada. No Latin American country was among the EC major trading partners at that time and, as will be further developed in the next section, Latin American courts' approach to the GATT/WTO agreements are largely ignored in the international trade debate.

Finally, the ECJ's opinion on the *Portuguese Republic v. Council* case is relevant because it provides a restrictive application of the exceptions that would allow private invocability of WTO agreements in the above mentioned *Germany v. Council* case. As documented, in *Germany v. Council* and *Nakajima*, the ECJ had provided an exception to the interpretation that Member States could not directly invoke WTO agreements as a basis to invalidate a Council Decision on condition that the Community's measure aimed to implement a specific WTO agreement or if the measure expressly refers to a particular WTO provision. In the *Portuguese Republic v. Council*, the ECJ considered that the measure at hand did not constitute an implementing legislation of the WTO agreements, rejecting therefore Portugal's argument.

---

[93] Case C-149/96, *Portuguese Republic v. Council of the European Union*, 1999 E.C.R. I-8395.

4.3.4.1 The Domestic Litigation

The Council Decision 96/386/EC approved by majority two Memoranda of Understanding, one with Pakistan, another with India, on arrangements in the area of market access for textile product, both of which were concluded after the signature of the WTO agreements in 1994.

Portugal challenged the Council Decision 96/386/EC before the ECJ arguing that it breached various principles of the WTO law, particularly the GATT 47, the Agreement on Textiles and Clothing (ATC) and the Agreement on Import Licensing Procedures. To support its claim, Portugal sustained that the ECJ should review the validity of the Council Decision 96/386/EC vis-à-vis the WTO agreements, because, according to previous ECJ case law, it is possible to challenge a Community measure based on alleged breaches of international trade agreements if such measure specifically refers to or aims at implementing the international agreement in question. According to Portugal's argument, the Council Decision was adopted following the conclusion of the Uruguay Round and constituted the implementing regulation of the WTO agreements, including the GATT and the ATC. Portugal argued that the WTO agreements were significantly different from the GATT, particularly considering the strengthened mechanism of dispute settlement.

4.3.4.2 The Decision of the European Court of Justice

Even though the ECJ agreed with Portugal's claim that the WTO agreements significantly differed from the previous GATT regime, the ECJ considered that the WTO agreements still gave considerable weight to negotiations between the signatory parties. Consequently, the ECJ decided that the WTO agreements, due to their nature and structure and in light of their subject matter and purpose, are not in principle among the rules upon which the Court may review the legality of measures adopted by the Community institutions.[94] The ECJ held that, similarly to the GATT, the WTO agreements were also based on the principle of negotiations to attain reciprocal and mutually advantageous arrangements. The ECJ cited several dispositions of the WTO Understanding on Rules and Procedures Governing the Settlement of Disputes (DSU) to demonstrate the importance of negotiations under the WTO legal framework:

> 37. Although the main purpose of the mechanism for resolving disputes is in principle, according to Article 3(7) of the Understanding on Rules and Procedures Governing the Settlement of Disputes (Annex 2 to the WTO), to secure the withdrawal of the measures in question if they are found to be inconsistent with the WTO rules, that understanding provides that where the immediate withdrawal of the measures is impracticable compensation may be granted on an interim basis pending the withdrawal of the inconsistent measure.

---

[94] Ibid., paragraph 47.

4.3 ECJ Cases

38. According to Article 22(1) of that Understanding, compensation is a temporary measure available in the event that the recommendations and rulings of the dispute settlement body provided for in Article 2(1) of that Understanding are not implemented within a reasonable period of time, and Article 22(1) shows a preference for full implementation of a recommendation to bring a measure into conformity with the WTO agreements in question.
39. However, Article 22(2) provides that if the member concerned fails to fulfill its obligation to implement the said recommendations and rulings within a reasonable period of time, it is, if so requested, and on the expiry of a reasonable period at the latest, to enter into negotiations with any party having invoked the dispute settlement procedures, with a view to finding mutually acceptable compensation.[95]

In examining the DSU provisions, which allow temporary compensation or mutually agreed solutions due to inconsistent actions with WTO rules, the ECJ found that if courts were to invalidate domestic legislation that were not consistent with the WTO agreements, the legislative or executive organs of all signatory parties would be deprived from the possibility accorded by the DSU to find a negotiated arrangement, even if only temporary.[96] In addition, the ECJ pointed out that the most important trading partners of the EU decided that WTO Agreements were not applicable when their domestic courts review the legality of domestic law.[97] In this sense, the ECJ considered that lack of reciprocity of the major trading players in recognizing the direct application of the WTO agreements could lead to disuniform application of such obligations. The ECJ therefore concluded that courts could not directly apply WTO rules because it would not allow the executive bodies of the Community to have the necessary scope for maneuver enjoyed by other contracting parties to reach mutually agreed solutions.

To support its rationale, the ECJ also considered the preamble of the Council Decision 94/800 which approved the Uruguay Round regarding the portion that falls under the competence of the EU. The preamble of the Council Decision 94/800 stated that the Agreement establishing the WTO, due to its nature, was not susceptible to be directly invoked before courts of the Community or Member States.[98]

Finally, after establishing that the WTO agreements did not have direct effect in the European legal order, the ECJ rejected Portugal's claim that the Council Decision 96/386/EC constituted an implementing regulation of the WTO agreements, because it was not designed to implement any particular WTO obligation, and did not expressly mention any provision of these agreements.

---

[95] Ibid., paragraphs 37–39.

[96] Ibid., paragraph 40.

[97] Ibid., paragraph 43.

[98] Council Decision 94/800/EC, of 22 December 1994, concerning the conclusion on behalf of the European Community, as regards matters within its competence, of the agreements reached in the Uruguay Round multilateral negotiations (1986–1994).

4.3.4.3 The Assessment of the Case

In *Portugal v. Council*, the ECJ extended its position previously taken in relation to the GATT to the WTO agreements. In this case, the lack of direct effect of WTO agreements reveals the ECJ's consistent self-restraint in judicial review of cases involving international trade law (other than association agreements, as earlier noted). This opinion also exposes the judicial deference towards the executive branch. Here, the ECJ opinion found that it was not possible for courts to substitute the legislative and the executive bodies in negotiations that involve policy choices on temporary compensation and mutually agreed solutions for WTO inconsistent measures. Indeed, public policy choices are inherent to the domain of the political branches.

The most important aspect of this opinion is the relevancy of the role of reciprocity in the ECJ's ruling. When the ECJ makes reference to the Community's trading partners that do not bestow WTO agreements with self-executing character, it is necessary to look at these trading partners. It can be argued that the ECJ was mostly concerned with the United States, as the importance of the United States for European exports has been widely known. The fact that the U.S. Congress has deprived the WTO agreements from any effect in their domestic legal system has certainly played a role in the ECJ's concern with reciprocity. The influence of the United States in the legal effects of the WTO agreements in domestic legal orders will be further developed in Chap. 5.

Finally, the ECJ's opinion on the *Portuguese Republic v. Council* case is relevant because it provides a restrictive application of the ruling in the above mentioned *Germany v. Council* case. In *Germany v. Council*, the ECJ had provided an exception to allow Member States to directly invoke WTO agreements as a basis to invalidate a Council Decision if the Community's measure aimed to implement a specific WTO agreement or if the measure expressly refers to a particular WTO provision. In the *Portuguese Republic v. Council*, the ECJ considered that the measure at hand—resulting from negotiations on textiles initiated in parallel during the Uruguay Round but concluded afterwards with two countries—did not constitute an implementing legislation of the WTO agreements on market access. It showed therefore how restrictive is the definition of what constitutes an implementing legislation. The Court rejected therefore Portugal's argument that the validity of the Council Decision should have been confronted with WTO rules.

4.3.5 Léon Van Parys v. Council

The *Van Parys* case[99] is a significant decision because the ECJ addressed the legal effects of WTO Dispute Settlement Body (DSB) rulings in the European legal order, and whether private parties may rely on such rulings to challenge Community legislation. Here, the case involves the long-standing banana dispute, already mentioned in Sect. 4.3.3. This time, however, instead of an EU Member country as applicant, a Belgian importer was the interested party. The *Van Parys* case becomes relevant because the ECJ explicitly refused to invalidate Community law even when the DSB had already found such legislation incompatible with WTO law, and excluded the application of the *Nakajima* exception in relation to Community legislation that implemented DSB rulings.

4.3.5.1 The Domestic Litigation

After importing bananas from Ecuador for 20 years, Van Parys—a Belgian banana importer—questioned the imposition of quotas on imports of bananas from Ecuador and Panama, as the Belgian Intervention and Refund Board (BIRB) refused to issue import licenses. Van Parys challenged the Council Regulation 404/93 and subsequent amending and implementing regulations establishing the common organization of the market in bananas with ACP states, in light of GATT Article I and XIII and the Framework Agreement on Cooperation between the European Economic Community and the Cartagena Agreement Article 4. The questions on Community law were referred to the ECJ by Belgian courts. As mentioned in Sect. 4.3.3 *Germany v. Council* case, Council Regulation 404/93 and subsequent regulations provided for a differentiated tariff quota system of banana trade, giving differentiated treatment between traditional imports from ACP countries, non-traditional imports from ACP countries, and imports from third states.

4.3.5.2 The Decision of the European Court of Justice

In what concerns the argument that the Belgian authorities' refusal to issue banana import licenses from Ecuador and Panama was unlawful because Council Regulation 404/93 and subsequent measures were not valid in light of Article I and XIII of the GATT 1994, the ECJ first decided to assess whether the WTO law provides Community citizens with a right to rely on such agreements before domestic courts

---

[99] Case C-377/02, *Léon Van Parys NV v. Belgisch Interventie- en Restitutiebureau (BIRB)*, 2005 E.C.R. 1499.

to challenge the validity of Community legislation when the WTO DSB findings concluded that the Community legislation and subsequent legislation adopted to comply with the WTO agreements were not consistent with such rules.[100] The ECJ then restated its settled case law that WTO agreements, due to their structure and nature, do not have direct effect and that the only exceptions are when the Community intended to implement a particular WTO obligation, or the measure makes express reference to precise rules of WTO agreements. In relation to the DSB rulings, the ECJ stated:

41. In the present case, by undertaking after the adoption of the decision of the DSB of 25 September 1997 to comply with the WTO rules and, in particular, with Articles I (1) and XIII of GATT 1994, the Community did not intend to assume a particular obligation in the context of the WTO, capable of justifying an exception to the impossibility of relying on WTO rules before the Community Courts and enabling the Community Courts to exercise judicial review of the relevant Community provisions in the light of those rules.
42. First, it should be noted that even where there is a decision of the DSB holding that the measures adopted by a member are incompatible with the WTO rules, as the Court has already held, the WTO dispute settlement system nevertheless accords considerable importance to negotiation between the parties (*Portugal v Council*, paragraphs 36 to 40).
43. Thus, although, in the absence of a resolution mutually agreed between the parties and compatible with the agreements in question, the main purpose of the dispute settlement system is in principle, according to Article 3(7) of the understanding, to secure the withdrawal of the measures in question if they are found to be inconsistent with the WTO rules, that provision provides, however, that where the immediate withdrawal of the measures is impracticable, compensation may be granted or the application of concessions or the enforcement of other obligations may be suspended on an interim basis pending the withdrawal of the inconsistent measure (see, to that effect, Portugal v Council, paragraph 37).
44. It is true that, according to Articles 3(7) and 22(1) of the understanding, compensation and the suspension of concessions or other obligations are temporary measures available in the event that the recommendations and rulings of the DSB are not implemented within a reasonable period of time, the latter of those provisions showing a preference for full implementation of a recommendation to bring a measure into conformity with the WTO agreements in question (*Portugal v Council*, paragraph 38).
45. However, Article 22(2) provides that, if the Member concerned fails to enforce those recommendations and decisions within a reasonable period, if so requested, and within a reasonable period of time, it is to enter into negotiations with any party having invoked the dispute settlement procedures with a view to agreeing compensation. If no satisfactory compensation has been agreed within 20 days after the expiry of the reasonable period, the complainant may request authorization from the DSB to suspend, in respect of that member, the application of concessions or other obligations under the WTO agreements.
46. Furthermore, Article 22(8) of the understanding provides that the dispute remains on the agenda of the DSB, pursuant to Article 21(6) of the understanding, until it is resolved, that is until the measure found to be inconsistent has been 'removed' or the parties reach a 'mutually satisfactory solution'.

---

[100] Ibid., paragraph 38.

4.3 ECJ Cases

47. Where there is no agreement as to the compatibility of the measures taken to comply with the DSB's recommendations and decisions, Article 21(5) of the understanding provides that the dispute shall be decided 'through recourse to these dispute settlement procedures', including an attempt by the parties to reach a negotiated solution.
48. In those circumstances, to require courts to refrain from applying rules of domestic law which are inconsistent with the WTO agreements would have the consequence of depriving the legislative or executive organs of the contracting parties of the possibility afforded by Article 22 of that memorandum of reaching a negotiated settlement, even on a temporary basis (*Portugal v Commission*, paragraph 40).[101]

The ECJ then concluded that, if judicial review were to be conceded in light of WTO law upon the expiry date of a DSB ruling's implementation process, the Community negotiation efforts to find a mutually agreeable solution to the dispute would be compromised. Also, the ECJ considered that judicial review in the circumstances of the case would prevent the reconciliation of the WTO and ACP obligations and the requirements for common agricultural policy. Therefore, according to the ECJ, a Community measure adopting a DSB ruling cannot be interpreted "*as measures intended to ensure the enforcement within the Community legal order of a particular obligation assumed in the context of the WTO.*"[102]

4.3.5.3 The Assessment of the Case

The ECJ excludes from the possibility of judicial review a Community measure clearly aiming at addressing the DSB recommendations regarding the establishment of the common organization of the market in bananas. The Court's opinion, while following its case law on the lack of direct effect of WTO agreements, was very strict in stating that the a Community measure adopting a DSB ruling would not fall under the category of "*a particular obligation assumed in the context of the WTO.*" Therefore, although in theory the ECJ had considered in the *Nakajima* case that WTO agreements could have direct effect if there would be implementing legislation of "*a particular obligation,*" this possibility seemed hard to predict. What would fit in the concept of "*a particular obligation*" is not clear. In this case, the rational choice theory approach of the ECJ seems to be exacerbated with a very restrict possibility of having an implementing regulation of a particular obligation.

When the ECJ valued the possibility of negotiations—which were in place at that time though not very successfully—the Court strengthened the dispute settlement mechanism to find a mutually satisfactory solution at the international level. Moreover, the ECJ considered the potential implications of judicial review based on the WTO recommendations when there was a conflicting obligation based on another international treaty that was not concluded within the WTO context. The ECJ's rationale necessarily reinforces the diplomatic powers of the executive

---

[101] Ibid., paragraphs 41–48.
[102] Ibid., paragraph 52.

bodies of the Community to adjust their conduct when facing conflicting obligations at the international level.

4.3.6 Ikea Wholesale Ltd. v. Commissioners of Customs & Excise

The *Ikea* case[103] is relevant because the ECJ was faced with an importer claim for reimbursement of antidumping duties collected under the "zeroing" methodology (described below) in light of WTO DSB recommendations and rulings, which considered such method of assessment as inconsistent with the Antidumping Agreement. This case restates that the ECJ has granted broad discretion to EU institutions in the field of external relations by giving a strict interpretation of the *Nakajima* exception—whereby the ECJ may review an EU measure in light of the WTO agreements only if such measure specifically refers to or expressly aims at implementing a WTO obligation. The ECJ considered that the measure in question *"did not in any way intend to give effect to a specific obligation assumed in the context of the WTO."*[104]

However, despite its refusal to assess the EU measure at hand in light of the WTO DSB ruling and the Antidumping Agreement, the ECJ found that the Community institutions committed a manifest error of assessment vis-à-vis Community basic regulations of antidumping. Such case therefore can be considered as the Court had implicitly applied the doctrine of consistent interpretation with the WTO rules and the DSB ruling.

4.3.6.1 The Domestic Litigation

The main issue of this case involved the affirmative determination of dumping based on a methodology that incorporated the practice of "zeroing," and a calculation of the amounts corresponding the administrative, selling and general costs and profits on imports of cotton-type bed linen imports from Egypt, India and Pakistan. The zeroing practice had been used in calculating the rate of dumping for products under investigation by counting as "zero" any negative dumping amounts.[105] The WTO DSB considered that the zeroing practice was inconsistent

---

[103] Case C-351/04, *Ikea Wholesale v. Commissioners of Customs & Excise*, 2007 E.C.R. I-7771.
[104] Ibid., paragraph 35.
[105] The "zeroing" practice was described by the Panel Report on *European Communities—Anti-Dumping Duties on Imports of Cotton-Type Bed Linen from India*, WT/DS141/R, paragraph 6.102, as follows:

> 6.102 The practice of "zeroing" arises in situations where an investigating authority makes multiple comparisons of export price and normal value, and then aggregates the results of these

4.3 ECJ Cases

with the Antidumping Agreement in the *EC—Bed Linen* case,[106] because it did not establish a margin of dumping based on the weighted average normal value with the weighted average of prices of all products, as required by Article 2.4.2.[107] At the WTO, however, rulings and recommendations of the DSB have prospective nature, that is, they refer to future and do not provide for retroactive effects.

Council Regulation 1515/2001 prescribed that the Council may take appropriate measures with regards to DSB recommendations regarding antidumping, which measures are to take effect from their entry into force and do not provide for the reimbursement of duties collected prior to that date, unless otherwise specified.[108] With consideration of these rules, the Community amended Council Regulation 2398/97—imposing definitive anti-dumping duty on imports of cotton-type bed

---

individual comparisons to calculate a dumping margin for the product as a whole. In this case, the European Communities compared weighted averages of export prices and normal value for each of several models or product types of bed linen. (...) The comparisons for the different models in some cases showed the export price to be lower than the normal value, and in some cases showed the export price to be higher than the normal value. The results of the latter comparisons are referred to as "negative" margins. The European Communities then calculated a weighted average dumping margin for the product at issue, cotton-type bed linen, on the basis of the results obtained in the comparisons by model. In the course of this part of the calculation, the European Communities summed up the total value of the dumping – the total "dumping amount" – on the investigated imports. The European Communities calculated the dumping amounts by multiplying the value of the imports of each model by the margin of price difference for each model. The European Communities counted as zero the dumping amount for those models where the margin was negative. The European Communities then divided the total dumping amount by the value of the exports involved, including the value of those models for which the individual margin was negative, and the dumping amount was thus counted as zero. It is this aspect of the calculation, the assigning of a value of zero to the comparisons yielding a "negative" margin, which constitutes the challenged practice of zeroing which is the subject of India's claim under Article 2.4.2.

[106] WTO, *European Communities—Anti-Dumping Duties on Imports of Cotton-Type Bed Linen from India*, WT/DS141/AB (adopted 12 March 2001).

[107] Agreement on Implementation of Article VI of the General Agreement on Tariffs and Trade 1994 (Anti-Dumping Agreement), Article 2.4.2

2.4.2 Subject to the provisions governing fair comparison in paragraph 4, the existence of margins of dumping during the investigation phase shall normally be established on the basis of a comparison of a weighted average normal value with a weighted average of prices of all comparable export transactions or by a comparison of normal value and export prices on a transaction-to-transaction basis. A normal value established on a weighted average basis may be compared to prices of individual export transactions if the authorities find a pattern of export prices which differ significantly among different purchasers, regions or time periods, and if an explanation is provided as to why such differences cannot be taken into account appropriately by the use of a weighted average-to-weighted average or transaction-to-transaction comparison.

[108] Council Regulation 1515/2001, Article 3:

Any measures adopted pursuant to this Regulation shall take effect from the date of their entry into force and shall not serve as basis for the reimbursement of the duties collected prior to that date, unless otherwise provided for.

linen originating in Egypt, India and Pakistan—and suspended its application through subsequent Council Regulations 1644/2001, 160/2002, and 696/2002. However, there was no provision for reimbursement of antidumping duties previously collected.

Based on the DSB ruling, Ikea Wholesale Ltd., a retailer based in the United Kingdom, requested the reimbursement of antidumping duties previously collected under the Council Regulation 2398/97 on its cotton-type bed linen imports. This request was denied by the customs authorities and Ikea seized the United Kingdom courts. During the proceedings, the High Court of Justice of England and Wales referred the questions of Community law in light of the findings of the WTO DSB to the ECJ for a preliminary ruling.

4.3.6.2 The Decision of the European Court of Justice

Reaffirming its case law according to which the WTO agreements do not have direct effect, the ECJ refused to answer the question of whether, in light of the findings of the DSB rulings, Council Regulation 2398/97 was incompatible with the Antidumping Agreement. The ECJ considered that

> [...] the legality of Regulation 2398/97 cannot be reviewed in the light of the Antidumping Agreement, as subsequently interpreted by the DSB's recommendations, since it is clear from the subsequent regulations that the Community, by excluding repayment of rights under Regulation No. 2398/97, did not in any way intend to give effect to a specific obligation assumed in the context of the WTO.[109]

The ECJ however examined the validity of the practice of "zeroing" in light of Article 2 (11) of the Council Regulation 384/96 on protection against dumped imports from countries not members of the European Community.[110] Because of the broad discretion the Community institutions need to face complex economic,

---

[109] Case C-351/04, *Ikea Wholesale v. Commissioners of Customs & Excise*, 2007 E.C.R. I-7771, paragraph 35.

[110] Article 2 (11) of the Council Regulation 384/96 on protection against dumped imports from countries not members of the European Community reads:

Article 2 – Determination of dumping (...)
D. DUMPING MARGIN
11. Subject to the relevant provisions governing fair comparison, the existence of margins of dumping during the investigation period shall normally be established on the basis of a comparison of a weighted average normal value with a weighted average of prices of all export transactions to the Community, or by a comparison of individual normal values and individual export prices to the Community on a transaction-to-transaction basis. However, a normal value established on a weighted average basis may be compared to prices of all individual export transactions to the Community, if there is a pattern of export prices which differs significantly among different purchasers, regions or time periods, and if the methods specified in the first sentence of this paragraph would

4.3 ECJ Cases

political and legal situations, the ECJ considered that the judicial review of choice of methods for calculating dumping margins is limited to verification of whether a manifest error of assessment has been committed vis-à-vis Community law. The ECJ explained:

> Furthermore, it is settled case-law that the choice between the different methods of calculating the dumping margin, such as those set out in Article 2(11) of the basic regulation, together with the assessment of the normal value of a product or the determination of the existence of harm require an appraisal of complex economic situations and the judicial review of such an appraisal must therefore be limited to verifying whether relevant procedural rules have been complied with, whether the facts on which the contested choice is based have been accurately stated, and whether there has been a manifest error in the appraisal of those facts or a misuse of powers (see, to that effect, Case 240/84 *NTN Toyo Bearing and Others* v *Council* [1987] ECR 1809, paragraph 19; Case C-156/87 *Gestetner Holdings* v *Council and Commission* [1990] ECR I-781, paragraph 63; and Case C-150/94 *United Kingdom* v *Council* [1998] ECR I-7235, paragraph 54).[111]

In assessing the validity of the "zeroing" methodology, the ECJ found that the practice of counting as zero the negative price differences to calculate dumping margins in the products under investigation was incompatible with Community rules which required Community authorities to make a fair comparison between the export price and the normal value.

4.3.6.3 The Assessment of the Case

A distinctive feature of the Ikea ruling is the restrict interpretation of what does not constitute a Community measure that would be considered as implementing a particular obligation assumed in the context of the WTO, which in principle allow for judicial review of such measure in light of WTO agreements. The *Ikea* case provides an example of how this hypothetical jurisprudential statement is strictly interpreted. It turned out that the ECJ took a very restrictive interpretation of the ECJ jurisprudence and set aside the possibility of challenging the Council Regulation 2398/97 in light of the Antidumping Agreement. Here, the ECJ considered that the Council Regulations 1644/2001, 160/2002, and 696/2002 did not intend to give effect to any WTO obligation even though, at the WTO level, the EC stated that "*by adopting Regulation 1644/2001 it has fully implemented the DSB*

---

not reflect the full degree of dumping being practiced. This paragraph shall not preclude the use of sampling in accordance with Article 17.

[111] Case C-351/04, *Ikea Wholesale v. Commissioners of Customs & Excise*, 2007 E.C.R. I-7771, paragraph 41.

recommendations and rulings in the dispute "EC – Anti-Dumping Duties on Imports of Cotton-Type Bed Linen from India.""[112] The point of interest here is that, because the WTO Dispute Settlement Body does not give retroactive effects to their recommendations, there is no WTO obligation to repair past injuries. Consequently, although all such Resolutions made express reference to the WTO *EC— Bed Linen* case, they excluded repayment of rights. The Court found that these Resolutions did not intend to implement a particular WTO obligation.

The ECJ did not elaborate much on this reasoning, but such position had already been expressed in the *Van Parys* case analyzed in the previous Sect. 4.3.5. In *Van Parys*, the ECJ stated that Community measures issued to implement a DSB ruling did not qualify as measures intended to implement a particular WTO obligation because it would still be possible to enter into negotiations to reach a mutually satisfactory solution.

While not considering Council Regulations 1644/2001, 160/2002, and 696/2002 as implementing a WTO obligation in the *EC—Bed Linen* case, the ECJ decided to address the question of whether zeroing was valid under Community law and whether it would be possible to reimburse previously collected antidumping duties when, in fact, less dumping had actually taken place. It turned out that, by invalidating the zeroing methodology under Community law, the ECJ provided more rights to the complaining party under Community law than those afforded by the WTO *EC—Bed Linen* dispute.

In what concerns its role regarding the WTO agreements, the ECJ reinforced its rational choice theory perspective by restating the lack of direct effect of WTO Agreements and by providing a restrictive interpretation of what constitutes "a *particular obligation assumed in the context of the WTO.*"[113] At the same time, however, in addressing the issue in light of Community law, the ECJ also found the zeroing methodology as invalid.

The ECJ position may therefore be subsumed under the doctrine of consistent interpretation. It can be reasonably considered that the ECJ interpretation on the *Ikea* case was influenced by the outcome of the dispute at the WTO DSB, to avoid inconsistent interpretations vis-à-vis WTO law.[114] Under this assumption, without the *EC—Bed Linen* ruling, the ECJ would have not reached the same conclusion on the merits of the practice of zeroing. As safe as this assumption can be, it obviously cannot be proved. Nevertheless, the doctrine of consistent interpretation seems fairly applicable in this example.

With this decision, besides strengthening its own powers vis-à-vis the WTO and providing more guarantees to the importer, the ECJ also strengthened its position

---

[112] *See* WTO, *European Communities—Anti-Dumping Duties on Imports of Cotton-Type Bed Linen from India*, WT/DS141/11, 21 September 2001—Understanding between India and the European Communities Regarding Procedures under Articles 21 and 22 of the DSU, paragraph 4.

[113] Case C-351/04, *Ikea Wholesale v. Commissioners of Customs & Excise*, 2007 E.C.R. I-7771, paragraph 30.

[114] Bronckers (2008b), p. 258.

before the Community executive bodies, which had their discretionary powers curbed for manifest illegality and were obliged to make repayments. Here, as far as judicial deference towards the executive is concerned, the ECJ made clear that, although complex economic situations entitle a limitation on judicial review of determinations of dumping margins, the Court will not tolerate manifest errors of assessment.

4.3.7 FIAMM v. Council

Also derived from the already mentioned long-standing dispute known as the "Banana case," the joined judgments *FIAMM v. Council* and *Fedon v. Council*[115] before the ECJ provide a case on a relevant topic on the WTO agreements: the effects of non-compliance with WTO DSB rulings in the European internal legal order.

4.3.7.1 The Domestic Litigation

FIAMM and Fedon, European producers of stationary batteries and spectacle cases, appealed against a decision of the Court of First Instance that denied compensation from the European Council and Commission for alleged damages suffered from the increase of customs duties levied on their products in the United States. The applicants based their claim on the EC Treaty Article 288 (2) that provides for the non-contractual liability of the Community,[116] in conjunction with Article 235, that bestows the Community institutions with powers to attain any Community's objectives.[117] The WTO DSB authorized the United States to impose retaliatory measures on these products following the Community's lack of compliance with the ruling on the *EC—Bananas* case concluding that the common organization of the market for bananas was not compatible with WTO rules.

---

[115] Joined Cases C-120/06 P and C-121/06 P, *Fabbrica italiana accumulatori motocarri Montecchio SpA (FIAMM) and others* [FIAMM Technology, Giorgio Fedon & Figli SpA and Fedon America Inc.] *v. Council of the European Union and Commission of the European Communities*, 2008 E.C.R. I-6513.

[116] Ex-Article 288 (2) TEC (now Article 340) reads:
In the case of non-contractual liability, the Community shall, in accordance with the general principles common to the laws of the Member States, make good any damage caused by its institutions or by its servants in the performance of their duties.

[117] Ex-Article 235 TEC (now Article 308) reads:
If action by the Community should prove necessary to attain, in the course of the operation of the common market, one of the objectives of the Community and this Treaty has not provided the necessary powers, the Council shall, acting unanimously on a proposal from the Commission and after consulting the European Parliament, take the appropriate measures.

After having their actions for damages dismissed by the Court of First Instance of the European Communities, FIAMM and Fedon appealed to the ECJ, where their cases were joined for judgment.

Among other arguments, FIAMM and Fedon claimed that the Community institutions acted unlawfully and therefore incurred in non-contractual liability for unlawful conduct, because that the Community institutions had not adopted the necessary measures to bring the common organization of the market for bananas in conformity with the DSB recommendations within the accorded time-limit. The applicants contended that the Community institutions violated the principle of *pact sunt servanda*, the principles of the protection of legitimate expectations and of legal certainty, the right to property and pursuit of an economic activity, and the principle of proper administration. In the alternative, the applicants argued that there would be the possibility of Community liability for lawful acts.

4.3.7.2 The Decision of the European Court of Justice

In this case, the ECJ addressed the legal effects of the DSB rulings and recommendations in the European internal legal order after the reasonable period of time for implementation expired. Here, after the DSB found that the Community regime on banana imports was not compatible with the WTO rules, the ECJ concluded that such ruling is not capable of conferring individual rights that private parties could rely on to challenge Community legislation before the judiciary. The ECJ considered that decisions of the WTO dispute settlement mechanism, even after the expiry date of the implementation period of a DSB ruling, had the same nature of the WTO agreements and were characterized by reciprocity and flexibility. The ECJ considered that *"the Community institutions continue in particular to have an element of discretion and scope for negotiation vis-à-vis their trading partners with a view to the adoption of measures intended to respond to the ruling or recommendation, and such leeway must be preserved."*[118]

Accordingly, the ECJ refused to impose a non-contractual liability on the Community for not complying with a recommendation from the DSB. By making reference to the DSU Article 3 (2)—whereby recommendations and rulings of the DSB cannot add to or diminish the rights and obligations provided in the WTO agreements—the ECJ affirmed that *"a decision of the DSB finding an infringement of such an [WTO] obligation cannot have the effect of requiring a party to the WTO agreements to accord individuals a right which they do not hold by virtue of those agreements in the absence of such a decision."*[119] The ECJ stated that there was not

---

[118] Joined Cases C-120/06 P and C-121/06 P, *Fabbrica italiana accumulatori motocarri Montecchio SpA (FIAMM) and others* [FIAMM Technology, Giorgio Fedon & Figli SpA and Fedon America Inc.] *v. Council of the European Union and Commission of the European Communities*, 2008 E.C.R. I-6513, paragraph 130.

[119] Ibid.

4.3 ECJ Cases

a distinction between the legal nature of the WTO rules and of the DSB rulings, and both did not have direct effect in the Community internal legal order.

The ECJ considered that the system of Community liability requires an unlawful act or an omission of the Communities institutions and, therefore, the Community could not be liable for legislative activity of public authorities as a result of choices of economic policy *"unless a sufficiently serious breach of a superior rule of law for the protection of the individual has occurred"*[120] provided that such rule intended to confer rights on individuals. Finally, the ECJ concluded that, as the WTO agreements do not have direct effect, *"no liability regime exists under which the Community can incur liability for conduct falling within the sphere of its legislative competence in a situation where any failure of such conduct to comply with the WTO agreements cannot be relied upon before the Community courts."*[121]

In what concerns the allegations of breach of the right to property and freedom to pursue a trade, the Court admitted that such rights can be restricted according to their social function and the general interest to establish a common organization of the market in bananas was not disproportionate or intolerable restriction, and such rights cannot be extended to protect mere commercial positions. Moreover, the Court explained that there was not a right to market share, which constituted of a momentary economic position subject to risks of changing circumstances. In the ECJ's words:

> An economic operator whose business consists in particular in exporting goods to the markets of non-member States must therefore be aware that the commercial position which he has at a given time may be affected and altered by various circumstances and that those circumstances include the possibility, which is moreover expressly envisaged and governed by Article 22 of the DSU, that one of the non-member States will adopt measures suspending concessions in reaction to the stance taken by its trading partners within the framework of the WTO and will for this purpose select in its discretion, as follows from Article 22(3)(a) and (f) of the DSU, the goods to be subject to those measures. [122]

By asserting that the Court of First Instance erred in law, the ECJ concluded that there is no liability regime for legislative conduct of Community institutions where failure in complying with the WTO agreements cannot be invoked before Community courts.

---

[120] Ibid., paragraph 172.
[121] Ibid., paragraph 176.
[122] Ibid., paragraph 186.

4.3.7.3 The Assessment of the Case

In the *FIAMM v. Council* decision, the ECJ clarified the effects of non-compliance with the DSB rulings in the European internal legal order. This issue had previously been brought before the ECJ in *Biret v. Council*,[123] where the Court ultimately refused to recognize a claim of a French meat trader for damages due to the EU failure to implement the WTO ruling on the *EC—Hormones* case.[124] In *Biret v. Council*, however, the ECJ relied on procedural grounds based on the fact that the company had gone out of business years before the WTO DSB recommendations were adopted and the reasonable period of time for implementation had expired. Therefore, the ECJ had avoided addressing the main question of the effects of non-compliance with the DSB rulings, which ultimately was addressed in *FIAMM v. Council*.

In *FIAMM v. Council*, the ECJ opinion confirmed its rational choice theory approach by denying the possibility of Community institutions' liability for economic and trade policy choices. In the rational choice theory perspective on role of domestic courts regarding international law, it is not for courts to assess the validity of political choices. With the previous case law of the ECJ in mind, the *FIAMM v. Council* decision was not a surprise, but the expectations were high due to the Court of First Instance opinion holding that there existed a Community system of liability for lawful acts, although not applicable in the circumstances of the case at hand. The ECJ was sharp in setting aside the court of First Instance's finding. However, the ECJ left the door open only if there is serious breach of individual rights, where market share enjoyed by a private company in the United States does not qualify under such hypothetical reference. After all, the ECJ notes, uncertainties are part of the risks of the economic activity and *"an economic operator cannot claim a right to property in a market share which he held at a given time, since such a market share constitutes only a momentary economic position, exposed to the risks of changing circumstances."*[125]

The decisive factor for the ECJ's position was that the DSU authorizes that negotiated solutions be reached in the dispute, even after the adoption of a DSB rulings. Therefore, the circumstance that the reasonable period of time for implementation of the DSB ruling had already expired was irrelevant. Accordingly, the ECJ provided the Community institutions with the power to continue negotiating to find a mutually agreed solution. In the Court's view, the flexibility provided in the WTO agreements seemed to be particularly relevant for the role of domestic courts

---

[123] Cases C-93/02 P, 2003 E.C.R. I-10497, and C-94/02, 2003 E.C.R. I-10565, *Biret International SA and Etablissements Biret et Cie. SA v. Council of the European Union*.

[124] Ibid. In this case, a French company in liquidation filed an action for compensation based on alleged damages suffered from the EU import ban on hormone-treated beef. The EU did not implement the Appellate Body Report on the case *European Communities—Measures Concerning Meat and Meat Products (Hormones)*, WT/DS26/AB/R, adopted 13 February 1998, until 25 September 2009.

[125] Ibid., paragraph 185.

regarding international law. Moreover, there were other international treaties involved in the dispute, and conflicting international obligations could arise from such diverse international treaties. In the present case, the ECJ provided the Community with room for maneuver to reconcile its WTO obligations with the ACP states commitments.

In the *FIAMM v. Council* case, the principle of reciprocity was again a major fundament of the ECJ's decision. The most important trading partners of the Community had never recognized the possibility of domestic courts review domestic measures in light of WTO agreements—much less DSB rulings—due to the nature of the WTO rules.

Here, the doctrine of direct effect was again not applied by the ECJ in a consistent way as per its previous case law. Similarly, the ECJ once again provided deference to the executive, by reaffirming the Community institutions powers to negotiate conflicting international obligations at the international level and to preserve their role in setting public policy in the internal order.

After examining several cases where the ECJ was confronted with the GATT/WTO rules and established the lack of direct effect of such agreements, attention is turned to whether domestic courts of EU Member States have confirmed or not the ECJ case law. To understand the impact of the ECJ case law on the GATT/WTO agreements in the European territory, it is necessary to examine the degree of cooperation that national courts of the EU Member States due to the unique features of the EU legal order. The next section will therefore examine the degree of cooperation of national courts of the EU Member States through the lens of constitutional pluralism.

4.4 Constitutional Pluralism: The Relationship Between the ECJ and National Courts Regarding WTO Agreements

After examining several cases where the ECJ was confronted with the GATT/WTO rules, a following point to address is how national constitutional courts of the European Union members responded to the ECJ case law. Constitutional courts of European Member States may occasionally be offered the opportunity to confront ECJ case law in domestic litigation, and their responses to confirm or not the ECJ decisions are therefore relevant. The national constitutional courts' perspective is also relevant due to these courts' prior jurisprudence on the GATT, and how such jurisprudence evolved with the supervening exclusive competence of the ECJ on international trade in goods. As mentioned earlier, the GATT was already in force in the national legal systems before the Community replaced the European Member States regarding the GATT in 1968. Therefore, such replacement gave rise to a struggle of power between the ECJ and national constitutional courts, a relationship nowadays explained by the theory of constitutional pluralism. Accordingly, due to the unique features of the EU legal order, the degree of cooperation of national courts with the ECJ's case law on the GATT/WTO agreements is an important aspect to consider through the lens of constitutional pluralism.

Constitutional pluralism aims at explaining the relations in the European integration process, which brought about a new context under which new arrangements were necessary to articulate the constitutional order of different countries. In constructing such new arrangements, the assumption under the Westphalian age that the centers or units of constitutional authorities were solely the states was challenged.[126] Indeed, conceptual frameworks tried to answer the question of how supranational governance has been constructed[127] and the consequent pressing questions to assess and coordinate the legal problems arisen in the integration process, such as intergovernmentalism, neofunctionalism[128] and constitutionalism.[129]

The debate on such conceptual frameworks in the context of the European integration process is extensive,[130] although some scholars also tested a more general macro theory of integration.[131] Yet, the European Union legal nature is still contested.[132] Nevertheless, the constitutional narrative is the dominant ideology in the scholarly debate for constructing the European integration since 1990s.[133] The European order developed its structure beyond "inter-*national*"[134] law and made its own independent constitutional claims, which exist alongside the states' constitutional authority.[135] On one hand, the national judicial systems of the EU member countries understand that the primacy of EU law is found in their respective national constitutions.[136] On the other hand, the European Court of Justice interprets the European legal order as having supremacy over national law.[137] De Witte clarifies that

> In light of this two-dimensional reality, whereby both the EU legal order, as interpreted by the Court of Justice, and the constitutional orders of the Member states, as interpreted by their highest courts, claim ultimate supremacy for themselves in the case of a conflict on

---

[126] Walker (2002), p. 337.

[127] Stone Sweet and Sandholtz (1997).

[128] Ibid.

[129] Maduro (2004).

[130] There is an enormous body of sophisticated doctrine on European integration. Nevertheless, discussing the origins and theories of integration processes in Europe are not the purpose of this study. Instead, this study will focus on the consequences of the European integration processes from the viewpoint of the role of courts and how integration have affected the way courts decide cases based on WTO law.

[131] Fligstein and Stone Sweet (2002), pp. 1236–1239.

[132] Avbelj (2008), p. 1.

[133] Ibid., pp. 1–2.

[134] Walker (2002), p. 337.

[135] Ibid.

[136] De Witte (2011), p. 356.

[137] Ibid.

4.4 Constitutional Pluralism: The Relationship Between the ECJ and National...

'important matters', a current in the legal literature has proposed to adopt a 'pluralist' reading of the relations between EU law and national law, which accepts that there are inherently different viewpoints and that the search for a perfect hierarchical ordering between legal norms and across legal systems may therefore be futile; and that one should accept that the relationship between the EU and national legal orders is, and remains, a heterarchical one.[138]

Constitutional pluralism therefore is the main legal theory that explains the relationship between the European order and its Member States, although there is not much consensus on what it conceptually means.[139] Constitutional pluralism may be defined as *"a plurality of constitutional sources which creates a context of potential constitutional conflicts between different constitutional orders to be solved in a non-hierarchical manner."*[140] In the context of constitutional pluralism, Maduro argues that courts should render their decisions with institutional awareness of the relationships with other actors and jurisdictions, with some form of mutual engagement.[141] Walker highlights that the debate on constitutional pluralism endemically involves the dispute for final authority,[142] and recognizes that there are many different constitutional sites in a heterarchical order, rather than in a hierarchical disposition.[143] In addition to a framework of principles whereby EU law should generally prevail in case of conflict with national law with few exceptions, Kumm goes further on constitutional pluralism and bring into question the way constitutional authority is based, urging for a paradigm shift to construct the foundations of constitutional authority.[144]

Although recognizing that constitutional pluralism has become the predominant concept in the European academic literature on the relationship between different legal systems, Eeckhout highlights that such theory has not managed to solve all legal issues.[145] According to him, there are more aspects involving the relationship between EU law and national law than mutual respect for constitutional identity,[146] and point out that, when it comes for national law to respect EU law, the answer is not respect for the EU's constitutional identity but all of EU law prevails over national law.[147] De Witte has also noted that *"the ECJ missed a few opportunities, recently, to recognize the special role and importance of national constitutional law in the EU legal order, despite invitations by its Advocate General to do so."*[148] In

---

[138] Ibid., pp. 356–357.
[139] Avbelj and Komárek (2008).
[140] Maduro (2007).
[141] Avbelj and Komárek (2008).
[142] Ibid.
[143] Walker (2002).
[144] Avbelj and Komárek (2008).
[145] Eeckhout (2010), p. 1518.
[146] Ibid., p. 1519.
[147] Ibid.
[148] De Witte (2011), p. 357.

his views, after entry into force of the Treaty of Lisbon, it may occur that the role of national constitutional law in the ECJ jurisprudence increases due to Article 4(2) of the Treaty of European Union[149] which, by guaranteeing national identity and making a reference to national constitutional law, can be interpreted as implicitly limiting the primacy of EU law.[150] Such development, however, is yet to be seen.

Under the current scenario, constitutional pluralism tries to adjust and coordinate different legal systems—the EU law and national law of its Member States—and is the mainstream legal theory in the European context. Although a fascinating and still unsettled discussion, the debate on the theory of European integration is not the aim of this research. This study therefore takes constitutional pluralism as the basic legal framework when analyzing the object of this research—the relationship between WTO law and domestic courts—in the European context, with particular attention to what the supremacy of European law means for its relationship with WTO law.

While the European Court of Justice established the primacy of European law over all national law, national constitutional law included, *"most national courts have not accepted outright the position of the ECJ. Instead many insisted that there are national constitutional red lines, guarded by national constitutional courts, which EU must not cross in order for it to be implemented nationally."*[151] Maduro has pointed out that *"the acceptance of the supremacy of EU rules over national constitutional rules has not been unconditional, if not even, at times, resisted by national constitutional courts. This confers to EU law a kind of contested or negotiated normative authority."*[152]

Therefore, as a consequence of constitutional pluralism at the European Union context, the analysis of the degree of cooperation of national courts with the European Court of Justice in relation to its case law on WTO agreements is an important aspect to consider. According to Schermers and Waelbroeck, the attitude of national judiciaries is that, in general, *"the judiciaries of monist member states accepted readily the views of the Court of Justice."*[153] In Germany, Italy, Denmark, Greece, and Spain, national constitutional courts have asserted or discussed the possibility of judicial review of European law.[154] In Portugal, although the control of constitutionality of European law has not been developed, this possibility is open

---

[149] Article 4(2) of the Treaty on European Union reads:

> The Union shall respect the equality of Member States before the Treaties as well as their national identities, inherent in their fundamental structures, political and constitutional, inclusive of regional and local self-government. It shall respect their essential State functions, including ensuring the territorial integrity of the State, maintaining law and order and safeguarding national security. In particular, national security remains the sole responsibility of each Member State.

[150] De Witte (2011), p. 357.
[151] Kumm (2011), p. 2.
[152] Maduro (2007), p. 1.
[153] Schermers and Waelbroeck (2001), p. 164.
[154] Mayer (2001), p. 29.

because the Portuguese Constitution set boundaries to European integration.[155] In some European Member States, however, claims of constitutional review of decisions of the European Court of Justice are not likely to happen due to their constitutional law's structural circumstances, as well as their community-friendly jurisprudence.[156] This is the case of Luxemburg and Finland, where national courts cannot review European law, and the Netherlands, where international treaties supersede even the Constitution and there is no constitutional court.[157]

Because the analysis of all domestic courts of all 27 European member countries would be beyond this research's scope and objectives, the German and Italian courts will be studied as representatives of the national courts of European Member States which have already conceded judicial review of European law. The choice of both Germany and Italy also derives from the fact that these two countries were the only founding member states of the Community that had constitutional courts[158] and, consequently, such courts' decisions provide the groundwork for evaluating whether the European Court of Justice's rulings are being reviewed. In addition, Germany and Italy are dualist countries with complete systems of human rights protection,[159] where their constitutional courts have found that there can be a violation of the national constitutional order in case the European Union law exceeds on its competences.[160] Therefore, the German and Italian courts' stance in relation to the lack of direct effect of WTO agreements is relevant for the purposes of investigating the application of these agreements within the European Union. Moreover, commentary has noted that the behavior of German-Italian constitutional courts vis-à-vis the primacy of EU law consubstantiate the default position in the majority of European countries.[161] Accordingly, this study will know proceed to examine the influential German jurisprudence.

4.4.1 The German Jurisprudence

In 2009, the German Constitutional Court [*Bundesverfassunsgericht*], while deciding whether the Treaty of Lisbon was within the boundaries of the sovereign powers accorded to the European institutions by way of conferral, stated that

---

[155] Ibid., p. 30.

[156] Ibid., pp. 30–31.

[157] Ibid.

[158] Laderchi (1998), p. 155.

[159] Keller and Stone Sweet (2008), p. 685. *See* also Schermers and Waelbroeck (2001), p. 151. Schermers and Waelbroeck classify the system in Italy and Germany as a mitigated dualism, because the international treaty, as soon as it is adopted, becomes part of the domestic legislation.

[160] Mayer (2001), p. 31.

[161] De Witte (2011), p. 355.

the exercise of this review power [on the Treaty of Lisbon], which is rooted in constitutional law, follows the principle of the Basic Law's openness towards European Law (*Europarechtsfreundlichkeit*), and it therefore also does not contradict the principle of sincere cooperation (Article 4.3 Lisbon TEU); otherwise, with progressing integration, the fundamental political and constitutional structures of sovereign Member States, which are recognized by Article 4.2 first sentence Lisbon TEU, cannot be safeguarded in any other way. In this respect, the guarantee of national constitutional identity under constitutional and under Union law goes hand in hand in the European legal area.[162]

Speaking about this judgment, a commentator concluded that the German Constitutional Court "*signaled that should European law continue to threaten the core of the German constitutional settlement – the German "social state" – that court would be obliged to disapply European law.*"[163] Other scholar concluded that, in this judgment, the German Constitutional Court decision implied that the "*European Union is an association of sovereign states and, hence, a secondary political area.*"[164] Scholars also note that the German Constitutional Court made the way for the enforcement of European law,[165] reiterating the "*Solange*" jurisprudence whereby the German Constitutional Court established that European Union law could be implemented within Germany only "*as long as*" it is compatible with the German Basic Law (constitution).[166] Halberstam and Möllers (2009) note that

---

[162] 2009 BVerfG, 2 BvE 2/08.

[163] Everson (2010).

[164] Schorkopf (2009), p. 1219.

[165] Halberstam and Möllers (2009), p. 1242.

[166] Being the English translation "*as long as*" doctrine, the *Solange* method was established in 1974, and has been reiterated in several judgments of the German Constitutional Court. *See* Petersmann (2007), p. 10. Petersmann explains the *Solange* method of conditional cooperation by national courts as follows:

- In its *Solange I* judgment of 1974, the German Constitutional Court held that "as long as" the integration process of the EC does not include a catalogue of fundamental rights corresponding to that of the German Basic Law, German courts could, after having requested a preliminary ruling from the ECJ, also request a ruling from the German Constitutional Court regarding the compatibility of EC acts with fundamental rights and the German Constitution. This judicial insistence on the then higher level of fundamental rights protection in German constitutional law was instrumental for the ECJ's judicial protection of human rights as common, yet unwritten, constitutional guarantees of EC law.
- In view of the emerging human rights protection in EC law, the German Constitutional Court held – in its *Solange II* judgment of 1986 – that it would no longer exercise its jurisdiction for reviewing EC legal acts "as long as" the ECJ continued to generally and effectively protect fundamental rights against EC measures in ways comparable to the essential safeguards of German constitutional law.
- In its *Maastricht* judgment (*Solange III*) of 1993, however, the German Constitutional Court reasserted its jurisdiction to defend the scope of German constitutional law: EC measures exceeding the limited EC competences covered by the German Act ratifying

4.4 Constitutional Pluralism: The Relationship Between the ECJ and National...

The Court pledges to adhere to the old Solange compromise and refrain from reviewing European secondary law and acts for their compatibility with fundamental rights *"as long as the European Union guarantees an application of fundamental rights that in substance and effectiveness is essentially similar to the protection of fundamental rights required unconditionally by the Basic Law."*[167] (Emphasis added)

Earlier, in the Maastricht decision,[168] the German Constitutional Court describes the relationship between national courts and the ECJ as a relationship of cooperation (*Kooperationsverhältnis*), and *"reserved for itself the right to review the exercise of competencies of European institutions in light of the German constitution."*[169] In other words, the Court accepted the expansion of Community's prerogatives, such as direct effect of community law, and, at the same time, retained the ultimate say on the constitutionality of community law within Germany.[170] The Maastricht decision triggered the constitutional pluralism movement in the scholarly debate,[171] which, as explained above, is the predominant concept of the relations between international and domestic law within the European sphere, where autonomous institutions are open to the others' claims of authority. In this context, Halberstam (2011) highlights that

> To be sure, as a matter of formal rhetoric, both the European Court of Justice, on the one hand, and national constitutional courts (such as the German *Bundesverfassungsgericht*), on the other, did each indeed lay claim to the ultimate supremacy of (its own interpretation of) its own legal order. But the judicial practice was, in fact, one of mutual accommodation.[172]

The theory of constitutional pluralism seems to be corroborated by the German Constitutional Court decision[173] involving the long-lasting dispute over the European regime for import of bananas within the community. As seen in Section 12.3, the EC gave a preferential market access to the imports of bananas cultivated in its former colonies—the African, Caribbean and Pacific countries (ACP)—in detriment to banana imports from Latin American countries.[174] The EC bananas regime

---

the EU Treaty [*ausbrechende Gemeinschaftsakte*] could not be legally binding and applicable in Germany.

[167] Halberstam and Möllers (2009), p. 1242.
[168] 1993 BVerfG, 2 BvR 2134/92 and 2 BvR 2159/92.
[169] Mayer (2001), p. 10.
[170] Halberstam (2011).
[171] Ibid., p. 8.
[172] Ibid.
[173] 2000 BVerfG, 2 BvL 1/97. For an overview of the case in English, *see* German Law Journal (2000).
[174] For a detailed account of the banana dispute, *see* Alter and Meunier (2006).

prompted litigation at three different levels: the GATT and WTO,[175] the European Court of Justice,[176] and German courts.[177]

In a case brought by importers of banana from Latin America contesting the import quotas allocated to them, the ECJ[178] decided on a preliminary ruling requested by the Frankfurt am Main Administrative Court (*Verwaltungsgericht*) to uphold the validity of the Council Regulation 404/93 on the common organization of the market in bananas based on its previous ruling *Federal Republic of Germany v Council of the European Union*[179] examined in Sect. 4.3.3. Upon this outcome, the plaintiffs requested the German Constitutional Court to declare the ECJ decisions, and the application of imports quotas to them as unconstitutional. Likewise, other German courts and tax tribunals started questioning the supremacy of European law, concerned that the ECJ refused to review the Bananas regulation under the GATT obligations, having in mind that both GATT and European law have binding effect in Germany.[180] In its own wording, the German Constitutional Court was seized to decide whether the application of the common organization of the market in bananas of the European Community in the Federal Republic of Germany was constitutional.[181] The German Constitutional Court decided that the EC banana regime was "generally" constitutional and, consequently, upheld the applicability of these norms within Germany. Petersmann (2007) explains that

> Following GATT and WTO dispute settlement rulings concerning EC import restrictions of bananas violating WTO law, and in view of an ECJ judgment upholding these restrictions without reviewing their WTO inconsistencies, several German courts requested the Constitutional Court to declare these EC restrictions to be *ultra vires* (*i.e.*, exceeding the EC's limited competences) and to illegally restrict constitutional freedoms of German importers. The German Constitutional Court, in its judgment of 2002 (*Solange IV*), declared the application inadmissible on the ground that it had not been argued that the required level of human rights protection in the EC had generally fallen below the minimum level required by the German Constitution.[182]

In discussing the German Constitutional Court decision, Alter and Mounier concluded that the German Constitutional Court "*refused to consider whether or not the regulation violated the German Constitution, arguing that so long as the*

---

[175] WTO, *European Communities—Regime for the Importation, Sale and Distribution of Bananas*, WT/DS16, WT/DS27, WT/DS105, WT/DS158, WT/DS361, and WT/DS364. For a brief chronology of the bananas dispute before the GATT and the WTO, *see* WTO Press Releases (2009).

[176] Case C-280/93, *Federal Republic of Germany v Council of the European Union*, 1994 E.C.R. I-4973.

[177] 2000 BVerfG, 2 BvL 1/97.

[178] Case C-466/93, *Atlanta Fruchthandelsgesellschaft mbH and others v. Bundesamt für Ernährung und Forstwirtschaft*, 1995 E.C.R. I-03799.

[179] Case C-280/93, *Federal Republic of Germany v Council of the European Union*, 1994 E.C.R. I-4973.

[180] Alter and Meunier (2006), p. 369.

[181] 2000 BVerfG, 2 BvL 1/97.

[182] Petersmann (2007), p. 23.

4.4 Constitutional Pluralism: The Relationship Between the ECJ and National...

ECJ is 'generally' ensuring respect for the Constitution, it would not consider whether specific European policies violate specific provisions of the German Constitution."[183] Indeed, the German Constitutional Court summarized its jurisprudence as follows:

> As long as the European Communities, in particular European case law, generally ensure effective protection of fundamental rights as against the sovereign powers of the Communities which is to be regarded as substantially similar to the protection of fundamental rights required unconditionally by the Basic Law, and in so far as they generally safeguard the essential content of fundamental rights, the Federal Constitutional Court will no longer exercise its jurisdiction to decide on the applicability of secondary Community legislation cited as the legal basis for any acts of German courts or authorities within the sovereign jurisdiction of the Federal Republic of Germany, and it will no longer review such legislation by the standard of fundamental rights contained in the Basic Law. References (of rules of secondary Community law to the Federal Constitutional Court) under Article 100(1) GG are therefore inadmissible (BVerfGE 73, 339<387>).[184]

In conclusion, the German Constitutional Court, although keeping its powers to review European law, imposed a high scrutiny level for challenging European regulation before German courts, and refused to admit a submission against the ECJ decisions on the bananas case. In an implicit assertion of its authority, the German Constitutional Court has not made any preliminary reference procedure to the European Court of Justice, although the German Constitutional Court has set out the conditions under which German courts must make such references.[185] Most importantly, the German Constitutional Court had the opportunity to overturn the ECJ decision on the bananas case, but preferred to find the claim inadmissible. Indirectly, the German Constitutional Court confirmed the ECJ's stance on WTO agreements, a treaty binding to both the European Union and Germany.

4.4.2 The Italian Jurisprudence

Historically, the Italian Constitutional Court [*Corte Costituzionale*] has ordered lower courts to make preliminary references to the European Court of Justice,[186] but the Court itself has first raised a preliminary question in 2008.[187] Similarly to its

---

[183] Alter and Meunier (2006), p. 369.
[184] 2000 BVerfG, 2 BvL 1/97.
[185] Mayer (2001), pp. 9–10.
[186] Ibid., pp. 10–11.
[187] Corte cos., Ordinanza n. 103, 13 February 2008.

German counterpart, the Italian Constitutional Court has reserved its power to review the legality of European law[188] in the Frontini,[189] Granital[190] and Fragd[191] cases. In the Frontini case, the Italian Constitutional Court established the counter-limits doctrine [*dottrina dei controlimiti*], by expressing that if there were an interpretation giving European bodies "*an unacceptable power to violate the fundamental principles of the Italian Constitution or the inalienable rights of man, the Italian Constitutional Court reserves the right to control the continuing compatibility of the Treaty as a whole with such fundamental principles.*"[192]

In 1984, in the Granital case, the Italian Constitutional Court ruled that Community regulation prevailed over conflicting national legislation:

> The system of the relationship between Community law and national legislation has been the subject-matter of several decisions by this Court and has undergone and evolution: the principle now is that EEC regulations prevail over conflicting provisions in national legislation. This has a variety of implications. First of all, as far as interpretation is concerned, national statutes must be presumed to be consistent with Community regulations. Thus, among all possible interpretations of the text of national legislation, the one that is consistent with obligations under Community law must prevail: this interpretation therefore also conforms with the provision in the Constitution which guarantees that the Treaty of Rome and the ensuing secondary legislations (see decisions n. 176 and 177 of 1981) will be respected.[193]

At the same time, the Italian Constitutional Court, in the very Granital case reaffirmed that it has competence to review the law implementing the Treaty "*with regard to basic principles of the Italian legal system and the respect for fundamental human rights.*"[194] In the subsequent Fragd case, the Italian Constitutional Court explicitly reiterated that Community law could not be enforced in Italy if it violates a fundamental principle of human rights protection of the Italian constitution, regardless the fact that the ECJ had validated the legality of rule.[195]

In what concerns the application of the GATT, prior to the establishment of the WTO, the Italian judiciary developed a doctrine of direct effect of GATT since late sixties up to 1981.[196] Differently from German courts, the Italian courts interpreted

---

[188] Rosenfeld (2006), p. 634; Mayer (2001), p. 29.

[189] Corte cos., *Frontini v. Ministero delle Finanze Giurisprudenza Constituzionale*, Sentenza n. 183, 27 December 1973, 1974 C.M.L.R. 372, paragraph 21.

[190] Corte cos., *Spa Granital v. Amministrazione delle Finanze dello Stato*, Sentenza n. 170, 8 June 1984.

[191] Corte cos., *Spa Fragd v. Amministrazione delle Finanze dello Stato*, Sentenza n. 232, 21 April 1989, Foro It. 1990, 1855.

[192] Corte cos., *Frontini v. Ministero delle Finanze Giurisprudenza Constituzionale*, Sentenza n. 183, 27 December 1973, 1974 C.M.L.R. 372, paragraph 10–11.

[193] Corte cos., *Spa Granital v. Amministrazione delle Finanze dello Stato*, Sentenza n. 170, 8 June 1984, 1984 C.M.L.R. 756, p. 758.

[194] Ibid., p. 764.

[195] Schermers and Waelbroeck (2001), p. 172.

[196] Sacerdoti and Venturini (1992), p. 340.

the GATT as a self-executing treaty, which granted private right of action to individuals.[197] During that period, Italian courts have granted protection of private traders who could invoke GATT provisions against government agencies' acts before domestic courts. Like in Brazil, Italy gave GATT an equal status to domestic law, and the principle of the *lex posteriori* principle would apply.[198] Similarly to Brazilian courts, the Italian courts are reluctant to declare that a supervening domestic law abrogates an international treaty,[199] as the country may incur in international responsibility and allegations of wrongdoing. Therefore, Italian courts applied interpretations that reconciled the GATT obligations with domestic law when they appeared to be in conflict.[200]

The Italian courts jurisprudence in regard to the self-executing character of GATT rules continued for some time after the ECJ established, for the first time, the lack of direct effect of GATT in the *International Fruit Company* case[201] in 1972. Sacerdotti and Venturini ponder that one of the reasons Italian courts kept admitting the private invocability of GATT rules before domestic courts was that the most controversial duty that originated court litigation had been abolished since 1971.[202] In 1974, however, the Italian Supreme Court [*Corte di Cassazione*] requested preliminary rulings to the ECJ involving the application of GATT provisions.[203] In *Societá Italiana per l'Oleodotto Transalpino (SIOT) v. Ministero delle Finanze and others*,[204] and the joined cases *Amministrazione delle Finanze dello Stato v. Societa Petrolifera Italiane SpA (SPI) and SpA Michelin Italiana (SAMI)*,[205] the European Court of Justice reiterated its previous rulings and denied direct effect to GATT rules, with the consequent declaration that private companies or individuals could not rely on these rules to support their claims. At that occasion, the Italian Supreme Court interpreted the ECJ decision as a "*a declinatory exception*"[206] in what concerns the application of GATT, and decided that GATT Article II "*could still be taken into account as a rule of construction of the domestic law*

---

[197] Cass., 21 May 1973, n. 1455, Foro It. 1983, 2453; Corte cost., *Spa. Legler Industria Tessile, s.p.a. Manifattura Festi Rasini e l'Amministrazione delle Finanze dello Stato*, Sentenza n. 96, 20 May 1982.
[198] Sacerdoti and Venturini (1992), p. 343.
[199] Ibid.
[200] Ibid., pp. 343–344.
[201] Joined Cases 21–24/72 *International Fruit Company NV and Others v Produktschap voor Groenten en Fruit*, 1972 E.C.R. 1219. For details on this case, *see* Sect. 4.3.1.
[202] Sacerdoti and Venturini (1992), p. 348.
[203] Cass. (Sez. Un.), 21 July 1981, n. 417; and Cass. (Sez. Un.), 21 July 1981, n. 417.
[204] Case C-266/81, *Societá Italiana per l'Oleodotto Transalpino (SIOT) v. Ministero delle Finanze and others*, 1983 E.C.R. 731.
[205] Joined Cases C-267/81, 268/81, 269/81, *Amministrazione delle Finanze dello Stato v. Societa Petrolifera Italiane SpA (SPI) and SpA Michelin Italiana (SAMI)*, 1983 E.C.R. 801.
[206] Sacerdoti and Venturini (1992), p. 354.

which instituted that duty and eventually maintained that the latter was not legally imposed upon goods originating from the GATT countries."[207] Sacerdotti and Venturini explain that this decision was ambiguous, which was supported by few decisions of the Italian Constitutional Court indicating that GATT could be possible grounds for challenging domestic legislation.[208] However, since 1982, the Italian Constitutional Court established that GATT does not prevail over domestic law and the doctrine of consistent interpretation replaced the former direct effect given to GATT in the Italian legal order.

In conclusion, constitutional courts of European Member States have shown that there are two possible grounds to challenge European Union law: violation of fundamental rights or exceeding of powers conferred to the European bodies.[209] The German–Italian jurisprudence is relevant not only within the German territory. Commentary has noted that constitutional courts of the post-communist Central and Eastern European countries have adhered to the Solange jurisprudence.[210] In this sense, Sadurski argued that these constitutional courts have questioned the principle of supremacy of EU law over the national constitution to strengthen their own position in their national system vis-à-vis other domestic political actors.[211] Similarly, De Witte (2011) explains that

> we do indeed find a number of new Constitutional Court judgments, in both old and new Member States, which confirm a general convergence around the Italian-German position of the 1990s, namely that Union law may prevail over conflicting national legislation, and possibly even over conflicting detailed rules of the national constitution, but not over the fundamental provisions of the constitution. Everywhere, the national constitution remains at the apex of the hierarchy of legal norms, and EU law is allowed to trump national law only under the conditions, and within the limits, set by the national constitution. In particular, the 2004 rulings of the French and Spanish Constitutional Courts relating to the Constitutional Treaty gave those courts an occasion to join the 'counterlimits' consensus. The 'domino effect' of the counterlimits doctrine is also visible in the newer Member States of Central and Eastern Europe, although with some interesting variations. In Poland and Lithuania, the Constitutional Courts have affirmed the supremacy of *all* constitutional provisions (not just the constitutional core) over EU law; and in Estonia, the constitution – as interpreted by the supreme court – operated a self-limitation which leaves room for the absolute primacy of EU law for as long as the constitution is not modified on this point.[212]

To sum up, constitutional courts of EU member countries have affirmed themselves as the guardians of the protection of human rights and democratic principles in their national legal orders. While corroborating the ECJ interpretation that GATT obligations do not have direct effect within their legal orders, the constitutional

---

[207] Ibid.
[208] Ibid.
[209] Bermann (2004).
[210] Sadurski (2008).
[211] Ibid.
[212] De Witte (2011), pp. 355–356.

courts of Italy and Germany left the door open for future review, if necessary—a jurisprudence that has fetched followers with the European context.

4.5 Conclusion

The rational choice theory approach has consistently marked the relations between WTO agreements and domestic courts in the European Union, despite that traditionalism has been accorded on the role of domestic judges regarding other areas of international law. This chapter has illustrated the mixed stance of the ECJ in relation to international trade agreements. The ECJ (1) has denied direct effect to the GATT/WTO agreements; (2) has granted judicial deference towards the executive; (3) has had recourse to the doctrine of consistent interpretation; and (4) has not applied the political question doctrine. As also documented, the ECJ however has allowed direct effect to international trade agreements concluded with European neighboring states and Turkey, and with former colonies. Association agreements exhibit relations of power whereby the EU exports EU rules to countries where the EU already had a dominant position or is willing to increase its presence. In this sense, direct effect of association agreements would not interfere with EU self-government of the EU, although the other way around may not be true for the remaining signatory parties. Accordingly, association agreements are not international trade agreements as envisioned in the world trade system.

Although heavily criticized by Conforti,[213] the ECJ jurisprudence on the lack of GATT/WTO agreements direct effect the ECJ position may be subsumed under Sykes' theoretical perspective on the function and objective of international trade agreements, and includes the principle of popular sovereignty and democratic self-government in choosing how international trade obligations are discharged. By its case law, the ECJ case law has guaranteed that EU institutions accommodate public policies based on higher societal values—albeit very controversial—like the prohibition of importation of hormone beef and the conservation of preferential treatment with former colonies. When granting leeway to the executive to negotiate and preserve relevant public policy goals, the ECJ has ensured that trade obligations do not intrude and prevail over higher societal values.

Furthermore, the ECJ's self-restraint stance on WTO agreements maintained the balance of powers between the executive and the judiciary, as trade policy is not in the domain of courts. Moreover, the case law of the ECJ has also provided that international trade rules were not decided by numerous domestic judges which would most likely result in different and inconsistent rulings in the European legal order. In addition, the ECJ's stance on the question of reciprocity is paramount in the perspective on the WTO agreements. It is the practice of major WTO members not to allow WTO rules in domestic litigation and such practice was naturally a

---

[213] Conforti (1993).

major concern of the ECJ. The influence of the United States is certainly perceived, as the U.S. Congress clearly prohibited any invocability of WTO rules at the domestic level. It seems to be a fair assumption that the EU competition with the United States on market access would certainly be affected if European courts were to allow challenges of public policy based on WTO rules before domestic courts.

In what concerns the DSB rulings, the ECJ took the view that, like the WTO agreements, DSB rulings have no effect in the EU internal legal order. The ECJ however has implicitly applied the doctrine of consistent interpretation in the *Ikea* case. Furthermore, under constitutional pluralism theory, the ECJ case law has been so far corroborated by the national domestic courts of the EU Member States through judicial dialogue, although the door was left open for potential but unlikely changes in the European Member States national courts' perspective.

From the above analysis, it can be concluded that the most important outcome from the ECJ position in denying direct effect of WTO agreements was that the Court avoided what Bronckers referred to as the pervasive scope of the WTO agreements.[214] The regulatory autonomy of the EU and any other WTO member state should not be jeopardized as it is the very place where the principle of self-government is exercised by choosing how international trade obligations are discharged. Therefore, the ECJ allowed the EU institutions to pursue relevant policy goals to defend higher societal values.

References

Alter K, Meunier S (2006) Nested and overlapping regimes in the transatlantic banana trade dispute. J Eur Public Policy 13(3):362–382

Avbelj M (2008) Questioning EU constitutionalisms. German Law J 9:1–26. http://www.germanlawjournal.com/index.php?pageID=11&artID=883. Accessed 4 Sept 2014

Avbelj M, Komárek J (eds) (2008) Four visions of constitutional pluralism – symposium transcript. Eur J Legal Stud 2(1):325–370. http://www.ejls.eu/4/61UK.pdf. Accessed 4 Sept 2014

Berkey JO (1998) The European court of justice and direct effect for the GATT: a question worth revisiting. Eur J Int Law 9:626–657

Bermann G (2004) Marbury v. Madison and European Union "constitutional review". Geo Wash Int Law Rev 36:557–566

Bronckers M (2007) The relationship of the EC Courts with other international tribunals: non-committal, respectful or submissive? Common Market Law Rev 44:601–627

Bronckers M (2008a) From 'direct Effect' to 'muted dialogue': recent developments in the European courts' case law on the WTO and beyond. J Int Econ Law 11:885–898

Bronckers M (2008b) Private appeals to the WTO: an update. J World Trade 42:245–260

Cass D (2005) The constitutionalization of the World Trade Organization: legitimacy, democracy, and community in the international trade system. Oxford University Press, Oxford

Conforti B (1993) International law and the role of domestic legal systems. Martinus Nijhoff, Dordrecht

---

[214] Bronckers (2008a), p. 887.

Cottier T (2009) International trade law: the impact of justiciability and separations of powers in EC law. Eur Const Law Rev 5:307–326

Cottier T, Schefer K (1998) The relationship between World Trade Organization law, national and regional law. J Int Econ Law 1:82–122

Craig P, De Búrca G (2008) The EU law – text, cases and materials. Oxford University Press, Oxford

De Búrca G (2010) The European court of justice and the international legal order after Kadi. Harv Int Law J 51:1–49

De Witte B (2011) Direct effect, primacy, and the nature of the legal order. In: Craig P, de Búrca G (eds) The evolution of EU law. Oxford University Press, Oxford

Eeckhout P (1997) The domestic legal status of the WTO agreement: interconnecting legal systems. Common Mark Law Rev 34:11–58

Eeckhout P (2004) External relations of the European Union, legal and constitutional foundations. Oxford University Press, Oxford

Eeckhout P (2010) The growing influence of European Union law. Fordham Int Law J 33:1490–1521

European Union European External Action Service (2014) Association agreements. http://eeas.europa.eu/association/index_en.htm. Accessed 4 Sept 2014

Everson M (2010) Is the European Court of Justice a legal or political institution now? The Guardian, 10 August 2010. http://www.theguardian.com/law/2010/aug/10/european-court-justice-legal-political. Accessed 4 Sept 2014

Fligstein N, Stone Sweet A (2002) Constructing polities and markets: an institutionalist account of European integration. Am J Soc 107:1206–1243

German Law Journal (2000) Federal Constitutional Court concedes the applicability of European Community law in the Banana Case. German Law J 1. http://www.germanlawjournal.com/index.php?pageID=11&artID=9. Accessed 4 Sept 2014

Guzman A, Pauwelyn J (2009) International trade law. Aspen, New York

Halberstam D (2011) Local, global, and plural constitutionalism: Europe meets the world. U. Mich. Pub. L. Legal Theory Working Paper Series n. 176. http://ssrn.com/abstract=1521016. Accessed 4 Sept 2014

Halberstam D, Möllers C (2009) The German constitutional court says "Ja zu Deutschland!". German Law J 10:1241–1258

Holdgaard R (2008) External relations of the European community: legal reasoning and legal discourses. Kluwer Law International, The Netherlands

Keller H, Stone Sweet A (2008) Assessing the impact of ECHR on national legal systems. In: Keller H, Stone Sweet A (eds) A Europe of rights: the impact of ECHR on national legal systems. Oxford University Press, Oxford

Kuijper PJ, Bronckers M (2005) WTO law in the European court of justice. Common Mark Law Rev 42:1313–1355

Kumm M (2011) How does European Union law fit into the world of public law? Costa, Kadi and three conceptions of public law. N Y U Pub L Legal Theory Working Papers n. 11–16:1–36. http://ssrn.com/abstract=1781985. Accessed 4 Sept 2014

Laderchi R (1998) Report on Italy. In: Slaughter AM, Stone Sweet A, Weiler JHH (eds) The European courts and national courts – doctrine and jurisprudence. Hart, Oxford

Lang R (2012) Quite a challenge: Article 263(4) TFEU and the Case of the Mystery Measures. Paper presented at the 9th session of the Jean Monnet Seminar in Dubrovnik on advanced issues of European Law – the first year of the treaty of Lisbon – consolidation and enlargement. http://www.pravo.unizg.hr/_download/repository/11-04-03_Dubrovnik_paper.doc. Accessed 4 Sept 2014

Maduro MP (2004) How constitutional can the European Union be? The tension between intergovernmentalism and constitutionalism in the European Union. Jean Monnet Working Paper 5/04. http://ssrn.com/abstract=1576145. Accessed 4 Sept 2014

Maduro MP (2007) Interpreting European law: judicial adjudication in a context of constitutional pluralism. Eur J Legal Stud 1(2):1–21. http://www.ejls.eu/2/25UK.pdf. Accessed 4 Sept 2014

Mayer F (2001) The European constitution and the courts: adjudicating European constitutional law in a multilevel system. Jean Monnet Working Paper 9/03. http://www.jeanmonnetprogram.org/archive/papers/03/030901-03.pdf. Accessed 4 Sept 2014

Mendez M (2010) The legal effect of community agreements: maximalist treaty enforcement and judicial avoidance techniques. Eur J Int Law 21:83–104

Nollkaemper A (2009) Rethinking the supremacy of international law. Amsterdam Center for International Law Working Papers. http://papers.ssrn.com/sol3/papers.cfm?abstract_id=1336946. Accessed 4 Sept 2014

Petersmann EU (2006) Multi-level judicial trade governance without justice? On the role of domestic courts in the WTO legal and dispute settlement system. EUI Working Paper Law n. 2006/44. http://ssrn.com/abstract=964136. Accessed 4 Sept 2014

Petersmann EU (2007) Do judges meet their constitutional obligation to settle disputes in conformity with 'principles of justice and international Law'? Eur J Legal Stud 1:1–38

Rosenfeld M (2006) Comparing constitutional review by the European court of justice and the U.S. Supreme Court. Int J Const Law 4:618–651

Ruttley P (1998) The effect of WTO agreements in EC law: how private parties can use WTO agreements in litigation before the EC courts and the national courts of EC member states. In: Ruttley P, Macvay I, George C (eds) WTO and international trade regulation. Cameron May, London

Sacerdoti G, Venturini G (1992) GATT as a self-executing treaty in the Italian case law. In: Adjudication of international trade disputes in international and national economic law. University Press of Fribourg, Fribourg

Sadurski W (2008) "Solange, Chapter 3": Constitutional Courts in Central Europe—Democracy—European Union. Eur Law J 14:1–35

Schermers H, Waelbroeck D (2001) Judicial protection in the European Union. Kluwer Law International, The Netherlands

Schorkopf F (2009) The European Union as an association of sovereign states: Karlsruhe's ruling on the Treaty of Lisbon. German Law J 10:1219–1240

Stone Sweet A, Sandholtz W (1997) European integration and supranational governance. J Eur Public Policy 4:297–317. http://works.bepress.com/alec_stone_sweet/20. Accessed 4 Sept 2014

Von Bogdandy A (2008) Pluralism, direct effect, and the ultimate say: on the relationship between international and domestic constitutional law. Int J Const Law 6:397–413

Walker N (2002) The idea of constitutional pluralism. Mod Law Rev 65:317–359

WTO Member Information (2014) The European Union and the WTO. http://www.wto.org/english/thewto_e/countries_e/european_communities_e.htm. Accessed 4 Sept 2014

WTO Press Releases (2009) Press 591 – Lamy hails accord ending long running banana dispute. http://www.wto.org/english/news_e/pres09_e/pr591_e.htm. Accessed 4 Sept 2014

Chapter 5
Comparing the Role of Domestic Courts in International Trade Agreements

This chapter compares the Brazilian and EU courts' perspectives on the domestic application of the WTO agreements by elaborating on the main similarities and divergences between them, and the consequences of traditionalism and the rational choice theory approach. Thinking beyond the Brazilian experience, this chapter reveals patterns of emerging economies in Latin America, as they have adopted the direct effect of international trade agreements, namely Mexico and Argentina. This chapter finally suggests that the findings of the Brazilian experience may also be relevant to these Latin America countries, with due reservation to each country's social history.

5.1 The Main Similarities and Divergences Between Brazilian and European Union Courts in International Trade Agreements

In broad terms, the comparative study of Brazilian and EU courts' decisions provides the similarities and divergences in the understanding of the GATT/WTO agreements by the judiciary in the domestic legal order of both Brazil and EU territory. Because both Brazilian and EU legislation are silent about the status of international trade agreements, the judiciary gets to decide on the legal effects of the GATT/WTO agreements in the domestic legal order. However, such common ground on the power to establish the domestic legal status of international trade agreements by the judiciary has generated diverging positions. While the Brazilian courts settled the question that international trade agreements have the same status of ordinary federal law and in principle have direct effect in the domestic legal order, the ECJ has ensured the supremacy of international trade law but denied direct effect of WTO agreements.

The main divergence between Brazilian and European Union courts regarding the application of WTO agreements (or lack of application) shows how the diverse levels of judicial review can disparately affect governmental trade policies. The ECJ ensured the executive with flexibility to administer the changeability of trade policy, and denied private invocability of trade rules before European courts. Conversely, Brazil has given WTO rules direct effect and therefore opened the door for private corporations to impact on public policy goals through the judiciary. Indeed, the views of the Brazilian judiciary on WTO agreements are different from the European case law. As this book argues, direct enforcement of WTO law in domestic legal systems is a very controversial topic due to the function and objective of the agreements as well as the questions it raises on popular sovereignty and self-government in choosing how to discharge international obligations.

A diverging characteristic between the Brazilian and EU courts that seems to affect why judges give (or not) direct effect to WTO agreements, although not specific to trade law, is the composition of the courts. The Brazilian judiciary has a mixed method of judicial selection, composed by career judges at the lower courts, with reputation judges at the higher courts. In this sense, the Brazilian judiciary contrasts with the membership of the EU courts, which are composed of recognition judges only, carefully nominated by EU Member States, who have more awareness of the international impact of their decisions. Generally speaking, judges in the developed world are mostly very reluctant to adjudicate on governmental trade policy, as they have more professional experience and are nominated later in their careers. Moreover, the lack of judicial self-restraint in Brazil based on the constitutional prominence given to access to courts also plays an indirect role in the direct effect of WTO agreements. Indeed, in Brazil, after the dictatorship ended in 1984, courts have not adopted the political question doctrine as a means to avoid deciding on complex governmental policy decisions. The Brazilian judiciary, on the contrary, has been most activist in assessing highly politically controverted matters,[1] international trade included. The new democratic Constitution of 1988, aiming at enhancing access to the judiciary, determined in Article 5, XXXV, that *"the law shall not exclude any injury or threat to a right from the consideration of the Judicial Power."*

As anticipated in the international legal scholarship, in what concerns the Brazilian experience in adopting traditionalism, diverse and conflicting judicial decisions were rendered, a flood of cases reached the domestic judiciary neutralizing trade measures, and the domestic interpretation of trade rules was different from the international understanding of such rules. As documented in Chap. 3, the impact and amount of diverse judicial decisions interpreting trade rules jeopardized the Brazilian stance before the WTO with the threat of retaliation for lack of compliance with WTO rules up to when the Brazilian Supreme Court, while not giving any legal effect to the WTO ruling, settled the controversy in a implicit consistent interpretation approach vis-à-vis the WTO Appellate Body. In the meantime, the

---

[1] Rodrigues (2009), Taylor (2004), Ballard (1999), and Faro de Castro (1997).

5.1 The Main Similarities and Divergences Between Brazilian and European Union...   179

ECJ has avoided such consequences and lack of legal certainty by not allowing private litigation against public policies over economic interests and better bargains.

Divergence between Brazilian and EU courts also is found on the issue of reciprocity of GATT/WTO agreements. Brazilian domestic courts have never considered the question of reciprocity in relation to international trade agreements. Contrastingly, the ECJ has bestowed a great level of importance to reciprocity with regards to GATT/WTO agreements having in mind the prevalence of the rational choice theory approach in the role of domestic courts in the United States. The original intent in the conception of the GATT, and United States leadership in adopting the rational choice theory approach in the role of domestic courts has much influenced the ECJ, as can be perceived in the cases studied. Nevertheless, when it comes to association agreements, the ECJ took a different position regarding reciprocity, which, as mentioned, gives out power relations between the EU and their former colonies or potential new members.

The divergences between Brazilian and EU courts indicate that the political and economic incentives seem to play a fundamental role on whether international trade agreements have direct effect. The ECJ focused on the question of reciprocity from its major trading partners to secure the EU room of maneuver in trade negotiations and disputes. In this sense, a political motivation to maintain the same power level of other rich economies, mainly the United States, certainly played a role in the ECJ's adoption of the rational choice theory in relation to the WTO agreements. On the other hand, in what concerns the Brazilian Supreme Court position, it seems that incentives to interpret the WTO/GATT agreements in a more liberal perspective was also caused by concerns on abiding to international rules for the lack of competitive power conditions in trade relations. After all, as Conforti argues, traditionalism advances the idea that *"[a] State can greatly enhance its position within the international community by establishing its conformity to international law rules."*[2]

With reference to the direct effect of WTO agreements, however, enhancing a country's position in trade relations by claiming more compliance with GATT/WTO rules may seem to be overestimated. The political benefits in traditionalism regarding WTO agreements do not seem to constitute a strong argument against the most powerful trading players—the EU and the US—which adopted the rational choice theory approach. The direct effect of WTO agreements seems much more linked to a subservient perspective arisen in a former imperial dominion than grounded on a more realistic observation of the international contemporary standards. Although Brazil has a long path to attain the standards of living and infrastructure found in developed economies, the argument that allowing private companies to challenge governmental public policy based on WTO state-to-state commitments on market access would improve Brazilian stance before the contemporary international trade milieu seems to be largely unrealistic. The WTO

---

[2] Conforti (1993), pp. 10–11.

members have never agreed on providing the WTO agreements with direct effect, and have never asserted that private companies' interests should prevail over domestic public policy goals. Hence, the lack of direct effect in the majority of WTO members' domestic legal orders.

Beyond the controversial positions on the policy debate on whether private invocability of WTO rules is desirable, there is a point of convergence between the Brazilian and European perspective. Neither the Brazilian nor the EU courts have considered the WTO rulings as being directly enforceable in their territories. Even though both Brazilian and EU courts have not enforced WTO rulings in their jurisdiction, analysis reveals certain interesting parallels in substance of the decisions rendered. In Brazil, WTO rulings were qualified as part of Brazil's international obligations, not as having any domestic legal status in relation to their enforceability. Indeed, they are not legally enforceable in the Brazilian territory. Similarly, in the EU, the ECJ has stated that, although it is possible to challenge the legality of a community measure that implements WTO rules, there is no right enabling private actors to ask European courts to question the EU implementation of WTO rulings.[3]

---

[3] Reiterating its original case law on WTO rules, the ECJ stated in the *Van Parys* case (2005 E.C.R I-1465, Summary of judgment):

> Given their nature and structure, the WTO agreements are not in principle among the rules in the light of which the Court is to review the legality of measures adopted by the Community institutions. It is only where the Community has intended to implement a particular obligation assumed in the context of the WTO, or where the Community measure refers expressly to the precise provisions of the WTO agreements, that it is for the Court to review the legality of the Community measure in question in the light of the WTO rules.
>
> By undertaking after the adoption of the decision of the WTO Dispute Settlement Body (DSB) to comply with the rules of that organisation and, in particular, with Articles I(1) and XIII of GATT 1994, the Community did not intend to assume a particular obligation in the context of the WTO, capable of justifying an exception to the impossibility of relying on WTO rules before the Community Courts and enabling the latter to exercise judicial review of the relevant Community provisions in the light of those rules.
>
> First, even where there is a decision of the DSB holding that the measures adopted by a member are incompatible with the WTO rules, the WTO dispute settlement system nevertheless accords considerable importance to negotiation between the parties. In those circumstances, to require courts to refrain from applying rules of domestic law which are inconsistent with the WTO agreements would have the consequence of depriving the legislative or executive organs of the contracting parties of the possibility afforded in particular by Article 22 of the Understanding on rules and procedures governing the settlement of disputes of reaching a negotiated settlement, even on a temporary basis.
>
> Secondly, to accept that the Community Courts have the direct responsibility for ensuring that Community law complies with the WTO rules would deprive the Community's legislative or executive bodies of the discretion which the equivalent bodies of the Community's commercial partners enjoy.
>
> Therefore, an economic operator cannot plead before a court of a Member State that Community legislation is incompatible with certain WTO rules, even if the DSB has stated that that legislation is incompatible with those rules.

5.1 The Main Similarities and Divergences Between Brazilian and European Union... 181

Convergence is also found in that both Brazilian and EU courts have made use of judicial deference towards the executive, although in different degrees. Under Conforti's typology, judicial deference towards the executive branch is understood as a judicial avoidance technique, implying that the governmental action does not conform with international law. Depending on the context, however, judicial deference to the executive may in fact stand for the appropriate enforcement of international trade rules. The Brazilian case on the imports of thermo bottles from China is an example where the Superior Court of Justice deferred to the executive to review the applicability of antidumping duties to an individual exporter. This ruling in fact favors the implementation of the Antidumping Agreement,[4] which requires members to maintain judicial review of administrative actions relating to "final determinations," and not, as happened at the Brazilian first instance level, to substitute the administrative agencies that would first analyze the individual request of non-application of antidumping duties to certain specific transactions.

Therefore, judicial deference towards the executive does not necessarily mean that international trade rules are not being respected by the executive. It could also mean that the executive has more adequate resources to evaluate whether a specific product is being dumped, rather than the judicial branch. However, this can be the case for countries where the political configuration provides a more self-restrained judiciary in reviewing governmental policies. Accordingly, instead of considering that judicial deference to the executive translates into a judicial avoidance technique against the application of international law, this study shows that in fact, there are instances where deference to the executive qualifies as compliance with international trade rights. Therefore, the assumption that the role of domestic courts regarding international trade rules is necessary and beneficial for international law requires the analysis of the context of the political institutions and the role of the judiciary in a specific country.

Another point of convergence in the way Brazilian and EU courts understand the WTO agreements is that, in a general perspective, both Brazilian and EU courts give a high value to the presumption of consistency of domestic law with international law. Although not recognizing the legal effect of WTO rulings in their respective legal orders, both Brazil and the European Union have interpreted litigation brought before them in a consistent way with WTO rulings, as seen in the *Retreated Tires*[5] case, before the Brazilian Supreme Court, and the *Ikea*

---

[4] Antidumping Agreement, Article 13 reads:

Article 13: Judicial Review

Each Member whose national legislation contains provisions on anti-dumping measures shall maintain judicial, arbitral or administrative tribunals or procedures for the purpose, *inter alia*, of the prompt review of administrative actions relating to final determinations and reviews of determinations within the meaning of Article 11. Such tribunals or procedures shall be independent of the authorities responsible for the determination or review in question.

[5] STF, Argüição de Descumprimento de Preceito Fundamental 101-DF, Relatora: Ministra Carmem Lúcia, 24.6.2009, D.J.U. 4.6.2012.

Wholesale[6] case before the ECJ. In the *Retreated Tires* case, the Brazilian Supreme Court's decision reached a similar outcome to the WTO ruling, but the legal grounds were based on domestic constitutional law and international treaties other than the WTO agreements. In the *Ikea Wholesale* case, the ECJ rejected the request for reimbursement of antidumping duties collected on imports of cotton-type

---

[6] Ikea Wholesale Ltd. v. Commissioners of Customs & Excise, 2007 E.C.R. I-07723. The ECJ stated:

> 29. It must be recalled, as a preliminary point that, according to settled case-law, given their nature and structure, the WTO agreements are not in principle among the rules in the light of which the Court is to review the legality of measures adopted by the Community institutions (Case C-93/02 P Biret International v Council [2003] ECR I-10497, paragraph 52, and Case C-377/02 Van Parys [2005] ECR I-1465, paragraph 39 and the case-law cited).
> 30. It is only where the Community has intended to implement a particular obligation assumed in the context of the WTO, or where the Community measure refers expressly to the precise provisions of the WTO agreements, that it is for the Court to review the legality of the Community measure in question in the light of the WTO rules (Case C-149/96 Portugal v Council [1999] ECR I-8395, paragraph 49; Biret International v Council, paragraph 53; and Van Parys, paragraph 40 and the case-law cited).
> 31. In accordance with Article 1 of Regulation No 1515/2001, the Council may, following a report adopted by the DSB, and depending on the circumstances, repeal or amend the disputed measure or adopt any other special measures which are deemed to be appropriate in the circumstances.
> 32. Regulation No 1515/2001 applies, according to its Article 4, to reports adopted after 1 January 2001 by the DSB. In the present case, the DSB adopted the report of the Appellate Body on 12 March 2001 together with that of the Panel as amended by the Appellate Body's report.
> 33. Pursuant to Article 3 of Regulation No 1515/2001, any measures adopted pursuant to that regulation are to take effect from the date of their entry into force and may not serve as basis for the reimbursement of the duties collected prior to that date, unless otherwise provided for. Recital (6) in the preamble to the regulation provides in that connection that the recommendations in reports adopted by the DSB only have prospective effect. Therefore, 'any measures taken under [Regulation No 1515/2001] will take effect from the date of their entry into force, unless otherwise specified, and ... do not provide any basis for the reimbursement of the duties collected prior to that date'.
> 34. In this case, having regard to the provisions of Regulation No 1515/2001 and to the DSB's recommendations, the Council first of all adopted Regulation No 1644/2001 on 7 August 2001. Next, on 28 January 2002, it adopted Regulation No 160/2002, and finally, on 22 April 2002, Regulation No 696/2002 confirming the definitive anti-dumping duty imposed by Regulation No 2398/97, as amended and suspended by Regulation No 1644/2001.
> 35. It follows from all of the foregoing that, in circumstances such as those in the main proceedings, the legality of Regulation No 2398/97 cannot be reviewed in the light of the Anti-dumping Agreement, as subsequently interpreted by the DSB's recommendations, since it is clear from the subsequent regulations that the Community, by excluding repayment of rights paid under Regulation No 2398/97, did not in any way intend to give effect to a specific obligation assumed in the context of the WTO.

5.1 The Main Similarities and Divergences Between Brazilian and European Union... 183

bed linen under the zeroing methodology as interpreted by the WTO Dispute Settlement Body in the *EC-Bed Linen*[7] case. At the same time, however, the ECJ granted the relief sought by the plaintiff based on an autonomous interpretation of the European regulation on antidumping. Table 5.1 provides a summary of the main divergences and similarities in the role of Brazilian and EU courts, and Table 5.2 the main consequences of their perspectives as discussed in Chaps. 3 and 4.

Table 5.1 Synopsis of divergences and similarities between Brazilian and EU courts regarding WTO agreements

	Brazil	European Union
Divergences	1. Traditionalism 2. WTO agreements equal to federal law 3. Private corporations may impact public policy based on WTO rules 4. Judiciary may decide on international trade obligations 5. No reciprocity required	1. Rational choice theory 2. Supremacy of WTO agreements 3. No possibility of interference in public policy choices based on WTO rules 4. The EU executive bodies decide how to discharge international trade obligations 5. Reciprocity is needed from other major trading partners
Similarities	1. Domestic legislation is silent on the domestic status of international trade agreements 2. Judicial deference to the executive, although in variable extents 3. No domestic legal status of WTO rulings, but use of consistent interpretation	

Table 5.2 The main consequences of the Brazilian and EU courts' perspective on the domestic legal effect of the WTO agreements

Brazil	European Union
1. Private parties may have recourse to courts to secure their economic position or increase profits	1. Private companies cannot challenge domestic public policy over their economic interests or market share
2. A flood of individual cases to revert unfavorable governmental trade policy, potentially neutralizing trade policies	2. Private companies have to support loss of market access or sales over governmental public policy, without recourse to courts
3. Diverse and inconsistent rulings among domestic courts within Brazil	3. Uniformity of interpretation of WTO rules in the EU territory by the EU executive
4. Domestic courts' interpretation of WTO rules differs from the international and foreign interpretation	4. Executive bodies are in charge of interpreting WTO rules and finding negotiable solutions for conflicting international obligations or foreign interpretations
5. Disequilibrium in international trade's concessions and rights among WTO members	5. International trade's balance of concessions and rights are under WTO review
6. Shift of decision-making on governmental public policies from the political powers to the judiciary	6. Empowerment of executive bodies to make public policy decisions that benefit society

---

[7] WTO, *European Communities—Anti-Dumping Duties on Imports of Cotton-Type Bed Linen from India*, WT/DS141/AB/R, adopted on 12 March 2001.

From the point of view of the general implementation of international law, the supremacy of international trade agreements, coupled with lack of direct effect of international trade rules in the European case, contrasts with the non-primacy of international law with the potential application of the *lex posteriori* principle in Brazil. Indeed, this research provides evidence that formal considerations on hierarchical primacy of international law, per se, do not necessarily translate into a more favorable role of domestic courts regarding international trade agreements. Likewise, the ordinary status of federal law given to international trade rules, when interpreted by domestic judges in a way that requires a clear intent of the legislator to revoke an international rule, may also provide stronger compliance with international law at the domestic level. What really seems to guarantee that WTO law is respected in domestic systems is, after all, the willingness of courts to construe domestic norms in a consistent way with the WTO agreements. Such approach towards international law seems to be the case in both Brazilian Supreme Court and the ECJ.

As earlier advanced, this research argues that the function and objective of WTO Agreements and the principle of popular sovereignty and self-government do not create individual rights at the domestic level. The reasons considered by the European Union courts, in line with other major economies, such as the United States, Japan, Canada, India and China, to consider WTO agreements as non-self-executing or as not having direct effect seem compelling. Furthermore, the implementation of the WTO agreements at the domestic level seems to be more effective when courts are willing to make use of the doctrine of consistent interpretation, which, indeed, has occasionally happened in both Brazil and the European Union. This conclusion is even more convincing in relation to the Brazilian standpoint due to the flood of individual claims filed against governmental trade measures, with the consequent hindrance of its objectives. Lastly, despite punctual economic crisis, the world trade will intensify and more complex cases may arise. Domestic courts may be not the optimal venue for deciding trade conflicts, as there is always the possibility of negotiating and finding a better solution among the countries involved, which are for the executive to assess and balance the alternatives available.

As a result, the WTO dispute settlement mechanism provides a more appropriate venue for deciding disputes and unifies the application of WTO rules to all member states. In fact, the international trade system has an effective dispute settlement at the international level and the primary argument for traditionalism—the lack of international mechanisms to make member states comply with international law—turns out to be not so relevant in the case of the world trade system.

With the main similarities and divergences between the understanding of the Brazilian and EU courts regarding the GATT/WTO agreements in mind, the next section will suggest that the findings of the Brazilian experience regarding the GATT/WTO agreements can be extended to a high degree to other emerging economies in Latin America, with due reservation to each country's social history.

5.2 Thinking Beyond Brazilian Perspectives: The Patterns of Emerging Economies in Latin America

As the world economy has been undergoing massive changes and the importance of emerging markets has been growing, the findings of this study can also be relevant to other emerging countries in Latin America that have adopted traditionalism in their domestic court's approach to international trade agreements. The Latin American emerging economies' courts approach on international trade law becomes of increasing significance because of their potential impact as international trade increases in the region.

The term "emerging markets" is a terminology created in the 1980s by Antoine van Agtmael to identify developing world countries with higher economic growth rates to promote foreign investment in markets with expansive consumer demands.[8] The term emerging markets however does not have a common and consistent definition in international institutions. For instance, the International Monetary Fund, in its World Economic Outlook Database,[9] divides the world into two major groups: (1) advanced economies and (2) emerging market and developing economies. This list however does not identify which countries are considered emerging countries out of the developing economies. Other institutions and international investment agencies make their own assessments and definitions. As a matter of fact, there is no clear consensus about which countries are considered emerging economies.[10]

Despite the lack of a consistent concept of emerging countries, the growing attention on the Latin American markets has made the role of domestic courts regarding international trade agreements in their domestic jurisdictions increasingly relevant. Because this study focuses on international trade, it will consider for the definition of emerging economies in Latin America the membership of the Group of Twenty (G-20),[11] all of which are members of the WTO. In addition to Brazil, Mexico and Argentina are the Latin American members of the G-20. The G-20 is currently one of the most relevant negotiation groups at the multilateral level, which aggregates the major developing and developed countries. In addition, according to the 2013 World Bank ranking table of countries' GDP,[12] Brazil, Mexico and Argentina ranked 7th, 15th and 21st, respectively, which show their economies' weight in Latin America.[13]

---

[8] Van Agtmael (2007), pp. 4–5.

[9] International Monetary Fund (2014), p. 180.

[10] Kvint (2008).

[11] The G-20 members are: Argentina, Australia, Brazil, Canada, China, France, Germany, India, Indonesia, Italy, Japan, Mexico, Russia, Saudi Arabia, South Africa, Republic of Korea, Turkey, United Kingdom, and the United States of America.

[12] World Bank (2014).

[13] Venezuela and Chile respectively ranked 27th and 38th in the 2013 table. *See* World Bank (2014).

The Latin American emerging economies become more relevant in the international arena as the world economy has been undergoing massive changes and the importance of emerging markets has been growing. Besides their membership to the WTO, Latin American emerging economies are also members of other significant regional trade agreements, with potential for overlapping obligations and conflicting rules and rulings. Brazil and Argentina are members of the Common Market of the South (MERCOSUL), and Mexico is member of North American Free Trade Agreement (NAFTA). This study will therefore assess, in relation to Mexico and Argentina, the domestic status of international treaties and their traditionalist perspective of these countries' domestic courts.

In relation to the domestic status of international treaties in the domestic law, the Mexican Constitution provides that international treaties, along with laws of Congress, are the supreme law of the Union.[14] This provision however has raised great controversies. In the last two decades, the Mexican Supreme Court [*Suprema Corte de Justicia de la Nación*] has taken different positions on this issue.[15]

A prominent position of the Mexican Supreme Court was taken in the case *Amparo de Revisión n. 120/2002*.[16] In this case, McCain Mexico, a subsidiary of Canadian company McCain Foods, challenged the imposition of a 20 % ad valorem safeguard duty on imported frozen potatoes from Canada. This safeguard duty was based on several provisions, being the most relevant a presidential Decree that fixed, for the year of 2001, the import tax of goods from North America and other countries. McCain Mexico argued that the safeguard duty was unconstitutional because the NAFTA established an import tax of zero percent and other rules of lesser hierarchy could not take precedence over an international treaty.

The Mexican Supreme Court then decided that international treaties are hierarchically above general statutory laws from all spheres of government, that is, they are superior to all state, federal, and local laws. The Mexican Supreme Court stated that international treaties are nevertheless not equal to Mexican constitutional rules. The Mexican Supreme Court made a systematic interpretation of Article 133 of the Mexican Constitution in balance with other international law principles prescribed in the Constitution, and concluded that international treaties are below the Federal Constitution and above all federal, state and municipal laws.

---

[14] Mexican Constitution, Article 133 reads:

This Constitution, the laws of the Congress of the Union that emanate therefrom, and all treaties that have been made and shall be made in accordance therewith by the President of the Republic, with the approval of the Senate, shall be the supreme law of the whole Union. The judges of each State shall conform to the said Constitution, the laws, and treaties, in spite of any contradictory provisions that may appear in the constitutions or laws of the States.

[15] Mexico, Suprema Corte de Justicia de la Nación, Amparo en Revisión 2069/91, considering that international treaties have the same hierarchical status of federal law; Amparo en Revisión 1475/98, stating that international treaties are situated above federal law and below the Constitution.

[16] Mexico, Suprema Corte de Justicia de la Nación, Amparo en Revisión 120/2002. Mc Cain México, S.A. de C.V. 13 de febrero de 2007, Semanario Judicial de la Federación y su Gaceta XXV, Abril de 2007, Tesis: P. IX/2007.

5.2 Thinking Beyond Brazilian Perspectives: The Patterns of Emerging Economies... 187

Nevertheless, constitutional reforms in 2011 brought about new constitutional provisions that affect the domestic status of international treaties in Mexico. Among several changes, these new constitutional amendments modified Article 1 of the Mexican Constitution which now provides that that every person in Mexico shall enjoy the guarantees granted not only by the Mexican Constitution but also by the international treaties to which the Mexican State is party, which cannot be restricted or suspended except in such cases and under such conditions provided by the Constitution itself.

In interpreting this new constitutional amendment in the case *Contradicción de Tesis 293/2011*,[17] the Supreme Court of Mexico, by a 10–1 vote, decided that human rights, regardless of their source, have constitutional status. In practice, the Court granted international human rights treaties the same status as the Constitution. However, whenever the Constitution provides any restriction to such international human rights, the Constitution prevails. Moreover, in this decision, the Mexican Supreme Court, by a 11–6 vote, ruled that the case law of the Interamerican Court of Human Rights is binding to the Mexican judiciary in case it is more favorable to individuals and consistent interpretation is not possible.

In what concerns Argentina, the Argentinean Constitution establishes as a general rule that international treaties signed with other countries or international organizations are hierarchically superior to general laws. The Constitutional Reform of 1994 introduced the constitutional rule establishing the supremacy of international treaties over domestic laws in the Argentinean system.[18] At that occasion, several international human rights treaties[19] were elevated to constitutional hierarchy.[20] Article 75, 22 of the Argentinean Constitution also created the possibility that other international treaties on human rights, after their approval by Congress, may be granted constitutional hierarchy with the vote of two-thirds of all members of each House. Most importantly, the Argentinean Constitution opened a door to the possibility of transferring sovereign power to international integration treaties in Latin America, if approved with absolute majority of members of each House.

---

[17] Mexico, Suprema Corte de Justicia de la Nación, Contradicción de Tesis n. 293/2011 suscitada entre el Primer Tribunal Colegiado en Materias Administrativa y de Trabajo del Décimo Primer Circuito y el Séptimo Tribunal Colegiado en Materia Civil del Primer Circuito, 2 y 3 de septiembre de 2013.

[18] Argentinean Constitution, Art. 75, XXII.

[19] According to Article 75, XXII, of the Argentinean Constitution, the human rights treaties with constitutional hierarchy are: the American Declaration of the Rights and Duties of Man; the Universal Declaration of Human Rights; the American Convention on Human Rights; the International Pact on Economic, Social and Cultural Rights; the International Pact on Civil and Political Rights and its empowering Protocol; the Convention on the Prevention and Punishment of Genocide; the International Convention on the Elimination of all Forms of Racial Discrimination; the Convention on the Elimination of all Forms of Discrimination against Woman; the Convention against Torture and other Cruel, Inhuman or Degrading Treatments or Punishments; and the Convention on the Rights of the Child.

[20] Argentinean Constitution, Art. 75, XXII.

In relation to countries outside Latin America, the Argentinean Constitution also permits integration agreements with the same qualified Congress vote, but only after Congress pass a previous "declaration of advisability" to allow such treaty to be considered for approval.[21] The possibility of sovereign power transfer to other countries that are not around Argentinean territorial limits showed the willingness of Argentina to develop a higher level of integration process within MERCOSUL and triggered tensions with Brazil. The Brazilian Constitution had not been amended to include a similar provision and there has been no clear inclination from the Brazilian political branches to do so.

Table 5.3 provides a comparative summary of the domestic legal status of international treaties in Brazil, Mexico and Argentina.

Table 5.3 The domestic legal status of international treaties in Brazil, Mexico and Argentina

Hierarchy of treaties	Brazil	Mexico	Argentina
Equal to federal law	International treaties (trade included)	No	No
Above federal law but below the constitution	International human rights treaties	International treaties (trade included)	International treaties (trade included)
Equal to constitution	International human rights treaties with qualified vote for approval	All international human rights treaties to which Mexico is party	1. Certain treaties on human rights; 2. Other human rights treaties with qualified vote
Sovereignty transfer to integration treaties	No	No	1. In Latin America: absolute majority 2. Other countries: absolute majority after the declaration of advisability

---

[21] Argentinean Constitution, Art. 75, XXIV, reads:

> To approve treaties of integration which delegate powers and jurisdiction to supranational organizations under reciprocal and equal conditions, and which respect the democratic order and human rights. The rules derived therefrom have a higher hierarchy than laws.
> The approval of these treaties with Latin American States shall require the absolute majority of all the members of each House. In the case of treaties with other States, the National Congress, with the absolute majority of the members present of each House, shall declare the advisability of the approval of the treaty which shall only be approved with the vote of the absolute majority of all the members of each House, one hundred and twenty days after said declaration of advisability.
> The denouncement of the treaties referred to in this subsection shall require the prior approval of the absolute majority of all the members of each House.

5.2 Thinking Beyond Brazilian Perspectives: The Patterns of Emerging Economies...

Like Brazil, Mexico and Argentina have also a tradition of giving direct effect to international treaties, including WTO agreements. In Argentina, WTO agreements have direct effect and precedence over domestic law.[22] Due to the constitutional rank of international treaties, any domestic judge in Argentina may, if requested in a case, *"declare the unconstitutionality of any measure adopted in breach of rules contained in an international treaty, such as the WTO Agreement."*[23]

According to Mexican law, once an international treaty is ratified by the Senate, it becomes domestic law with self-executing character.[24] Therefore, in Mexico, WTO agreements have direct effect, and international agreements have a status higher than ordinary federal law.[25] As a result, in case of conflict with domestic law, WTO agreements prevail. In fact, Mexico and Argentina confer individuals the right of action to challenge domestic law based the WTO agreements.

The Judicial Power of Mexico is composed by the Supreme Court of Justice of the Nation [*Suprema Corte de Justicia de la Nación*], the Electoral Court, the collegiate and unitary circuit courts, and district courts.[26] The Federal Judicial Council oversees of the administration of the judiciary, except in relation to the Supreme Court of Justice, and selects district judges. Federal courts adjudicate on matters involving the enforcement and application of international treaties.[27] The Supreme Court of Justice of the Nation may exercise abstract judicial review against international treaties.[28] In Mexico, the structure of state courts is defined by local law and, with some variations, is divided into state superior court of justice [*tribunal superior de justicia*] and courts of first instance [*tribunales de justicia del fuero común/primera instancia*].[29]

In Mexico, trade litigation between private parties and government authorities is decided by the federal administrative court [*Tribunal Federal de Justicia Fiscal y Administrativa*] with technical autonomy to adjudicate on cases involving international trade treaties and the Foreign Trade Law.[30] Final decisions of this administrative court may be reviewed by federal courts.[31]

---

[22] WTO, *Argentina—Measures Affecting Imports of Footwear, Textiles, Apparel and Other Items*, WT/DS56/R, paragraph 3.214, circulated on 25 November 1997.

[23] Ibid.

[24] Miranda and Partida (2013), p. 56.

[25] The direct effect of WTO agreements, and the fact that they prevail in conflict with domestic legislation in Mexico, was used as a defense before the WTO dispute settlement mechanism in *Mexico—Definitive Anti-Dumping Measures on Beef and Rice*, WT/DS295/R, circulated on 6 June 2005.

[26] Mexican Constitution, Art. 94.

[27] Mexican Constitution, Art. 104.

[28] Mexican Constitution, Art. 105, II, b, c, g.

[29] Kossick Jr (2000), pp. 27–28.

[30] Mexico, Ley Orgánica del Tribunal Federal de Justicia Fiscal y Administrativa, D.O.F. 6.12.2007, Art. 14, X and XIII.

[31] Hernández (2003) p. 161.

In Argentina, the Supreme Court of Justice of the Nation [*Corte Suprema de Justicia de la Nación*] and federal lower courts constitute the federal judiciary.[32] The Argentinean Constitution gives autonomy to Argentinean provinces regarding the administration of justice[33] and, as a result, each Argentinean province has a particular court system. The Judicial Council is in charge of the selection of judges as well as of the administration of the judiciary.[34] Federal courts have the attribution to decide on cases involving international treaties with foreign countries.[35] For instance, in 1999, the federal judge of Concepción del Uruguay ordered the limitation of chicken imports from Brazil into Argentina until Argentinean authorities reanalyzed a request for antidumping measures made by Argentinean poultry producers.[36] Nevertheless, tax and customs authorities decisions can be challenged before an administrative court [*Tribunal Fiscal de la Nación Argentina*], which provides an independent technical venue for questioning government authorities decisions on such matters. However, this administrative court cannot review the constitutionality of any customs and tax laws and regulations, except if the Argentinean Supreme Court, whose interpretation should be followed, has already decided the issue.[37]

There are numerous decisions involving international trade agreements such as the NAFTA and MERCOSUR before the Mexican and the Argentinean judiciaries, but not as much in relation to WTO agreements. For instance, the Argentinean Supreme Court of Justice has rendered more than 55 cases involving MERCOSUR, while the lower courts have decided on 420 cases.[38] However, there is not much domestic litigation based on the WTO agreements. To illustrate, although Argentinean authorities initiated 325 antidumping investigations in the period between 1995 and 2010, "*only a few were subjected to judicial review.*"[39] The Argentinean Constitution provides all citizens with right of access to courts, but the case law of the Argentinean Supreme Court requires that, in most cases, an administrative review be first filed over a dispute against an administrative act.[40] Commentary has noted that the lack of use of judicial review of trade remedies may be due to the requirement of administrative remedies' exhaustion and the time-length of court proceedings.[41]

---

[32] Argentinean Constitution, Art. 108.
[33] Argentinean Constitution, Art. 5.
[34] Argentinean Constitution, Art. 114.
[35] Argentinean Constitution, Art. 116.
[36] La Nación (1999).
[37] Argentina, Ley 11.683, Art. 185.
[38] De Klor and Perotti (2009), pp. 93–94.
[39] De Artaza (2013), p. 131.
[40] Ibid., p. 134.
[41] Ibid., p. 151.

5.2 Thinking Beyond Brazilian Perspectives: The Patterns of Emerging Economies... 191

With regards to Mexico, in a search of the Mexican Supreme Court database, five cases related to WTO trade remedies were found.[42] An important case to mention is the one that the Mexican Supreme Court considered the WTO Appellate Body ruling as an additional reason to maintain a disputed governmental trade measure. The plaintiff in this case challenged a presidential decree that raised to 20 % the import taxes under the NAFTA on American wine and distilled beverages.[43] This tariff raise was issued in retaliation to the United States lack of compliance with the WTO ruling on the *US—Offset Act (Byrd Amendment)*, as authorized by the WTO DSS.[44] In order words, the WTO authorized retaliation over products protected under a different trade agreement, although such agreement was between the same dispute parties. The plaintiff argued that the federal executive could not modify the preferential tariff quotas enshrined in the NAFTA, alleging several constitutional grounds.[45] The Mexican Supreme Court considered that the

---

[42] The search was made at the Mexican Supreme Court case law database [*Jurisprudencia y Tesis Aisladas*] under the words "acuerdo general aranceles," with three results on antidumping; "OMC" and "GATT" with no results, and finally "Organización Mundial del Comercio" with two results in 2013.

[43] Mexico, Amparo en revisión 196/2007. Unión de Grandes Marcas, S.A. de C.V. 20 de junio de 2007. Ponente: Juan N. Silva Meza. Novena Época, Primera Sala, Semanario Judicial de la Federación y su Gaceta XXVI, Septiembre de 2007, Página: 374, Tesis: 1a. CLXXXVIII/2007, Tesis Aislada.

[44] WTO, Decision by the Arbitrator, *United States—Continued Dumping and Subsidy Offset Act of 2000, Original Complaint by Mexico—Recourse to Arbitration by the United States under Article 22.6 of the DSU*, WT/DS234/ARB/MEX, 31 August 2004, DSR 2004:X, 4931.

[45] The most relevant constitutional argument was that the presidential decree violated Article 131, 2nd paragraph, of the Mexican Constitution, which reads:

> The Executive may be empowered by the Congress of the Union to increase, decrease, or abolish tariff rates on imports and exports, that were imposed by the Congress itself, and to establish others; likewise to restrict and to prohibit the importation, exportation, or transit of articles, products, and goods, when he deems this expedient for the purpose of regulating foreign commerce, the economy of the country, the stability of domestic production, or for accomplishing any other purpose to the benefit of the country *The Executive himself, in submitting the fiscal budget to Congress each year, shall submit for its approval the use that he has made of this power*. (emphasis added).

In his view, the plaintiff interpreted Article 131 as prescribing that the extraordinary powers of the executive on foreign trade was conditioned to the previous approval of Congress through regular legislative proceedings. In this case, the Presidential decree modifying the tariffs was not informed to Congress. The Mexican Supreme Court of Justice rejected the plaintiff's argument, and clarified that the President may enact decrees modifying tariffs based on Article 131 of the Constitutional, and considered that the respective authorization of Congress's had already been granted by the Foreign Trade Law (Mexico, Ley de Comercio Exterior, D.O.F. 27.6.2003, Art. 4). The Court added that the fact that the President had not informed Congress of such decree does not turn the decree invalid and, as mentioned above, that he President may modify preferential tariff rate quotas of NAFTA more so if he is enforcing a WTO rulings.

The Mexican Supreme Court of Justice considered that the Mexican Constitution Article 131, 2nd paragraph, allows the executive to face situations that impair the national economy with Congress permission in a timely and efficient manner, because it is the executive branch that may respond to the dynamism of international trade. The Court clarified that the interpretation

Executive needed mechanisms to respond to the dynamics of international trade, and to face conflicting international obligations originated from diverse international trade agreements. Like in the Brazilian *Retreated Tires* case, the Mexican Supreme Court decision validating the presidential decree originated from a WTO authorization to retaliate may also be understood as the judicial inclination to apply the doctrine of consistent interpretation. Although the WTO rulings did not have legal effect in their domestic legal order, the Brazilian and Mexican Supreme Courts implicitly validated the WTO rulings' outcome. Conversely, in these cases, both MERCOSUL and NAFTA did not prevail over WTO agreements.

It is most likely that particular interpretations and characteristics of the Brazilian courts' experience on the domestic application of WTO agreements may not be entirely shared by the Argentinean or Mexican judiciaries. Nevertheless, the crucial point here is that all these Latin American emerging economies have considered, at least in principle, that WTO agreements are to be enforced by domestic courts. Accordingly, the conclusion of this study to bring into question the level of domestic judicial protection given to international trade rules may also be extended to these Latin American emerging economies, with due respect to each country's particularities. More field research is required to understand the context of the political institutions and the role of the judiciary in these countries. However, Latin American emerging economies have in principle restrained their own policy autonomy at the domestic level by adopting traditionalism in the role of domestic courts regarding international trade agreements. As earlier noted, major trading players of the world adopt the rational choice perspective and do not give up their power to set domestic policy according to their own higher societal values. Therefore, international trade agreements should be distinguished from other international treaties and should not have direct effect in WTO member states domestic legal orders. Whenever necessary, the doctrine of consistent interpretation may be applied through guidance of the Supreme Court to avoid incurring the country into international responsibility.

The question that remains to be answered is whether Latin American emerging economies would be willing to keep this additional restraint infringed by traditionalism in their domestic public policy to achieve public interest goals to favor private companies' interests based on WTO rules, out of a political incentive to improve their reputation of abiding to international law, or would they want to make domestic public policy choices by themselves.

---

sought by the complainant, that is, the need of Congress approval through regular legislative process, would render the constitutional provision ineffective. Based on the principle of useful effect, the Mexican Supreme Court of Justice interpreted that the last part of Article 131, 2nd paragraph of the Mexican Constitution, conferring the possibility of extraordinary powers to the executive, created a speedily and exceptional system to evaluate the changing circumstances and adopt measures in international trade matters in accordance with Mexican state's objectives. The Mexican Supreme Court of Justice expressly referred to the dynamism of trade relations, globalization and, more importantly, the multiplication of international trade agreements that, in the Court's opinion, escape from Congress and are clearly perceivable by the executive.

5.2 Thinking Beyond Brazilian Perspectives: The Patterns of Emerging Economies... 193

Meanwhile, at the international level, developed countries have managed to increase their regulatory capacity through litigation at the WTO dispute settlement system.[46] This research therefore suggests that Latin American emerging economies should, like the overwhelming majority of WTO members, protect their public policy autonomy to purse public interest goals based on legitimate societal values by not allowing private companies to invoke WTO rules before the domestic judiciary to impair public policy choices.

Therefore, the contrasting perspectives between the Latin American countries vis-à-vis major developed economies of the world give rise to an issue of power. Commentary remarked that weaker countries tied their hands more easily than powerful economies in relation to international trade law.[47] This seems to be a safe assumption to explain why Latin American countries have given direct effect to WTO law. In principle, as the Latin American economies grow, and their stance at the international trade system increases, it may be reasonably expected a move from traditionalism to the rational choice theory approach in Latin American countries, as it happened in European courts and American courts. However, this potential shift is yet to be seen in future years. So far, Brazilian courts' tendency has been to address highly politically complex issues, not the opposite.

To be sure, any potential lack of compliance with the WTO obligations is to be questioned and discussed through the WTO dispute settlement system, which is the forum for settlement of disputes between states. This book advances the idea that, instead of adopting traditionalism regarding WTO agreements, Latin American emerging economies should be focusing their attention on WTO rights and obligations at the international level by having recourse to the WTO dispute settlement system whenever needed. As argued by Santos, through lawyering and litigation before the WTO DSS, developing countries may use their legal capacity to further development goals by influencing changes in WTO rules' interpretation.[48] Santos notes that there are examples at the WTO dispute settlement system where a WTO member has succeeded in making such changes by expanding WTO exceptions.[49] In this sense, by focusing on the WTO dispute settlement system, Latin American emerging economies may strive for securing sovereign policy space for their regulatory objectives.[50] After all, international trade is not an end in itself, but it is at the service of the peoples of the world for their benefit and welfare[51] to allow sustained economic development.

---

[46] Santos (2012).

[47] Guzman and Pauwelyn (2009), p. 77.

[48] Santos (2012).

[49] Ibid. Santos notes that the United States has managed to gradually expand the boundaries of the GATT Article XX exceptions regarding extraterritorial effects of U.S. regulatory measures on environment protection, starting from full prohibition in the case *Tuna Dolphin I* up to permission in the *Shrimp Turtle II* case.

[50] Ibid.

[51] Azevedo (2013).

5.3 Conclusion

This chapter provided comparative studies on how the European and Brazilian judiciaries have adjudicated on domestic litigation based on WTO agreements. Based on the original intent of the GATT, this chapter elaborated on the main similarities and divergences between Brazilian and EU courts regarding the domestic effects international trade agreements and provided the consequences of each approach. It concluded that the function and objective of international trade agreements conjoined with the principle of popular sovereignty and democratic self-government require the adoption of the rational choice theory approach regarding the WTO agreements. Finally, this chapter suggested the findings of this research may also be extended to other emerging economies in Latin America, namely, Argentina and Mexico.

In the comparison between Brazilian and EU domestic courts, a common ground between them is that the domestic legislation is silent on the domestic status of international trade agreements. Consequently, it is for the highest courts of each jurisdiction to decide on the domestic status of international trade agreements. Another similarity among Brazilian and EU courts is that, when confronted with WTO DSB rulings, both jurisdictions did not grant any domestic legal status for such rulings. Nevertheless, in the cases analyzed, both Brazilian and EU courts applied the technique of consistent interpretation and ruled in a consistent way with the DSB recommendations, despite the fact that the lack of domestic effect of WTO rulings, as shown in the *Retreaded Tires* case and in the *Ikea* case. In other cases, however, the ECJ did not use the doctrine of consistent interpretation and did not recognize the possibility of domestic courts reviewing domestic public policies in light of WTO rulings, such as in the *FIAMM* case. Another point of convergence between Brazilian and EU courts, though in very different extents, is the use of the doctrine of judicial deference to the executive.

With regard to the divergences, the most outstanding is the adoption of traditionalism by Brazilian courts, with the legal status of federal law to WTO agreements, whereas the EU courts implicitly adopted the rational choice theory approach along with supremacy of WTO agreements. As a result, private companies or individuals may interfere with public policy choices based on WTO rules in Brazil, while there is no such possibility in the EU domestic legal order. Another point of divergence derived from such contrasts is that the Brazilian judiciary may unilaterally decide on the content of international trade obligations, when the EU courts ensure that the executive bodies are the proper venue for deciding how international trade obligations are to be discharged. Divergence between Brazilian and EU courts is also found in the question of reciprocity, where Brazilian courts have never required reciprocity from other WTO Member States, while the EU courts considered reciprocity as needed from major trading partners.

With this main divergences in mind, attention is drawn to why the Brazilian judges have considered international trade agreements as creating private rights of

5.3 Conclusion

action domestically, as also it is also documented in relation to Mexico and Argentina, while EU courts have decided in an opposite way.

Developing countries in Latin America have a long settled tradition of enforcing international treaties, trade agreements included, in their domestic systems. Generally, Latin American emerging countries do not distinguish the GATT/WTO agreements from other international treaties. The volume of trade of Latin American countries largely depend on trade with developed countries, therefore it seems that it is an incentive for Latin American countries' economies to follow WTO agreements in a more visible and clear way, more so with the extensive scholarship on the influence of the rule of law on economic development and prosperity. Indeed, there are some possible economic, cultural, and social reasons why Brazilian courts, and to a greater extent Latin American courts in general, give direct effect to international trade rules.

The first possible explanation from an economic viewpoint for why Latin American emerging economies give direct effect to all international treaties, WTO agreements included, could be that developing countries compete with each other to attract more investment from the developed countries. Therefore, to enhance their position as other similarly positioned countries, developing countries would want to enhance their standards of protection.[52] International pressure, particularly from major economies, combined with economic strains, encourages a developing country to demonstrate at all levels its commitment to international obligations to attract foreign investment.

Another possible reason for why developing countries in Latin America give direct effect to international trade rules and do not distinguish them from other international treaties may be grounded on these countries' legal culture. In what concerns Brazil, and Latin American countries in general, respecting and enforcing international treaties is embedded in their legal culture. In these countries, international law is mostly perceived as being more advanced because it promotes cooperation between nations, in a Kantian concept of international law as promoting peace in the world.[53] In fact, applying internationally agreed rules at the domestic level is perceived as a progress of cooperation between nations, where courts do not question whether there is effective reciprocity from the other signatory countries to enforce international trade treaties, and do not allow domestic law to trump international rules, as seen in the Brazilian codfish case, where the GATT was not invalidated even in the face of a constitutional change. Under this Kantian perspective, the firm commitment to international trade obligations at the domestic

---

[52] Sornarajah (2010), p. 173.

[53] *See* Kant (1795). While elaborating on the law of nations, which should be founded on a federation of free states, Kant affirms that states

> should give up their savage (lawless) freedom, adjust themselves to the constraints of public law, and thus establish a continuously growing state consisting of various nations (civitas gentium), which will ultimately include all the nations of the world.

level would arguably increase joint gains from international agreements,[54] and would maintain the reputation of compliance in international law. However, as earlier noted, such gains cannot be achieved by unilateral concession, as trade agreements are made in return for other states' concessions.[55]

In addition to the legal culture, social ties with the "motherland" (*madre patria*), particularly in Hispanic culture, may be a major factor for explaining the general enforcement of international treaties before domestic courts. As former European colonies, most Latin American countries have inherited colonial features that are used to receive rules imposed from abroad. With a strong historical background in abiding to impose rules coupled with strong social relations with economically powerful countries, former colonies with much more reason would be willing to enforce internationally agreed rules at the domestic level which are seen as a natural consequence of the ratification of an international treaty.

There may have been other reasons why WTO agreements are provided with direct effect in the Latin American emerging economies. Regardless of the historical context that brought about the current jurisprudence on the direct effect of WTO agreements, the reasons considered by the European Union, as well as other major economies, primarily the United States which conceptualized the international trade system, to consider WTO agreements as non-self-executing or as not having direct effect seem compelling, as new strategies are required to deal with the new developments in international trade.

An example of new developments can be taken from the effects of exchange rate variations on tariff protection, whereby tariffs concessions can be distorted by overvalued and by devaluated currencies.[56] To illustrate, one can look at the unfair increase of China's trade due to its undervalued currency. Before the G-20 summit at the end of 2010, the Brazilian Minister of Economy declared that a currency war had begun, whereby countries were trying to undervalue their exchange rates to strengthen their exports, turning into a de facto trade war.[57] As a result, the artificially low prices of Chinese imports into Brazil has made antidumping remedies ineffective, as even with these duties, the Chinese products still enter the Brazilian market with extremely low prices, therefore hurting the national industry. These new developments in trade after the 2008 financial crisis require state-to-state negotiations and collective solutions at the international level to deal with the impact of exchange rate misalignments, not domestic judicial adjudication of trade rules.

Be as it may, whereas some member countries do not give direct effect of WTO obligations and others do consider WTO agreements as self-executing at the national level, the imbalance of trade concessions through the application of international trade rules at the domestic level increases. Direct effect of WTO agreements may bring about a disproportionate cost to countries where private individuals or companies may seek courts to supersede a desirable trade policy

---

[54] Jackson and Sykes (1997), p. 462.
[55] Sykes (2005), p. 646.
[56] Thorstensen et al. (2014).
[57] Wheatley and Leahy (2011).

based on the public interest, to favor a most economically advantageous transaction for a private importer, as *the Retreated Tires* case showed.

Due to these imbalances, countries that grant direct effect to WTO agreements should consider these differences in future agreements and negotiations; either for anticipating the potential consequences of traditionalism, or for using it to actually enhance their leverage to attain more concessions, although the latter does not seem to be a powerful argument in diplomatic negotiations. Even in the remote possibility that all signatory members would give direct to WTO agreements, the diverse domestic courts' decisions from different countries would generate what Knop has identified as "fragmentation of meaning"[58] of international law whose benefits in the long term for the development of international law are contentious.

Although given direct effect to WTO agreements has been proved to be counterproductive and generated unintended consequences as shown in the Brazilian cases, more conclusive elements are required in relation to Mexico and Argentina. The lack of actual litigation involving WTO agreements has not allowed to deepen this research in relation to these countries. Although the Brazilian experience may not be fully representative of the Mexican and Argentinean perspectives, due to each state's particular social history and legal culture, the fact that Mexico and Argentina have granted direct effect to the WTO agreements shows that the potential for unintended consequences of traditionalism is always a possibility.

Therefore, this study suggests that the Brazilian findings with regard to traditionalism in WTO agreements may bring into question the desirability of the role of domestic courts in both Argentina and Mexico, as global coherence in the lack of direct effect of WTO agreements is necessary per the original intent of the contracting parties of the GATT/WTO agreements, in accordance with the function and objective of international trade agreements, and the principle of popular sovereignty and democratic self-government. This book's argument, however, does not exclude the possibility of application of consistent interpretation by the highest domestic court, if necessary to divert potential international responsibility for non-compliance with WTO rules.

References

Azevedo R (2013) Presentation to the WTO General Council by the Brazilian candidate to the post of Director-General of the WTO. http://www.wto.org/english/news_e/news13_e/roberto_e.doc. Accessed 4 Sept 2014

Ballard M (1999) The clash between local courts and global economics: the politics of judicial reform in Brazil. Berkeley J Int Law 17:230–276

Conforti B (1993) International law and the role of domestic legal systems. Martinus Nijhoff, Dordrecht

---

[58] Knop (2000), p. 517.

De Artaza M (2013) Argentina: a well-structured but unsuccessful judicial review system. In: Yilmaz M (ed) Domestic judicial review of trade remedies. Cambridge University Press, New York

De Klor AD, Perotti AD (2009) El rol de los tribunales nacionales de los Estados del MERCOSUR. Editorial Advocatus, Córdoba

Faro de Castro M (1997) The courts, law and democracy in Brazil. Int Soc Sci J 49:241–252

Guzman A, Pauwelyn J (2009) International trade law. Aspen, New York

Hernández AS (2003) Estructura y Funcionamiento del Tribunal Federal de Justicia Fiscal y Administrativa. Podium Notarial 28:160–174. http://www.juridicas.unam.mx/publica/librev/rev/podium/cont/28/pr/pr28.pdf. Accessed 4 Sept 2014

International Monetary Fund (2014) World Economic Output April 2014. Table A1- Summary of the World Output. p. 180. IMF Publication Services, Washington

Jackson J, Sykes A (1997) Questions and comparisons. In: Jackson J, Sykes A (eds) Implementing the Uruguay round. Clarendon, Oxford

Kant I (1795) Perpetual peace: a philosophical sketch. http://www.mtholyoke.edu/acad/intrel/kant/kant1.htm. Accessed 4 Sept 2014

Knop K (2000) Here and there: international law in domestic courts. N Y Univ J Int Law Polit 32:501–535

Kossick RM Jr (2000) Litigation in the United States and Mexico: a comparative overview. Univ Miami Inter Am Law Rev 31:23–91

Kvint V (2008) Define emerging markets now. Opinion, Forbes, 1 January 2008. http://www.forbes.com/2008/01/28/kvint-developing-countries-oped-cx_kv_0129kvint.html Accessed 4 Sept 2014

La Nación (1999) La Justicia Limitó la importación de pollos desde Brasil: El gobierno nacional deberá fijar un cupo para el ingreso de carne blanca. 22 November 1999. www.lanacion.com.ar/nota.asp?nota_id=162130. Accessed 4 Sept 2014

Miranda J, Partida JC (2013) Mexico: quasi-judicial review of trade remedy measures by NAFTA panels. In: Yilmaz M (ed) Domestic judicial review of trade remedies. Cambridge University Press, New York

Rodrigues I (2009) Judicialization of politics: constitutional review and intrastate litigiousness in contemporary Brazil. Paper presented at the annual meeting of the Southern Political Science Association on 7 January 2009. http://www.allacademic.com/meta/p275709_index.html. Accessed 4 Sept 2014

Santos A (2012) Carving out policy autonomy for developing countries in the World Trade Organization: the experience of Brazil and Mexico. Va J Int Law 52:551–632

Sornarajah M (2010) The international law on foreign investment. Cambridge University Press, Cambridge

Sykes A (2005) Public versus private enforcement of international economic law: standing and remedy. J Legal Stud 34:631–666

Taylor MM (2004) Working the courts: the Worker's Party and the judicialization of politics in Brazil. Paper presented at the annual meeting of the American Political Science Association, 2 September 2004. http://www.allacademic.com/meta/p61115_index.html. Accessed 4 Sept 2014

Thorstensen V, Marçal EF, Ferraz L (2014) WTO x PTAs – where to negotiate trade and currency. Working paper No. 2014/09 presented at the fourth biennial global conference of the society of international economic law, 16 June 2014. http://ssrn.com/abstract=2451292. Accessed 4 Sept 2014

Van Agtmael A (2007) The emerging markets century: how a new breed of world-class companies is overtaking the world. Free Press, New York

Wheatley J, Leahy J (2011) Trade war looming, warns Brazil. Financial Times, 9 January 2011. http://www.ft.com/intl/cms/s/0/6316eb4a-1c34-11e0-9b56-00144feab49a.html. Accessed 4 Sept 2014

World Bank (2014). World development indicators – gross domestic product ranking table 2013. http://databank.worldbank.org/data/download/GDP.pdf. Accessed 4 Sept 2014.

Chapter 6
Conclusion

The question of the most appropriate role of domestic courts regarding international trade agreements raises a very complex debate. The most relevant approaches in international legal scholarship in relation to the role of domestic courts are identified by this study as traditionalism and the rational choice theory. Essentially, traditionalism reflects conventional international law scholarship arguing that domestic courts should be applying and interpreting international law in domestic litigation, largely conceived due to the lack of enforcement mechanisms at the international level. Conversely, the rational choice theorists propound that domestic courts are not an appropriate venue for decision-making over domestic public policy choices that involve international rules.

Considering that there is no universal answer for the role of domestic courts in international law, this study argued that a substantial field approach is necessary to evaluate the values and limits of both traditionalism and the ration choice theory according to the type of international treaty involved. For example, extradition treaties preferably require domestic courts' intervention in assessing whether the extradition conditions are met, because it involves the forceful deliver of an individual to another state and directly affects individual liberty. Conversely, other areas regulated by international law with state-to-state obligations should be circumscribed to the international level only, and should not be enforced by domestic courts. Beyond any peremptory answers to the role of domestic courts regarding international law in general, this study narrowed the research to only one substantial field of international law, that is, international trade agreements.

The claims of traditionalism and the rational choice theory approach on the role of domestic courts regarding international trade agreements were analyzed against actual litigation before domestic courts in Brazil and in the European Union involving WTO agreements, namely the GATT and the Antidumping Agreement. The point of this comparative work was to both explore these two theoretical approaches to assess the consequences of their application and whether the traditional view that domestic judiciaries are an efficient venue where international law may achieve its full efficacy is valid for international trade agreements. It puts in question the core assumptions of traditionalism when applied to emerging economies in Latin America.

The analysis of Chap. 2 revealed that traditionalism has long been the dominant theoretical approach in Brazilian courts' practice, and its domestic courts have not to this date differentiated international trade agreements from other areas of public international law. As documented, traditionalism regarding WTO agreements generated several unintended and counterproductive consequences, foreseeable and anticipated by the international scholarly debate on the direct effect of WTO agreements. In the Brazilian cases studied, the following unintended and counterproductive consequences were found in domestic litigation involving the GATT and the Antidumping Agreement: (1) a flood of individual cases, (2) diverse and inconsistent rulings among domestic courts within Brazil, (3) domestic courts' interpretation of WTO rules different from the international and foreign interpretation of trade rules, and finally (4) disequilibrium in international trade's concessions and rights. For example, in the *Retreaded Tires* case, lower courts' injunctions almost gave rise to retaliation against Brazil before the WTO dispute settlement system. Eventually, such outcome was disallowed due to the Supreme Court's judgment reversing those courts' injunctions, implicitly applying the doctrine of consistent interpretation in relation to the WTO rulings and invalidating the conflicting MERCOSUL arbitral award.

Therefore, the core assumptions of traditionalism do not seem to be applicable to international trade agreements, particularly regarding emerging economies, as follows. First, traditionalism was largely conceived to respond to the lack of efficient sanctions or enforcement mechanisms at the international level. With regards to international trade agreements, however, this is not a concern as the WTO dispute settlement mechanism has been frequently used for solving trade disputes among WTO members, with a compliance rate of 90 %.[1] Although a lot should be improved at the WTO Dispute Settlement Understanding, retaliation is a possibility and therefore the lack of efficient ways for compliance with international trade rules is not a primary concern.[2] Indeed, there are various deficiencies in the WTO dispute settlement, but WTO members have been engaged in discussing improvements.[3] Despite the potential for improvement of the Dispute Settlement Understanding regarding compliance mechanisms, it is hardly the case that an emerging economy would be more pressured by courts' injunctions issued by its own domestic courts on private domestic litigation over trade rules, than the potential retaliation for lack of compliance with a WTO ruling at the international level. If not for the reputation consequences of non-compliance with WTO rules, certainly the suspension of concessions under the WTO covered agreements works

---

[1] WTO News: Speeches—DG Pascal Lamy (2011).

[2] *See* Colares (2011).

[3] The Dispute Settlement Understanding has been under review at the WTO for improving the dispute settlement system. For an overall account of these negotiations, *see* Evans and Tarso Pereira (2005).

as a stronger deterrence to non-compliance and have a larger effect on a WTO member state's economy as a whole than domestic courts' injunctions.

Second, traditionalism assumes non-compliance of WTO members with their international obligations. The perceived problem to which traditionalism presents itself as a solution is based on the concern that powerful states, when they want to, have been able to not comply with their international obligations. Indeed, with higher leverage in the trade world, powerful countries may occasionally refuse to abide to a WTO ruling, and there are famous cases where international trade obligations were not complied with, e.g., *US—Gambling*, *EC-Hormones*, and the *EC-Bananas*. Not coincidentally, in such cases, the non-compliant WTO members were the United States and the European Union, which are the major and most powerful economies of the world. These two WTO members, together with a handful of major players, seem to be the only ones that may be able to face retaliation and international pressure among more than 160 members of the multilateral trade system.[4] Nevertheless, these cases are indeed famous for they are exceptions. The United States has complied with other unfavorable WTO rulings, being the most prominent ones the Venezuelan oil case[5] and, most recently, the highly contentious zeroing cases.[6] As earlier mentioned, even these famous cases of refusal to adopt the recommendations of the DSB, the parties involved eventually reached a mutually satisfactory solution over the *EC-Hormones* case,[7] and in the *EC-Bananas* disputes,[8] which proves the WTO as a forum for solving trade disputes between states when they involved higher societal values that cannot be superseded.

Third, domestic interpretation of international law does not seem to do much to advance international law, for it generates various conflicting rulings, causes a mix between international and domestic law, and the resulting outcome does not seem to foster the function and objective of international trade agreements. Variations of traditionalism in international legal scholarship, as mentioned above, have considered these facts as beneficial to international law in what their normative inclinations have predicted an epistemic community of judges promoting international liberalism and creating international law. Although very sophisticated and refined normative proposals, these theories does not seem to be grounded on the actual consequences when domestic courts' interpretation of WTO rules are different from the international and foreign interpretation of trade rules, and provides for

---

[4] WTO, *Members and Observers* (2014).

[5] WTO, *United States—Standards for Reformulated and Conventional Gasoline*, WT/DS2/9, adopted 20 May 1996, implementation notified by the United States on 25 September 1997.

[6] WTO, *United States—Use of Zeroing in Anti-Dumping Measures Involving Products from Korea*, WT/DS402/R, adopted 24 February 2011, implementation notified by the United States on 19 December 2011.

[7] In 2011, the EU, the US and Canada notified the DSB that they reached a satisfactory solution to the disputes WT/DS26, DS48, DS320 concerning meat and meat products (Hormones), which had started in 1996.

[8] In November 2012, the parties notified the DSB that they reached a mutually agreed solution to the disputes WT/DS16, WT/DS27.

conflicting rulings within a WTO member domestic jurisdiction, as well as among WTO members themselves. Domestic courts unilaterally deciding the meaning of international trade rules impair legal certainty and provokes imbalance in the mutual commitments on market access. Traditional modes of international legal scholarship on the role of domestic courts regarding international law assume that more formal enforcement of international law by domestic courts will necessarily make international law stronger. The arguments that the mixture of domestic and international law brings about something that is neither domestic nor international, and the diversity of courts from different countries leads to fragmentation of meaning in international law,[9] with a consequent weakening of international trade law as it is beneficial to have common interpretations of meaning at the WTO level. From the cases studies in the Brazilian stance, this study showed that a plethora of domestic courts' decisions, and the mix of international law with local rules weakens international law, as in the *Radial Tires* case where a lower court had halted the collection of antidumping duties on sales contract made before such duties were imposed by interpreting WTO commercial defense rights in light of the domestic constitutional principle of non-retroactivity of laws.

From a formal perspective, if domestic courts were applying international rules, it would necessarily follow that international rules are being enforced and strengthened. However, from an empirical observation of the Brazilian courts, such unavoidable mixed outcomes may weaken the need of clear rules and reciprocal rights and obligations based on the consent of the countries involved at the WTO system. It is feasible and most likely that, in certain contexts, the enforcement of international law by domestic courts may create more trouble than if international rules are enforced through state-to-state international mechanisms, with room for a negotiated solution. Indeed, a highly significant contribution to the debate on the role of domestic courts in international law is to acknowledge and bring attention to the necessarily hybrid legal outcome of the mix between international and domestic law.[10]

Other than the unintended counterproductive consequences identified by this study in traditionalism regarding WTO agreements in the Brazilian experience, what traditionalism does not address is how a power shift within a country's domestic legal order will necessarily lead to better compliance with international law in countries where the executive complies with international law, and the power-related behavior of non-compliance with international law simply does not exist. Although with legitimate concerns in advancing the enforcement of international law, advocates of traditionalism do not consider that the lack of compliance with international trade obligations is neither an option nor desirable to the overwhelmingly majority of the countries of the world. Therefore traditionalism, offered as a general and uniform solution, burdens developing countries with internal trade disputes and judicial decisions that do not necessarily attain the

---

[9] Knop (2000), p. 517.
[10] Ibid., p. 506.

function and objective of international law, can even be responsible for causing a breach of international obligations, and restrain self-government and regulatory powers. In this sense, traditionalism may become a burden to the majority of developing economies as the executive is the most interested and engaged in ensuring that a country's international trade obligations are complied with.

The traditionalist account on the enforcement of international trade rules was however not adopted in relation to the WTO agreements in the European Union cases, as shown in Chap. 3. Although having a contentious mixed stance on international trade agreements, as agreements with former colonies and neighboring states were considered as granting private rights of action, the ECJ denied direct effect to the GATT/WTO agreements and refused to shift the balance of power from EU executive bodies to the judiciary. In the EU, executive bodies were therefore able to maintain higher societal values on health concerns such as not supplying hormone beef in the EU territory—a policy choice that was considered as inconsistent with the WTO rules—while eventually finding a mutually agreed solution with the complainant members.

Through the lens of constitutional pluralism doctrine in the European Union context, this study showed that there is a high degree of cooperation of national courts of EU Member States. The case law of the German and Italian courts corroborated the ECJ opinion on the GATT/WTO agreements, although such courts have not closed the door for any potential review of their position in the future, however unlikely this may seem. The ECJ interpretation of the lack of direct effect of WTO agreements was grounded on the principle of negotiations to attain reciprocal and mutually advantageous arrangements, and the lack of reciprocity from other major trading partners of the EU, mainly the United States.

The United States leadership in the creation of the GATT and in the international trade system as a whole, while at the same time not giving direct effect of WTO agreements at the domestic level, influenced the ECJ to adopt the same understanding. After all, supporting and advancing international law and institutions do not imply a surrender of self-government,[11] a solid argument when one considers that the WTO is a strong international system and the covered agreements are essentially inter-states rules. WTO agreements were not intended to create private rights enforceable before domestic courts to impose how, according to a private business's interests, trade obligations are to be discharged.

After proving the unintended consequences of traditionalism regarding international trade agreements, this study's main argument has two parts. First, this study argues that traditionalism does not conform with the function and objective of international trade rules to concede mutual government-to-government market access and, consequently, international trade law does not create individual rights that may be enforceable before domestic courts. Second, this study propounds that traditionalism in international trade agreements disregards the principle of popular

---

[11] Rubenfeld (2005), p. 289.

sovereignty and democratic self-government in choosing how international trade obligations are discharged.

As for the first part of this study's argument, the function and objective of international trade agreements is to make reliable government-to-government commitments for improving market access and consequently increase mutual political welfare.[12] Accordingly, international trade agreements are inter-states' obligations and concessions given between states under international law, not between states and corporations or private individuals. Thus, international trade agreements are not meant to create rights of private corporations and individuals because the reduction of trade barriers are exchanged in return of concessions from other states against which the domestic judiciary may not impose their solutions based on their domestic legislation and their interpretation of international trade agreements. Commentary noted that states do not make international trade agreements that lower the price of imported goods for no reason.[13] States reduce trade barriers and lower the price of imports as a concession that is made in return for other states' concessions.[14] By imposing a unilateral domestic judicial interpretation of international trade agreements, domestic courts in the traditionalist perspective would put businesses private interests over national public interest goals that are legitimately chosen by the executive and legislative, without any other state's concessions in return. Therefore, the mutual agreed rights and obligations for cooperation in the trade system as provided for in the related international trade agreement becomes imbalanced.

Consequently, private parties should not be entitled to invoke international trade rules before domestic courts to challenge legitimate public choices made by governments, which are the political filters for legal arguments in the enforcement action in case another state is not complying with its international trade commitments.[15] If the domestic judiciaries of all WTO members would be allowed to pass judgment on how trade rules should be interpreted and applied, future international trade agreements to achieve mutual gains on market access would be hindered as the legal uncertainty on the agreed commitments would be submitted to what a domestic court would understand them to be, with the corollary of diverging and conflicting rulings, not to mention the possibility of denunciation of the treaties in force. Indeed, as this study showed, treaty denunciation actually occurred in Brazil due to the impact of judicial implementation of the Termination of Employment Convention of the International Labor Organization (ILO Convention n. 158) in the Brazilian domestic legal system.

To be sure, in the cases studied, the Supreme Court of Brazil averted the imminent retaliation from the EU at the WTO level against the lower courts' injunctions on the retreated tires case in Brazil. Indeed, guidance from the Supreme

---

[12] Sykes (2005), p. 633.
[13] Ibid., p. 646.
[14] Ibid.
[15] Ibid., p. 633.

Court may provide for a solution on domestic litigation involving international trade agreements, particularly using the doctrine of consistent interpretation.

Nevertheless, higher courts' guidance on domestic litigation involving international trade may not do much in relation to potential conflicting rulings from regional trade agreements and WTO dispute settlement systems, or in relation to other WTO members' domestic courts opinions on the interpretation of trade rules. In these cases, domestic courts have no answer. It is for the executive to negotiate among other trading partners on how to overcome conflicting obligations from different trade regimes to find a satisfactory solution to all states involved, and a domestic judicial decision over the issue may potentially be impossible to overcome.

Furthermore, this study found that traditionalism should not be applied to international trade agreements because it disregards the principle of popular sovereignty and democratic self-government in choosing how international trade obligations are discharged. To be sure, every member state of the WTO agreements has rights and obligations before the other WTO signatory parties. Nevertheless, other parties may not impose their views on how should such trade commitments be discharged at the domestic level, and therefore each state has the right to choose how to discharge their international trade obligations. In this sense, the idea that domestic judges may circumvent deliberative law-making on trade public policy choices by applying and interpreting international trade rules seems to be a stretch that would not foster international trade law. International trade law are made by states and, consequently, states may not have their own regulatory autonomy hindered due to unaccountable domestic legal actors based on international trade obligations which are essentially non-self-executing or programmatic in nature and, in particular, come with mandatory international dispute settlement system in case of a member state finds that the agreement is not being complied with by another signatory party. More importantly, in case of disputes, such agreements still give preference to a mutually agreeable solution.[16]

It may be argued that domestic judges legitimize the processes of implementing international trade rules. Nevertheless, the interpretation and application of international trade agreements rules that affect domestic public policy choices without the engagement of the political branches provokes a shift of power from the domestic constituencies to the international community. This shift of power, perceived as beneficial by traditionalism proponents, however does not consider that the enforcement of international trade law is much more a matter of public policy than a legal choice.[17] As seen in the cases studied, the executive bodies of the EU were able to maintain their policy choices, although contentious, without interference of the judiciary. The idea that public interest should give leeway to

---

[16] WTO Understanding on Rules and Procedures Governing the Settlement of Disputes (DSU), Article 3.7.

[17] Posner (2009), p. 112.

commercial interests by recourse to domestic courts is an inversion of the fundamental democratic values over which western societies are founded.

Of course, any possible lack of compliance with the WTO agreements has consequences, as any potential violation may be addressed at the WTO dispute settlement system. As a method to constrain practices that are not in compliance with the WTO, the application and interpretation of trade rules by domestic judges seem to disregard the decisional capacity of political branches towards their international obligations, their redistributive social policies and their commercial defense rights to promote public interest. By empowering domestic judges, traditionalism largely ignored the ordinary processes of democratic law-making out of a legitimate aspiration for the full enforcement of international law. Nevertheless, the domestic enforcement of international trade rules for commercial bargains cannot be an end in itself. After all, international trade should be at the service of the improvement of living conditions of families.[18] In this sense, the intention of the contracting parties in the creation of the GATT/WTO agreements was to regulate a state-to-state relationship, as showed by this study, and never to have a direct effect in domestic legal orders as to impair public policy choices. Accordingly, WTO rules should not be directly imposed in domestic legal orders by domestic courts, as public policy choices are not domestic courts domain or responsibility, and was never the intention of the GATT/WTO members to give direct effect to trade rules. In fact, the lack of direct effect of WTO agreements is adopted by the majority of WTO members, with the Latin American exception being a peculiar position.

While legal culture contributes to the application of international treaties by the Latin American judiciary, the economic incentives and power relations play a fundamental role on whether international trade agreements have direct effect. The fact that Latin American emerging economies have different interests from the developed countries in international trade may seems to condition the different responses the Brazilian and the European Union courts have provided in relation to the direct effect of WTO agreements. For instance, in what concerns international trade interests, European countries are more interested in market access, while developing countries are keener on attracting foreign investment. Such different interests may possibly condition the diverse responses from the European and the Latin American judiciaries.

In addition, the diverse positioning of developed countries as opposed to Latin American states may also indicate that it would be very unlikely that the European Union would grant direct effect of WTO agreements based on reciprocity granted by these emerging economies. After all, the implementation of the WTO rules at the domestic level seems to be more effective when courts are willing to make use of the doctrine of consistent interpretation, which, indeed, is the case for both Brazil and the European Union. This conclusion seems to be even more convincing in relation to the Brazilian standpoint due to the flood of individual claims filed against

---

[18] Azevedo (2013).

Brazilian governmental trade measures, with the consequent hindrance of its objectives in detriment of public interest that benefits the country as a whole.

The contrasting perspectives between the Latin American countries and richer economies suggest that relations of power are an important factor in the adoption, or not, of direct effect of WTO agreements. As mentioned, weaker countries abide to international obligations more easily than powerful economies,[19] which may partially explain traditionalism in Latin America. As Latin American economies develop, and their role in the international trade system increases, one can reasonably expect a move from traditionalism to the rational choice theory in these countries, as in the European and American examples. If Latin American economies will continue to grow and a shift will occur, remains to be seen in the years to come. For now, Brazilian courts' trend is to not avoid highly political questions. Indeed, Brazilian courts take a very different stance to that of the United States courts which, as noted above in Sloss's observation, rarely use their powers to invalidate governmental acts based on international treaties' violations.[20]

If, for the sake of strengthening the domestic enforcement of international trade legal rules *per se*, traditionalism is chosen without consideration of powerful member states' interpretation, then the question becomes whether the enforcement and bindingness of the GATT would attain the *raison d'être* of traditionalism which is to bring power under law.[21] This study indicated that, instead of bringing power under law, judicial enforcement of trade rules by Latin American courts provoke more asymmetry in the world balance of power, and constrains more the weaker countries in their domestic policies, because rich WTO member states do not provide rights of action on trade rules at the domestic level.

In fact, powerful countries have more leverage in administering their own domestic policies and their WTO commitments. Exporters from powerful countries have access to Latin American domestic courts to challenge any governmental policy against their interests, while the exporters of Latin American countries do not have courts' access based on the WTO commitments in powerful WTO members. In this sense, instead of bringing about a constraint in the behavior of powerful countries, domestic enforcement of international trade law by Latin American countries in principle provokes more imbalance and unequal relations among states, widening the gap between north–south trade relations. Indeed, the equilibrium of mutual gains and advantages cannot be promoted or sustained by domestic courts.

At the global level, Latin American countries are more influenced by global pressures in international trade, and it seems that traditionalism generates even more constraints at the domestic level because it restricts the governmental trade policy-making and therefore impairs self-government in deciding how international trade rules are to be discharged. The role of domestic courts in enforcing WTO

---

[19] Guzman and Pauwelyn (2009), p. 77.
[20] Sloss (2010), p. 3.
[21] Nollkaemper (2011), p. 1.

agreements can bring more constraints to regulatory prerogatives and more liberal interpretations than the jurisprudence of the WTO, which is closely followed by the WTO membership. On the other hand, powerful and wealthier economies are inherently more able to resist potential pressures on trade matters[22] and are, most often than not, not constrained in their domestic realms by the local judiciary. As a result, when traditionalism for the enforcement of international trade rules by domestic courts is applied in developing countries, regardless of the balance of mutual concessions and lack of reciprocity from powerful member states, it does not strengthens an equal and fair international legal order. Instead, in the current description of the world, the impact of traditionalism in developing countries enhances the disequilibrium and inequality among nations with the benefit of the powerful countries. As a result, traditionalism in international trade agreements context seems to sparks the very imbalance of power that it seeks to avoid through the enforcement of international law by domestic courts in the field of trade law.

Lastly, despite the current economic crisis, the world trade will intensify and more complex cases with overlapping rules or jurisdictions may arise. Domestic courts are not the optimal venue for deciding on such conflicts, as there is always the possibility of negotiating an alternative solution among the countries involved to bring a country's position in conformity with conflicting international obligations. Alternative solutions are for the executive to diplomatically assess and domestically balance the interests involved. As a result, the WTO dispute settlement mechanism seems to provide a more appropriate venue for deciding disputes and finding mutually agreed solutions between member countries.

This book was an attempt to address an understudied issue on the application of international trade rules by emerging countries' courts, and complements the current studies on the interaction between international trade law and domestic courts. It benefits the international community in understanding better how Brazilian domestic courts decide on paramount international trade disputes, and the actual effect of the international dispute settlement mechanisms at the national level. This study also aimed at assisting the national judiciaries in learning how courts in other countries have decided on complex cases involving international trading systems and therefore can be a valuable input in judicial decision-making process when similar questions arise in another member country's judiciary. Stephen Breyer, a U.S. Supreme Court Associate Justice, based on the increasing number of domestic issues that involve foreign or international law, stated that foreign courts' decisions can be a useful tool in offering points of comparison and provides a practical experience in bringing solutions to a common legal issue.[23] Similarly, Justice

---

[22] Examples of long-standing disputes where powerful WTO members have refused to comply with WTO law, even after a ruling from the WTO dispute settlement system, are the *European Communities—Regime for the Importation, Sale and Distribution of Bananas*, WT/DS16, WT/DS27, WT/DS105, WT/DS158, WT/DS361, and WT/DS364, the *European Communities— Measures Concerning Meat and Meat Products* (Hormones), WT/DS26, and *United States— Measures Affecting the Cross-Border Supply of Gambling and Betting Services*, WT/DS285.

[23] Breyer (2003).

Ginsburg of the United States Supreme Court, also in favor of comparative foreign experience, stated that *"conclusions reached by other countries and by the international community should at times constitute persuasive authority."*[24] Hopefully, this book has enhanced the awareness that the prevailing international legal scholarship arguing for increased role of domestic courts regarding international law should not include international trade agreements, even if this perspective happens to be the central precepts of the dominant Latin American legal culture.

References

Azevedo R (2013) Presentation to the WTO General Council by the Brazilian candidate to the post of Director-General of the WTO. http://www.wto.org/english/news_e/news13_e/roberto_e.doc. Accessed 4 Sept 2014

Breyer S (2003) The Supreme Court and the new international law. Proc Annu Meet (Am Soc Int Law) 97:265–268

Colares J (2011) The limits of WTO adjudication: is compliance the problem? J Int Econ Law 14:403–436

Evans D, Tarso Pereira C (2005) DSU review: a view from the inside. In: Yerxa R, Wilson B (eds) Key issues in the WTO dispute settlement: the first ten years. Cambridge University Press, New York

Guzman A, Pauwelyn J (2009) International trade law. Aspen, New York

Knop K (2000) Here and there: international law in domestic courts. N Y Univ J Int Law Polit 32:501–535

Nollkaemper A (2011) National courts and the international rule of law. Oxford University Press, Oxford

Posner E (2009) The perils of global legalism. University of Chicago Press, Chicago

Rubenfeld J (2005) Two world orders. In: Nolte G (ed) European and US constitutionalism. Cambridge University Press, Cambridge

Sloss D (ed) (2010) The role of domestic courts in treaty enforcement: a comparative study. Cambridge University Press, London

Sykes A (2005) Public versus private enforcement of international economic law: standing and remedy. J Legal Stud 34:631–666

WTO Members and Observers (2014) http://www.wto.org/english/thewto_e/whatis_e/tif_e/org6_e.htm. Accessed 4 Sept 2014

WTO News: Speeches—DG Pascal Lamy (2011) As trade changes rapidly, you must help guide WTO, Lamy tells global business. http://www.wto.org/english/news_e/sppl_e/sppl192_e.htm. Accessed 4 Sept 2014

---

[24] *Lawrence v. Texas*, 539 U.S. 558, 572–573 (2003).

Printed by Printforce, the Netherlands